its usability or performance. In all cases, original manufacturer's recommendations, procedures, and instructions supersede and take precedence over descriptions herein. Specific component design and mechanical procedures – and the qualifications of individual readers – are beyond the control of the publisher, therefore the publisher disclaims all liability, either expressed or implied, for use of the information in this publication. All risk for its use is entirely assumed by the purchaser/user. In no event will Cartech®, Inc. or the author be liable for any indirect, special, or consequential damages, including but not limited to personal injury or any other damages, arising out of the use or misuse of any information in this publication.

This book is an independent publication, and the authors and/or publisher thereof are not in any way associated with, and are not authorized to act on behalf of any of the manufacturers included in this book. Chevrolet®, Chevy®, Chrysler®, Ford®, Mopar®, Pontiac®, Oldsmobile®, GMC Trucks®, and General Motors® are registered trademarks. The publisher reserves the right to revise this publication or change its content from time to time without obligation to notify any persons of such revisions or changes.

CHRYSLER PERFORMANCE ENGINES

BY FRANK ADKINS

ILLUSTRATIONS BY
ROB McCALL

EDITED BY
DAVID BOHON

PRODUCTION BY
RACHELLE RAPHAEL

COVER DESIGN BY
TAMARA BAECHTEL

OVERSEAS DISTRIBUTION BY:

BROOKLANDS BOOKS LTD.
P.O. BOX 146, Cobham, Surrey, KT11 1LG, England
Telephone 01932 865051 • FAX 01932 868803

BROOKLANDS BOOKS LTD.
1/81 Darley Street, P.O. Box 199, Mona Vale,
NSW 2103, Australia
Telephone 2 9997 8428 • FAX 2 9997 5799

ISBN 1-884089-54-2
Order No. SA67

CARTECH®, INC., 11605 KOST DAM RD., NORTH BRANCH, MN 55056

Acknowledgments

Few books such as this are written solely from the author's own resources, ambition, and knowledge. Along the way assistance, input, and moral support are usually offered by friends, colleagues, and family members. If the author has any humility or common sense whatsoever, he will graciously accept these offerings. He will also rely on the vital assistance and cooperation of professionals in related fields. Such was the case with this project.

I would like to offer my thanks to Alan and Susan Pedersen, Jack Lakatos, Doug Dutra, Russ Hart, Don Lindman, Mike Boswell, Barry Beck, Joe Pullella, Lee Pullella, Larry Charney, Joel Friedman, Jack Poehler, Bob Barry, Greg Rager at *High Performance Mopar* magazine, Renee Rogers at *Mopar Performance News*, David Elshoff and Art Ponder at DaimlerChrysler, and all of the parts vendors at car shows and swap meets (such as the Mopar Nationals and Chryslers at Carlisle) who allowed me to pick through their inventory and photograph the parts I needed for this book.

Thanks to "Mr. Super Stock Hemi" Ray Barton of Ray Barton Racing Engines in Wernersville, Pennsylvania and his staff of engine-building craftsmen. These guys tolerated my presence in their shop while I looked over their shoulders, asked questions, and photographed their works in progress.

Special thanks to Rob and Erin McCall, Steve and Leah Gray, and all the folks at CarTech® who were as supportive and helpful with the production of this project as they were with my first book, *Chrysler Performance Upgrades*.

Above all, I want to thank my wife Kristan, whose support and patience never wavered, and who never complained about the late nights and early mornings I spent wrenching in the garage or rapping on the computer keyboard, or the days I spent away from home in my quest for photographs and information for this book. Thanks, Dear!

About the Author

Frank Adkins developed a passion for Chryslers at an early age. He recalls as a youngster helping his father tune the family Dodge, listening earnestly while his father recounted his younger days behind the wheel of a 1957 Fury powered by a "dual quad" 318. At age 15 Frank purchased his first car, a 1964 Dodge Dart with a nearly grenaded Torqueflite, and by his 16th birthday he had replaced the car's automatic transmission with a manual one, complete with pedals and custom fabricated shifter linkage. Since then Frank has owned over 50 Chrysler vehicles, from restored musclecars and modified street cars to Slant Six-powered beaters and parts cars. Many of those machines have served as rolling research and development projects.

Frank is an honors graduate of the Automotive Training Center in Exton, Pennsylvania, and also holds an Associate's Degree in Automotive Technology from Delaware Technical and Community College. He has been an ASE certified Master Technician since 1986, and has an additional ASE certification in Advanced Level Engine Performance.

An active enthusiast, Frank belongs to four different car clubs and attends several car shows and drag race events each year. He is a two-time competitor in the Michelin Tire/*Car and Driver* magazine-sponsored "One Lap of America," a week-long event. In one competition he and teammate Steve Gray drove around the country in a modified 1970 Dodge Dart powered by a supercharged 360, competing at many racetracks along the way.

Frank has written for several automotive hobbyist magazines, and is the author of a previous CarTech® book, *Chrysler Performance Upgrades*.

TABLE OF CONTENTS

CHRYSLER PERFORMANCE ENGINES

Introduction

Being a Chrysler enthusiast can be tough. The root of our trouble stems from when our cars were new, for overall, in the 1960s and '70s Chrysler cars were built in far fewer numbers than comparable models from Ford or General Motors. To illustrate this point, think of your high school days. If you grew up in the '60s, '70s, or '80s, how many Camaros, Novas, Monte Carlos, Torinos, and Mustangs converged on the parking lot at school each day? Several, no doubt. How many Chargers, Dusters, or Barracudas were scattered among them? Probably not too many.

Today there are even fewer of these older Chrysler cars available to serve as project cars or parts cars. Used Chrysler parts have become scarce, and thus the prices of existing salvageable cars and useable parts have climbed dramatically over the last couple of decades.

To make matters worse, the interchangeability of parts between Chrysler engine families and car lines was not a major consideration when our cars were engineered. Knowing the similarities and differences between parts and whether or not they are interchangeable is crucial when you are planning an engine build-up or swap. For example, if you want to pull the tired 318 from your Satellite and replace it with a 360, can you simply drop in the 360 and take off? Or what if you want to build a 440, but you have a pair of heads from a 361. Will those heads fit a 440? And if they do fit, how well will they perform?

If you have not yet decided to purchase this book, you may be wondering for whom it was written. It can be frustrating to spend the better part of 20 bucks for a book, only to discover later that it doesn't contain the information you need or was written on a level that is either too basic or too advanced for your needs.

This book was written for those enthusiasts who have had at least some experience with the procedures involved in removing, disassembling, reassembling, and reinstalling engines. While there is some coverage of the various exotic pieces used in race engines (such as aftermarket cylinder heads), this book was certainly not written to showcase high dollar-race engines packed with parts that are cost prohibitive to the majority of us. Instead, this book takes a real-world approach, covering topics of interest to the active grassroots Chrysler enthusiasts. These are the guys and gals who show up at the drag strips and dirt tracks on weekends, and who enjoy participating in local cruises and car shows.

The author's first book, *Chrysler Performance Upgrades*, thoroughly covers engine swaps as well as suspension, brake system, rear axle, and electrical system retrofits and upgrades. *Chrysler Performance Engines*, on the other hand, covers information you will need for engine

This early polyspherical A engine can be identified by its distributor at the rear of the engine, two bolts retaining each rocker cover, and scalloped lower edge on each rocker cover.

The LA engine family is characterized by the distributor at the rear of the engine and five bolts retaining each rocker cover.

build-ups. This book will familiarize you with each of the different families of engines used in Chrysler rear-wheel-drive vehicles. Each engine within a family is discussed, and the similarities and differences between each of the engines is stressed. Furthermore, throughout the evolution of each of the engine families many changes took place. These changes are addressed as well.

Nearly all of us plan an engine build-up within the confines of a budget. In keeping within that budget we normally try to reuse as many of the original parts as possible, provided they are up to the task of delivering the desired horsepower we seek without sacrificing the durability of the engine. Of course, as horsepower levels rise many production pieces must give way to superior aftermarket pieces. As such, some aftermarket pieces are discussed in this book, but only as they relate to increasing power levels and engine durability beyond the capability of the production parts they replace.

Before planning any type of engine build-up or the purchase of a crate engine, it is important for you to have a clear and realistic vision of how the engine will be used. Is it a race-only engine? What type of racing? Will it see street use with a lot of low-speed driving and idle time? Is day-to-day

durability a concern? How about fuel economy? How stringent is the emissions testing in your area? Will the engine have to run on pump gas? How much money can you devote toward this engine build-up? Will other changes to the car be needed, such as exhaust, a high stall-speed torque converter, and numerically higher rear-axle gears? In what type of vehicle will this engine be used? These types of questions must be answered realistically *before* you plan your build-up.

It is important to remember that no engine can "do it all." Inevitably, performance, economy, emissions, and cost all seem to be at odds with each other. Achieving gains in one or more of these areas almost always means having to sacrifice in other areas. By setting realistic goals and having realistic expectations of what you wish to achieve with your engine, you can begin to make educated choices and select components that will work well together so that your overall engine package meets your needs. Of course, all of this requires a sound understanding of the various families of engines that have been manufactured by the Chrysler Corporation.

With all of this in mind, hold on as we plunge into the world of Chrysler Performance Engines!

The unmistakable Slant Six engine is inclined 30 degrees to the right.

Magnum small-block engines look similar to LA engines, but their rocker covers are retained by ten bolts each.

Casting dates are typically found on one side of the block on all engines. They are usually easy to read as long as you have an unobstructed view.

The B and RB engines, known as big-block engines, are characterized by the distributor located at the front of the engine and angled to the right side of the car.

The ID pad on small-block A, LA, and Magnum engines is located on the front side of the left cylinder bank.

The 426 Hemi distributor is located the same as on other big-block engines, but the spark plug wires pass through the wide rocker covers to reach the spark plugs.

The ID pad on B engines is located just ahead of the right side cylinder bank.

On V-8 engines, the displacement is typically …

… cast into the side of the block as well.

Engine identification numbers can be found stamped on this pad on Slant Six engines.

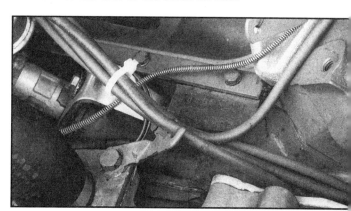

The ID pad on 426 Hemi and RB engines is located adjacent to the distributor.

BODY TYPE DESIGN

Body Type	Models
A-Body	1963-1976 Dart, 1964-1969 Barracuda, 1970-1976 Duster, all Valiant, Scamp, Demon, Dart Sport, and Swinger
B-Body	All Coronet, Belvedere, GTX, Super Bee, Charger (RWD), 1968-1975 Road Runner, 1977-1978 Monaco, (not Royal), 1978-1979 Magnum, 1962-1964 and 1975-1978 Fury, 1975-1979 Cordoba
C-Body	1965-1978 New Yorker, Newport, and 300, 1965-1974 Fury, 1965-1976 Monaco and Polara, 1975-1977 Gran Fury, 1977 Royal Monaco
E-Body	1970-1974 Barracuda and Challenger
F-Body	1976-1980 Aspen, Volare, Aspen R/T, Road Runner
M-Body	1977-1988 Diplomat, LeBaron (RWD), Caravelle (RWD), Fifth Avenue (RWD), 1982-1988 Gran Fury
J-Body	1980-1983 Cordoba and Mirada
R-Body	1979-1981 New Yorker, St. Regis, Newport, and 1980-1981 Gran Fury

Engine Type	Description
Slant Six Engines	All 170, 198, and 225 C.I.D. engines.
V-6 Engine	3.9 liter truck engine with carburetor (1987), throttle body fuel injection (1988-1991) and in Magnum form (1992-on).
A-Engines	277, 301, 313, and pre-1967 318 C.I.D. engines. Characterized by polyspherical combustion chambers, 2-bolt rocker covers, and distributor at rear of engine.
LA-Engines	All 273, 340, 1967-1991 318, and 360 through 1992 engines. Characterized by 5-bolt rocker covers and distributor at rear of engine.
Magnum Engines	1992 and later 318 and 1993 and later 360 C.I.D truck engines, and Mopar Performance crate engines based on the production 360 engine. Characterized by 10-bolt rocker covers and distributor at rear of engine.
B-Engines	350, 361, 1962 and later 383, and 400 C.I.D. engines. Characterized by distributor at front of engine and absence of engine ID boss adjacent to distributor.
RB-Engines	1960-1961 383, and all 413, 426 Wedge head, and 440 C.I.D. engines. Characterized by distributor at front of engine and engine ID boss adjacent to distributor.
Early Hemi Engines	Any of the 1958 and earlier V-8 engines with hemispherical heads. Characterized by wide rocker covers through which the spark plug wires pass and distributor at rear of engine.
426 Hemi Engine	1964-1971 Race Hemi and Street Hemi engines. Characterized by wide rocker covers through which the spark plug wires pass and distributor at front of engine.

CHRYSLER PERFORMANCE ENGINES

Slant Six Engines

With the dawn of the 1960s came a change in the attitude of the car-buying public. America's love affair with automotive excess was coming to an end, as consumers began trading in their road hogs, with long tail fins and lavish chrome, for smaller cars that were cheaper to operate and maintain. That demand prompted Detroit to come out with such cars as the Chevy II, the Corvair, and the Falcon.

Chrysler began catering to this segment of the market with its introduction of the Valiant and Lancer compacts. These new "econo-boxes" needed an updated power plant, for the V-8 engines would not fit easily, nor were they deemed economical, and the flat-head six was too heavy for these new fuel-sipping cars. Chrysler needed a smaller, lighter engine that would meet the power requirements and fuel mileage expectations of economy conscious consumers. Furthermore, the engine had to be of an overhead valve design, which would allow the engine to breathe more freely, producing more power. Overhead valves had become the automotive rage in the 1950s, and a savvy motoring public would accept nothing less in an all new car.

In response to these needs, Chrysler created its legendary slanted six-cylinder engine. The "Slant Six," as it was called from the beginning, was certainly an odd looking engine, canted 30 degrees to the right with an intake manifold that had comparatively long, sweeping runners. Chrysler engineers explained that tilting the engine not only made room for the long runner intake manifold, but also allowed for a lower hood line. Contemporary in-line six-cylinder engines from other manufacturers stood vertical and used intake manifolds that positioned the carburetor close to the cylinder head, dictating that cylinders three and four had extremely short runners, while cylinders one, two, five, and six all had longer runners with sharp bends.

Throughout the 1960s, Chrysler produced the Slant Six in both 170 and 225 cubic-inch versions. Both of these engines have a bore of 3.40 inches. The 170 has a stroke of 3.125 inches, while the stroke of the 225 measures 4.125 inches. Because of this difference in strokes, a low-deck version of the block was used for 170 engines, and a tall-deck version was used for 225 engines. To the casual observer, these two engines appear identical, but a trained eye quickly notes the

The 170 engine has a short-deck height and, therefore, uses a short bypass hose.

The 198 and 225 engines have a tall-deck height and require a longer bypass hose.

From the outside, aluminum blocks are easily identified by the vertical groove between each of the cylinders.

differences between them. The 170 uses a short bypass hose between the cylinder head and the water pump that measures just over an inch in length, while the 225 uses a bypass hose that is roughly twice as long. Nearly all components will interchange between a 170 and a 225. The only exceptions (in addition to the block and bypass hose) are the crankshaft, the connecting rods, and the push rods.

Chrysler did specify different camshafts and carburetors for these two engines, but the differences were subtle. In terms of fit and function, they are interchangeable. Thus, it is possible to replace a 170 engine with a 225, and vice versa. While a swap such as this usually goes without a hitch, you may experience some trouble with the exhaust head-pipe due to the difference in overall engine heights. If you replace a 225 with a shorter 170, it is possible that the pipe will interfere with the steering linkage, especially when accelerating in reverse. If you replace a 170 with a 225, the pipe may contact the torsion bar cross member, especially when accelerating forward.

Aluminum Slant Six

When Chrysler started the Valiant program in 1957, reducing vehicle weight was a major consideration for all domestic auto manufacturers. It seemed that every carmaker was working toward the development of an aluminum engine, and the folks at Chrysler were certainly

in the middle of that effort. From the beginning, Chrysler designed the Slant Six family so that the engines could be produced in either cast iron or aluminum. Aluminum not only offered the advantage of lower weight, but the metal could be machined faster than cast iron, so fewer machining lines would be needed, thus reducing machining costs.

At that time, there were actually four Slant Six engines in the works: the 170 and 225, both in cast iron and aluminum. The aluminum cylinder head design was similar to its cast-iron counterpart, but the aluminum head had larger head-bolt bosses, as well as provisions for valve-seat inserts. Unfortunately, at that time there were no high-volume foundries with experience in aluminum cylinder head casting. Also, early aluminum heads had shrinkage and porosity

problems, and so never made it into production.

Slant Six aluminum blocks also posed some challenges for Chrysler but despite delays for 1960, they did make it into production in 1961 and 1962. On aluminum blocks, iron cylinder liners (or sleeves) were cast in place. Although these liners were not intended to be serviceable, the cylinders could be bored oversize during an overhaul. The camshaft used no bearings, riding directly against the aluminum surface of the block, much like today's engines with overhead camshafts and aluminum cylinder heads.

The main bearing saddles used steel inserts, cast into the block, as a means of keeping the desired main bearing clearance in check throughout the range of operating temperatures (aluminum has a considerable thermal expansion and contraction rate). This made for better bearing retention and, overall, a stronger bottom end.

Because of the problems Chrysler encountered with manufacturing aluminum cylinder heads, all production aluminum block Slant Six engines use cast-iron cylinder heads that are interchangeable with those used on iron block engines. Unlike cast-iron blocks, which have a solid-deck surface, the water jackets of the aluminum blocks are open at the top, and require special head gaskets. Head gasket sealing is critical on aluminum block engines, for if a leak develops at the top of a water jacket, the coolant

The cylinder liners were cast in place and cannot be removed.

Iron main bearing saddles help to ensure bottom-end integrity.

can easily track into an oil return passage. Coolant in the crankcase will quickly destroy the bottom end.

Now a hotrodder might think that an aluminum block would make a great foundation for a performance engine build-up because of the significant weight saving over a cast-iron block.

Unfortunately, the limitations of an aluminum block are quickly realized in a high-performance application. An aluminum block's main saddle webbing will not take a great deal of punishment, and since the top of the block is completely open there is not nearly enough support for the tops of the

cylinders. Although aluminum blocks hold up fine under stock usage, they lack the strength and rigidity necessary for any type of serious high-performance application.

Hyper-Pak Engines

Throughout the 1960s, Chrysler equipped Slant Six engines with either Holley or Carter one-barrel carburetors. However, in the early '60s, a few Slant Sixes were equipped with a dealer-installed package known as the "Hyper Pak." Designed primarily for racing, the Hyper Pak featured a Carter AFB four-barrel carburetor, an intake manifold with much longer runners, a high lift (.430 inches), long-duration camshaft (276/268 degrees with 52 degrees overlap), valve springs with dampers, stiffer pushrods, 10.5:1 compression (this only in race engines destined for Daytona International Speedway), and dual exhaust manifolds. This package was available only on the 170 engine in 1960, but was available on both the 170 and 225 in 1961. Cars with the Hyper Pak engines were extremely rare nearly 40 years ago, when they were new. Today they are practically nonexistent.

Changes Over the Years

Chrysler made only a few changes to the Slant Six during the 1960s. Early engines were known to have ring sealing trouble, but Chrysler quickly remedied that malady. The 1960 Valiant came with the alternator mounted on the left side of the engine, the same as larger Dodge and Plymouth models. From 1961 on, all models had alternators mounted on the right side of the engine. In 1963 the crankcase road draft tube gave way to the first emissions control device, a positive crankcase ventilation (PCV) valve. Also, in 1964 the large diameter temperature sending unit that had been used up to that point was dropped in favor of the small temperature sender that is common today.

Perhaps the most noteworthy change to the Slant Six engine occurred with the 1968 model year.

The Hyper Pak engine package transformed this early Slant Six into a real performer. (Reprinted with permission of the DaimlerChrysler Corporate Historical Collection)

The large temperature sending unit, which was used through 1963 ...

... was replaced by a smaller sending unit in 1964.

From the beginning, the Slant Six crankshaft flange was of a six-bolt configuration. Like the crank flanges on Chrysler V-8 engines, the bolts are unevenly spaced so that the bolt holes in the flywheel or flex plate will line up in only one position. The bolt pattern is not quite the same between six- and eight-cylinder engines, however, for only five of the six holes are positioned alike. Therefore, it is impossible to interchange flywheels and flex plates between six- and eight-cylinder engines.

Also, Slant Six engines used through the 1967 model year have a much smaller flywheel/flex plate centering lip on the crank flange, and the torque converter pilot area is smaller than that on nearly all V-8 engines. For the 1968 model year, the flywheel/flex plate centering lip and torque converter pilot area were enlarged to the same size as those on the V-8 engines. The bolt pattern of the flange remained the same, and the small pilot hole in the center of the

crank used to support the input shaft of manual transmissions did not change, either.

As to interchangeability, if you are a) swapping an engine from 1967 or earlier into a car from 1968 or later, or b) swapping an engine from 1968 or later into a car from 1967 or earlier, you will encounter some interchangeability problems. If the vehicle has a manual transmission, you will need the correct flywheel for the engine you are using. Because the bolt pattern of the crank flange did not change, it is possible to bolt a 1968 or later flywheel to the flange of a 1967 or earlier engine. However, this is not advisable, because the hole in the middle of the flywheel is much larger than the centering ring on the flange. If the flywheel is not properly centered, it can throw the engine out of balance, resulting in a horrible vibration and damage to the crankshaft and bearings. You must remember to install a pilot bushing in the crankshaft of the new engine if there isn't one already there.

If the vehicle has an automatic transmission, things become a bit more complex. Not only will you need the proper flex plate for the engine you are using, but you will also have to change the torque converter due to the difference in size of the pilot recess in the crank flange. While it is physically possible to bolt a 1968 or later engine with the proper flex plate into a 1967 or earlier car, the small snout on the early torque converter will not center itself inside the large crank flange opening of the later engine. If the torque converter is not properly centered, the resulting imbalance can cause vibration and damage to the crankshaft, bearings, torque converter, and transmission pump.

It is possible to purchase a spacer that fills the void between the small torque converter hub and the larger opening in the crank flange, allowing the early torque converter to be properly mated to the later crankshaft. Contact Ed Yost at Wildcat Auto Wrecking in Sandy, Oregon (503-668-7786).

If you are installing a 1967 or earlier engine into a 1968 or later vehicle, there is no way (short of custom

machine work) to mate the late torque converter to the early crankshaft. Swapping in an early torque converter would seem to be a simple solution, but around the same time that the crankshaft flanges changed, the input shaft splines on the A-904 transmissions changed also, making it impossible to interchange between early and late torque converters. The only way around this dilemma is to use an early transmission, too. Keep in mind, however, that all Chrysler automatic transmissions used through the 1965 model year were cable actuated. It wasn't until 1966 that shift linkage replaced the cables, so your choices of transmission donors are limited. Perhaps an easier solution would be to install a crankshaft from 1968 to 1976 in the early Slant Six, then drop it into the car and bolt it up.

Some interesting changes came to the Slant Six engines in the 1970s. For the 1970 model year, the 170 cubic-inch engine was dropped and replaced by a 198 cubic-inch engine. The 198 shared the same block as the 225, so it was now impossible to be certain of the displacement without reading the numbers from the identification pad on the block. Like the 170 and 225, the 198 has a 3.4-inch bore, and its stroke measures 3.625 inches. Because the block is the same, the only pieces that are specific to either a 198 or a 225 cubic-inch engine are the crankshaft and connecting rods.

As any car buff knows, in the early 1970s the Environmental Protection Agency was beginning to make life difficult for carmakers. Although Slant Sixes are fairly clean running engines, Chrysler made some changes in the interest of complying with federal emissions regulations. By 1972 it was apparent that leaded gasoline was on the way out. Oil companies had added tetraethyl lead to gasoline primarily because it provided a cheap way for them to increase the gasoline's octane rating. As a side benefit, lead also provided lubrication for an engine's exhaust valves. Without this lead, the exhaust valves and their seats would wear more rapidly, and eventually the valves would most likely burn or recede into the heads.

In the 1972 model year, Chrysler began induction-hardening the exhaust seats in anticipation of the disappearance of lead from gasoline. A short while later, it added an exhaust gas recirculation valve, and electronic ignition was standard equipment from 1973 on. The camshaft profile was changed in the interest of lower emissions (but at the expense of performance), and a new Holley one-barrel carburetor replaced the carburetors used previously. In addition, Chrysler eventually dropped the 198, leaving the 225 as the only six-cylinder engine available.

For the 1975 model year, a new style cylinder head appeared on the Slant Six. Although Chrysler had used a few different cylinder head castings up to that point, the differences were subtle. This new head used 5/8-inch spark plugs instead of the larger 13/16-inch plugs used previously, and the removable aluminum spark plug tubes that had been used with all the earlier heads were also gone. Additionally, the rear-most rocker shaft bolt was now of a stepped design, with a 9/16-inch head and 3/8-inch shank, but 5/16-inch threads. The corresponding hole in the rocker shaft was drilled so that only this bolt could fit that hole, preventing the shaft from being accidentally installed backward and ensuring that the rocker arms would be sufficiently lubricated.

In 1977, more big changes came for the Slant Six. First, Chrysler introduced the Super Six engine. A new intake manifold allowed a recalibrated version of the Carter two-barrel carburetor from the 318 engine to be bolted to the Slant Six. Early two-barrel manifolds had been constructed from two pieces of aluminum. Porosity problems with this manifold were known to cause mysterious vacuum leaks, and a better quality cast-iron manifold replaced the aluminum. Special transmission kickdown linkage was needed for these Super Six engines.

The other major change centered on the crankshaft, but also involved the rods and block. All Slant Six engines used through the end of the 1976 model year had forged steel

crankshafts, but for 1977 cast crankshafts replaced the forged units. In order to strengthen the cast cranks, the rod and main journals were narrower than on the earlier crankshafts. Narrower rod journals meant that the rods and rod bearings had to be narrower, and narrower main journals necessitated blocks with narrower main saddles and narrower main bearings. As to interchangeability, any 1977 or later cast crank engine will interchange with any 1968 through 1976 forged crank engine with no troubles. However, individual pieces such as blocks, crankshafts, and rods cannot be interchanged.

It was also about this time that Chrysler changed the method of distributor retention. Early distributors, whether they were for points ignition or electronic ignition, had a steel plate bolted to the under side. The hold-down bolt passed through a slot in this plate and threaded into the block. Later a ring was bolted to the distributors in the same manner as the plate, and a fork-shaped hold-down bracket (similar to those used on V-8 engines) secured the distributor to the engine block. The early arrangement used a 1/4-inch diameter bolt, while the later style used a 5/16-inch diameter bolt. Early distributors can be used in later blocks and vice-versa, provided the proper distributor attaching hardware is used.

In 1981, more changes came to the Slant Six with the introduction of yet another cylinder head. All Slant Six rocker covers through 1980 can be interchanged, but this latest head required a new rocker cover that was not interchangeable with earlier covers. On 1981 and later engines, Chrysler calls for the use of a composition-style head gasket instead of the steel gasket used up to that point.

The big news for 1981 was the replacement of solid lifters and camshafts with hydraulic lifters and camshafts. Traditionally, hydraulic lifters receive oil from an oil gallery that passes through the lifter bores. Oil is fed from the lifters, up the pushrods, and finally to the rocker arms. However, in the Slant Six with hydraulic lifters, oil for the valvetrain comes from the rocker shaft, passes

through the rocker arms, and goes down the pushrods to the lifters.

Unfortunately, all good things must come to an end, and midway through the 1987 model year, Chrysler ceased domestic use of the Slant Six engine.

Cylinder Head Interchangeability

All Slant Six cylinder heads are interchangeable – that is, any Slant Six cylinder head can be bolted onto any Slant Six engine. All have the same intake and exhaust port configuration, and all use the same 1.62-inch intake and 1.35-inch exhaust valve diameters. Over the 28 years of Slant Six production, Chrysler used several different Slant Six cylinder head castings, which can be broken down into three basic groups: 1960 through 1974, 1975 through 1980, and 1980 through 1987.

1960 through 1974. This group was characterized by large 13/16-inch sized spark plugs that resided in removable aluminum tubes. Heads used through 1963 had large diameter temperature sending units (previously mentioned), while heads from 1964 and later used the small temperature sender that is commonly seen today. Through 1969, both heater hoses measured 5/8 inch in diameter, but from 1970 on one hose was 5/8 inch, while the other measured 1/2 inch in diameter, requiring that a smaller nipple be screwed into the cylinder head. The threaded hole in the head remained the same size as that used previously. Recall that Chrysler began

Cylinder heads used through the 1974 model year require these aluminum spark plug tubes. They use large 13/16-inch "N" series spark plugs.

induction-hardening exhaust valve seats in 1972 for added longevity in the absence of tetraethyl lead in gasoline. So if you are restoring an early Slant Six car, installing a 1972 through 1974 head with hardened exhaust seats will allow the engine to run trouble free on today's gasoline while maintaining an original appearance.

Also in 1972, Chrysler introduced a new head casting that had the provisions for air injection. Although this head was used primarily on vehicles that needed to meet California emissions standards, it saw use in other applications as well. If it was used on a vehicle with air injection, the air injection tube was connected to a hole in the head just behind the number six exhaust port. Air was injected into this hole and followed internal passages to each of the six exhaust ports. As was the case with later heads (all of which had provisions for air injection), if this head was used in an application that did not call for air injection, a block-off plate was bolted over the hole in place of the air injection tube.

1975 through 1980. All of the heads in this group were intended for use with unleaded fuel, all had provisions for air injection, and all used the smaller 5/8-inch tapered-seat spark plugs with no spark plug tubes. Unfortunately, the pushrods now passed through small holes in the head, making it impossible to remove the lifters with the cylinder head installed. Furthermore, these heads were additionally characterized by a different rocker shaft. Up to that point, the rocker shafts were retained by seven 3/8-inch diameter bolts. Oil was supplied to the cylinder head via pas-

Heads from 1975 and later do not have spark plug tubes. They use smaller 5/8-inch "BL" series spark plugs.

This special stepped rocker shaft bolt helps to ensure that the rocker shaft is installed correctly.

sages in the block, and was also routed through a drilling in the rear-most (number four) cam journal to limit the volume of oil flow to the head. Upon reaching the head, the oil passed into the rocker shaft around the rear-most rocker shaft bolt and through the shaft to the rocker arms. Oil then flowed through the rocker arms and lubricated the valve stems and pushrods.

In order for the holes in the rocker shaft to line up properly with the passages in the rocker arms, the rocker shaft had to be positioned properly on the cylinder head. Chrysler stated that the small flat found on one end of the shaft must be placed toward the front of the engine facing up. Since the shaft could be bolted to the head in any of four different positions, it sometimes happened that the rocker shaft was installed incorrectly. Beginning in 1975, the rocker shaft was attached to the head with six 3/8-inch diameter bolts, and a seventh bolt with a 3/8-inch diameter shank but a reduced thread diameter of 5/16 inch. The rear-most hole in the rocker shaft was drilled accordingly, so the rocker shaft would fit only one way (rendering it idiot proof). The pre-1975 rocker shaft can be used on 1975 and later cylinder heads, but a hardened 5/16-inch diameter bolt is needed at the rear-most attaching point.

If you are swapping between a 1960 through 1974 head and a 1975 through 1980 head, the main hardware considerations are the different rocker shaft and bolt configurations; the possible need of an air injection

The lower front corner of the rocker cover rail on all Slant Six cylinder heads used through 1980 is shaped like this. As such, all rocker covers through 1980 can be interchanged.

hole block-off plate; and the difference in spark plugs, spark plug tubes, and rubber spark plug tube seals. All other major components are the same.

1981 through 1987. This final group of heads saw a slightly redesigned valve cover, the use of a composition-style head gasket, and, in 1981, the introduction of hydraulic lifters in the Slant Six. Consequently, the pushrods and rocker arms were changed, too, since an adjustable valvetrain was no longer needed. A big plus with this new head was that, unlike the 1975 through 1980 head, lifter access was possible, albeit difficult. The pushrods still passed through holes in the head, but these holes were enlarged somewhat so that it was possible for a lifter to be passed through them. Production engines began using composition-style head gaskets at the time this

Cylinder heads from 1981 and later have the rocker cover rail shaped like this, requiring a different rocker cover than the earlier engines.

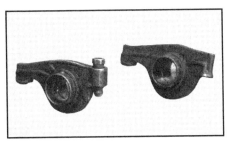

On the left is a 1960-1980 adjustable rocker arm. The non-adjustable rocker arm on the right was introduced in 1981 for use with the hydraulic lifter camshaft.

This block-off plate is used to cap off the air injection passage in the cylinder head.

Heads from 1981 and later have larger pushrod holes. With the head installed, lifter replacement is possible, though difficult.

head was introduced, but this change appears to have nothing to do with the head. I have used the thinner steel head gasket specified for 1980 and earlier engines with the 1981 through 1987 cylinder head and experienced no trouble at all.

When installing this head on a pre-1981 engine, you must use the 1981 and later rocker cover, and you must reuse the adjustable rocker arms and pushrods from the early engine. If you are installing the head on a pre-1975 engine, the same conditions that applied with the 1975 through 1980 head also apply here with regards to the rear-most rocker shaft bolt.

Crankshaft Interchangeability

Unlike some of the various families of V-8 engines, all Slant Six engines were internally balanced. In addition, there doesn't seem to be the trouble of manual transmission pilot holes that are either not drilled or are not finished to size. Every Slant Six crankshaft I have ever encountered has been drilled and finished to size for a pilot bushing. In fact, many times pilot bushings were installed in the crankshafts of engines that were ultimately mated to automatic transmissions. The odds of encountering a problem in this area are remote.

In terms of fit and function, a total of six different crankshafts were used in the Slant Six engine during its nearly three decades of production. From 1960 through 1967 there were essentially two crankshafts – one for the 170 cubic-inch engine with its 3.125-inch stroke, and one for the 225 cubic-inch engine with its stroke of 4.125 inches. A hardened, shot-peened version of the 225 crankshaft was used in some heavy-duty truck applications, but they are rare. Furthermore, they are interchangeable with the standard 225 crankshaft.

For the 1968 model year, the crankshaft flange pilot area was enlarged slightly on both 170 and 225 engines. Because of this, different flex plates and torque converters were used in automatic transmission applications from that point on, while manual transmission applications required different flywheels. However, there was no change to the manual transmission pilot hole or bushing. The new 225 crankshaft remained unchanged through 1976, while the new 170 crankshaft remained unchanged until

Because the 1960 through 1974 engines use spark plug tubes, lifter access on those engines is not much of a problem. Because 1975 through 1980 heads have small pushrod holes, the cylinder head must be removed to gain access to the lifters.

The crankshaft flange configuration used through the 1967 model year has a small 1.95-inch diameter centering ring and a 1.57-inch diameter torque converter hub recess. The centering ring and torque converter hub recess were enlarged in 1968 to 2.15-inch and 1.82-inch diameters respectively.

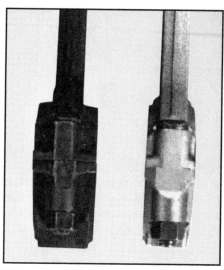

When the cast crankshaft was introduced in 1977, the main and rod journals were made more narrow. On the left is a 1960-1976 connecting rod, while the rod on the right is a 1977-up piece.

that engine was dropped at the end of the 1969 model year. Because there were no other significant changes made to either the 170 or the 225 engines at that time, it is possible to install a 1960 through 1967 crankshaft in a 1968 or later engine, or vice-versa, with respect to engine displacement.

Chrysler introduced the 198 cubic-inch engine in 1970. Its 3.625-inch stroke required yet another crankshaft, which remained unchanged until the demise of the 198 at the end of 1974. Since the engine block and pistons are the same on 198 and 225 cubic-inch engines, a 225 crankshaft can be used in a 198 as long as the 198 rods are replaced with the shorter 225 rods. Doing so will increase the displacement to 225 cubic inches.

From 1975 on, the Slant Six was only available in 225 cubic-inch displacement. Through the 1976 model year, all Slant Six engines used forged-steel crankshafts. Considering the length of an inline six-cylinder crankshaft, and the fact that Slant Six engines have only four main bearings, it might seem that the crankshaft would be a potential weak point in these engines. The fact is, however, that the forged-steel crankshafts found in Slant Six engines through the 1976 model year are stout pieces with rod and main journals of generous diameter and width.

Because the original design of the Slant Six called for aluminum engine blocks as well as cast iron, Chrysler engineers felt that beefy crankshafts would help to ensure the integrity of the bottom end in the aluminum engines, for aluminum is not as rigid as cast iron, and an aluminum block could not support a crankshaft as well as an iron block. Perhaps these crankshafts were a bit of overkill in iron-block engines, but because of this overkill, they are capable of withstanding a great deal of punishment.

In 1977 the forged crankshaft was discontinued from production and replaced with a cast crankshaft. The rod and main bearing journals retained the same diameters that all Slant Sixes had used up to that point, but all journals were made narrower in an effort to strengthen the crankshaft. Narrower rod and main journals required narrower rod and main bearings, as well as narrower rods and main bearing saddles in the block. Therefore, it is impossible to interchange crankshafts, blocks, or rods between forged crankshaft (pre-1977) and cast crankshaft (1977 and later) engines.

Cylinder Block Interchangeability

Although Chrysler produced a number of slightly different casting variations over the years, in terms of interchangeability there were a total of five

Slant Six engine blocks. Aluminum block engines were offered in 1961 and 1962, and were available in both low-deck (170 cubic-inch) and tall-deck (225 cubic-inch) versions. Variation number three was used for the low-deck cast-iron 170 cubic-inch engine. The fourth variation was used for the tall-deck iron 225 cubic-inch engine from 1960 through 1976, and was shared by the 1970 through 1974 198 cubic-inch engine. The final Slant Six block was introduced with the cast crankshaft in 1977 and was used through 1987. It was a tall-deck block that was available only in 225 cubic inches.

Rod and Piston Interchangeability

All Slant Six engines have the same 3.400-inch nominal bore size, and all use the same pistons. Connecting rods are a different story. Chrysler used four different rods in Slant Six engines. The 170 engine used rods measuring 5.707 inches from center to center. The 225 engine used rods that measured 6.699 inches center to center. The 225 rods can be interchanged from 1960 through 1976, but 1977 and later rods have a much narrower big end, a design change brought about by the cast crankshaft. The 198 shares the same tall-deck block as the 225, but because it has a half-inch less stroke, its rods are longer still, measuring 7.006 inches center to center. All Slant Six rods use pressed wrist pins.

Oil Pump Considerations

Stock replacement, high-volume, and high-pressure oil pumps are all available for the Slant Six. In many cases the original pump was retained by six bolts, while the replacement is retained by only five. If you find this to be the case, don't get alarmed. The five-bolt replacement pump should work just fine. When replacing an oil pump, however, you must always compare the new oil-pump gasket to the new pump, then compare it to the mounting flange on your block. There were a couple of variations for the mounting surface of the block, and not all aftermarket oil pumps will seal properly against all blocks.

When an improper seal occurs between the oil pump and the block, on the inlet side of the pump a small gap will allow air to be drawn into the pump along with the oil that is being pulled from the pick-up tube. The pump will develop enough pressure to keep the oil pressure warning light off, and it will appear that everything is okay. But as the pump churns the oil and air together, it is pumping foam through the engine. Since foam doesn't lubricate very well, within just a few miles the engine will be destroyed.

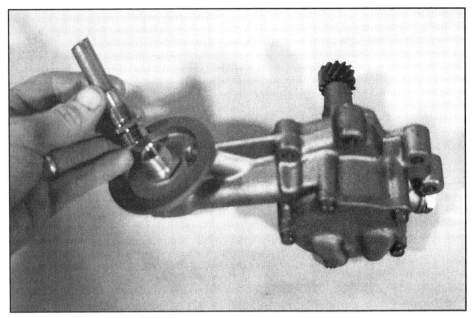

Most replacement oil pumps come with an oil filter nipple installed, but this should always be replaced with a standpipe.

Another critical point to keep in mind with Slant Six oil pumps is the standpipe – the tall pipe that protrudes upward from the oil pump onto which the oil filter is screwed. The standpipe's most obvious function is to provide a means of attaching the oil filter, but it also serves to keep oil in the filter when the engine is not in use. Since the oil filter is mounted upside down, the oil will tend to drain from the filter when the engine is not running. When the engine is first started, it will run for several seconds while the oil pump works to refill the filter. During this time, no oil is being supplied to the bearings or any other part of the engine. Only when the fil-

ter is full will oil begin to flow through the oil galleries to the critical points of the engine.

The standpipe helps to maintain the level of oil in the filter and reduce the effects of gravity on the oil. At the same time, a check valve in the bottom of the standpipe prevents the oil from draining backward from the oil galleries through the filter and pump and into the oil pan. Since most replacement oil pumps are fitted with a short nipple that has no check valve, when replacing an oil pump you should reuse the standpipe from the original pump. Better still would be to install a new standpipe, since over time the check valve often loses its ability to seal properly and block the oil from draining.

Slant Six Performance Modifications

Throughout the nearly three decades of Slant Six production, a few companies have offered high-performance parts for these engines. For example, the Mopar Performance line has catered to the Slant Six enthusiast with camshafts, high-compression pistons, ported cylinder heads, and a host of other goodies. However, the one company that stands at the forefront of six-cylinder performance, is Clifford Research in Corona, California (909-734-3310). Clifford's

When installing an aftermarket oil pump, be sure to check the gasket against both the oil pump and the block. A mismatch in the area shown sometimes occurs and can lead to engine failure.

numerical slogan, "6=8," truly represents the company's commitment to maximizing the potential of six-cylinder engines.

A number of camshaft vendors, including Mopar Performance, Crane, and Racer Brown, have offered a variety of Slant Six camshafts, designed to run the gamut from slightly warmer than stock to wild and woolly. Nearly all are of the solid-lifter variety, so if you intend to install one of these camshafts in a 1981 or later engine you will need to use the pushrods and rocker arms from an earlier engine.

As with any high-performance, big camshaft engine build-up, you should check the piston-to-valve clearance to be certain that there is sufficient clearance to avoid contact when the engine starts to wind up and things really begin to happen. This is seldom a problem with the 225 engine, though, since the pistons normally don't come anywhere near the tops of their bores.

When changing camshafts, it is important for you to know what year cylinder head your engine has. Cylinder heads from 1960 through 1974, and from 1981 through 1987, have large openings for the pushrods and oil returns. With these cylinder heads, it is possible to remove the lifters from the engine with the cylinder head in place. Cylinder heads used from 1975 through 1980 have small holes for the pushrods. These holes are not large enough to remove the lifters; consequently, if you need to remove the lifters, you must first remove the cylinder head.

The production two-barrel intake manifold would certainly be a performance upgrade from the one-barrel manifold used on most Slant Sixes, and this manifold is also available from Mopar Performance. Cast-aluminum four-barrel intake manifolds have been offered by Clifford Research and Offenhauser. The Offenhauser piece is based very closely on the production manifold, with runners which are identical in shape and size to the production model. The Clifford manifold is shaped differently than the factory manifold and offers a greater plenum volume. The Hyper Pak production four-barrel intake manifold was cast with long, nearly equal length runners, reminiscent of the long-ram 413s of the day. Doug Dutra in Sunnyvale, California reproduced a limited quantity of these manifolds a few years ago, and they have recently become available from Clifford as well.

Another noteworthy intake manifold was manufactured by Offenhauser and allowed two production one-barrel

The vast majority of Slant Sixes were originally equipped with one-barrel carburetors.

A 1977-1980 production two-barrel carburetor and intake manifold would offer a performance improvement. If you go this route, be sure to use the proper throttle cable and automatic transmission kickdown linkage.

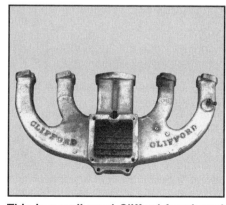

This is a well-used Clifford four-barrel intake manifold.

An Offenhauser four-barrel intake manifold allows a Carter Thermo-Quad to feed this engine. It exhales through a six-into-one header.

The "Dutra Duals" allow the rear three cylinders to breathe through the rear section of a production exhaust manifold and utilizes the entire original exhaust system. The front three cylinders are funneled through a separate manifold and exhaust pipe.

under side of the intake manifold plenum, warming it for better fuel vaporization in cold weather.

The production manifold does a satisfactory job of allowing the exhaust gasses to escape a stock engine, but it is certainly not up to the task of allowing free breathing on a performance engine. In my own experience, using a stock exhaust manifold on a mild street engine caused the power output to falter above 3,000 rpm. The obvious solution would be to install some sort of steel-tube header(s), but there are some real drawbacks that should be considered. What type of driving does the car see? In what type of climate is the car used?

When installing headers on a Slant Six, you can no longer use the factory automatic choke. Your choices are to install a manual choke, rig up an electric choke, or simply eliminate the choke if you live in a warm climate or don't mind a long warm-up time before you leave your driveway.

One way you could possibly have your cake and eat it too would be to purchase a manifold kit from Slant Six aficionado Doug Dutra in Sunnyvale, California. Doug starts with a production exhaust manifold, lops off the front portion just ahead of the exhaust outlet, and caps off the opening. This mates only cylinders number four, five, and six to a common exhaust pipe, while still providing the heat riser and automatic choke functions. He then fabricates a special manifold that mates cylinders number one, two, and three to another exhaust pipe. When "Dutra Duals"

carburetors to feed the engine. Although Chrysler never equipped the Slant Six with fuel injection, in keeping with the times Clifford Research now offers fuel injection for these engines.

The exhaust manifold of a Slant Six engine does more than just funnel the spent gasses from the cylinders into the exhaust pipe. It also provides a point of attachment for the automatic choke coil where it can pick up the heat necessary to time the opening of the choke. Another thermostatic coil located near the exhaust outlet controls the heat riser flapper which directs hot exhaust gas against the

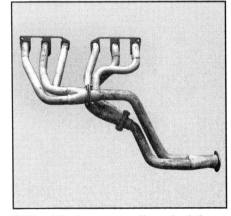

Clifford Performance offers dual three-into-one headers which can then be joined by a Y-pipe.

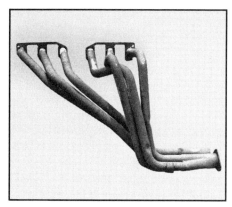
They also offer these long three-into-one headers.

are installed, the rear three cylinders feed into the existing exhaust system, so only one-half of the new dual exhaust system needs to be fabricated. This is a great system for vehicles that are used for daily transportation and have stock or nearly stock engines.

For more serious build-ups, however, steel tube headers are a must. Several of the larger manufacturers have offered headers in a variety of styles for several different car and truck chassis. However, Clifford Research has emerged as the leader. Clifford offers a kit that includes two three-into-one "shorty" style headers.

Dual exhaust can then be run from the collectors on these headers, or they can be joined by the Y-pipe that is included with the kit, and a large single exhaust can be run from its collector. Clifford also offers a package with two long three-into-one headers that extend well beneath the bottom of the firewall. This package performs extremely well, but ground clearance can be a concern and the headers are a tight fit in the area of the clutch linkage on cars with manual transmissions. Several header manufacturers have carried six-into-one headers as well.

Piston selection for Slant Six engines has never been good. For many years it seemed that unless you were willing to drop a large sum of money for specially made custom pistons, you could only choose between cast and forged construction in either the standard size or an appropriate oversize, depending on how far the cylinders needed to be bored. High-compression pistons simply were not available. You could only raise the compression ratio by milling the block deck surface and/or the cylinder head. Thankfully, the deck surface of the head was thick, and at one time Chrysler said that up

to 90/1,000 of an inch could be safely removed from the Slant Six cylinder head! The point is, even with poor piston selection, there is still a lot of room to work with the compression ratio.

When raising the compression ratio, regardless of the means, be sure to check the piston-to-valve clearance. Furthermore, if you are removing several thousandths of an inch from the head and/or block deck surface, and you are using a high-lift camshaft, check for binding between the rocker arms and the edge of the cups on the upper ends of the pushrods. If there is interference here, you could shim the rocker shaft upward. However, a better approach would be to make a set of slightly shorter pushrods using a kit from Mopar Performance. This would ensure sufficient clearance between the rocker arm and the pushrod cup while maintaining acceptable rocker arm geometry.

All of the Slant Six cylinder head groups respond well to performance modifications. Throughout the entire span of Slant Six production, the valve sizes remained unchanged. Intake valves were 1.62 inches in diameter, while the exhaust valves measured 1.35 inches. Early engineering data indicate that these valve sizes were adequate for the 170 cubic-inch engine, but smaller than optimum for a stock 225 cubic-inch engine. Needless to say, if you are planning a serious performance build-up of a Slant Six, you must include some cylinder head massaging. You can realize significant gains in flow by opening up and smoothing the bowl area of both the intake and exhaust ports. In fact, doing a little bowl work, and using the two-barrel carburetor and intake manifold from a 1977 through 1980 Super Six, will really wake up an otherwise stock engine.

The underside of the Slant Six intake manifold seals against the top of the exhaust manifold. Exhaust heat warms the intake manifold plenum. When headers are used the plenum is not heated, which can lead to poor cold-weather driveability. By attaching a flat plate with two fittings to the underside of the intake manifold, coolant can be circulated beneath the plenum.

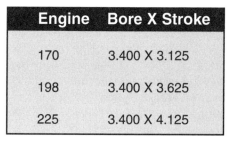

Engine	Bore X Stroke
170	3.400 X 3.125
198	3.400 X 3.625
225	3.400 X 4.125

CHRYSLER PERFORMANCE ENGINES
Early Small-Block A Engines

Chrysler's "small" 318 cubic-inch V-8 engine of the early and mid-1960s was actually spawned in the 1950s. Its design is the result of the evolution of what Chrysler called its "A engine" family. In 1956, the first year of the A engine, its 3.74-inch diameter bore and 3.12-inch stroke gave it a displacement of a modest 277 cubic inches. In 1957, Chrysler increased the bore diameter to 3.91 inches, and with the same 3.12-inch stroke the A engine now displaced 301 cubic inches.

In 1957, the Chrysler Corporation also introduced a 3.31-inch stroke crankshaft. When this new crankshaft was coupled with the larger 3.91-inch diameter bore size, the displacement was increased to 318 cubic inches, and it was in this form that the A engine was carried into the 1960s. If these bore and stroke dimensions look familiar to you, it is because they are the same bore and stroke of Chrysler's later 318 LA engine.

Wide Block 318

The large exterior dimensions of this early 318 cubic-inch engine are somewhat deceiving, considering its relatively small displacement. Although Chrysler dubbed this family of engines as the A engine, the early 318 is known to many as the "wide-block 318" or the "polyspherical 318," referring to the polyspherical shape of the combustion

chambers. Confusion sometimes exists between the A engine family and the LA engine family, with engines in the LA family often incorrectly referred to as "A" engines. DaimlerChrysler has certainly been guilty of this misreference. In much of the company's literature the LA engine is simply referred to as the A engine, and the true A engine as the "old style" A engine. In reality, the true Chrysler A engine was last

The polyspherical 318 is most often thought of in its two-barrel form.

From 1958 through 1962, the 318 was offered with a single four-barrel carburetor.

The polyspherical combustion chamber is certainly not of a conventional wedge design.

used in vehicles sold in the U.S. in 1966. Chrysler replaced it with the 318 cubic-inch LA engine for the 1967 model year. Any mention of an A engine built after the mid-1960s, or in a displacement larger than 318 cubic inches, is actually a reference to the LA engine family.

In the A engine, the rocker covers are retained by only two bolts and the distributor is located at the rear of the engine. All A engines are of the solid-lifter variety, and like all Chrysler engines of the day, the

blocks are meaty castings with forged-steel crankshafts. Most people think of this engine in its mundane two-barrel form, but it was offered with single four-barrel carburetion from 1958 through 1962, and in 1957 Chrysler introduced it in the Fury model with two WCFB four-barrel carburetors and an output rating of 290 horsepower!

The polyspherical head design lends itself well to free breathing and, consequently, to good horsepower potential. In looking at the

combustion chambers, one realizes quickly that this engine is not of a conventional wedge design. The valves are not on the same plane, and the chamber shape is somewhat rounded. This head is of a canted-valve arrangement, sometimes referred to as a "semi-Hemi." Because the valves oppose each other to some degree, this type of combustion chamber promotes excellent exhaust scavenging. Furthermore, angling the valves in this manner helps to straighten the

A dual four-barrel set-up was introduced on this engine in the 1957 Fury.

The canted valve arrangement of a polyspherical engine is obvious when one compares the orientation of the intake and exhaust valve springs.

Mounted on a common shaft, the intake and exhaust rocker arms swing in opposite directions.

Deep notches in the block provide clearance for the intake pushrods.

which feed oil to the cylinder heads. Oil then flows through the rocker shafts to the rocker arms. Spit holes in the rocker arms lubricate the pushrods and valve tips and stems.

The A engine was used through the 1966 model year in B-body intermediate and C-body full-sized cars, as well as in trucks. It was never offered in the A-body compacts, perhaps due in part to its weight, but most likely because of its large physical dimensions and the narrow confines of the early A-body engine compartment.

Despite the performance potential of the polyspherical combustion chamber and the straighter exhaust port it afforded, this engine was never accepted by the automotive community as a serious performance engine. Although it had proven itself in the Fury, the automotive aftermarket failed to offer a good variety of speed equipment for it.

Adding Performance

If you wish to hop up one of these engines, you have to start by scouring the swap meets and classified ads for a used four barrel or, if you really feel lucky, a two-four-barrel intake manifold. Unfortunately, an intake manifold is the only high-performance piece you are likely to find. High-performance camshafts were available from a couple of different cam grinders when this engine was current, but those sources dried up decades ago. If you wish to run steel-tube headers, you will need to have them fabricated from scratch. Due to the differences in exhaust port shape and manifold attaching points, exhaust manifolds and headers for the later LA engines will not fit the earlier A engines.

Through 1961 all V-8 engines were fitted with crankshafts having flat, eight-bolt flanges. In 1962 Chrysler introduced the familiar six-bolt, staggered-pattern flange. If you wish to replace a 1962 through 1966 A engine with a later LA engine, or vice versa, the two families of engines are fairly easy to interchange. The bellhousing bolt pattern and the bolt pattern on the crank flange of the A engine are the same as those on all LA engines, with the exception of the

ports, smoothing out the flow of the spent exhaust gases.

Because the A engines have camshafts with solid lifters, they are equipped with adjustable rocker arms and pushrods with cups on the upper ends. These pushrods are of the same style as those used in Slant Six, early 273, and 1970 340 T/A engines, although the pushrods in the 318 are of a different length than those used in any of these engines. Because of the canted-valve arrangement, the intake and exhaust rocker arms point in opposite directions. Oiling to the upper end of the engine is achieved via passages drilled through the block

This crankshaft flange was used through 1961; 1962 and later engines have crankshafts with the familiar six-bolt staggered pattern and a centering ring for the flex plate/flywheel.

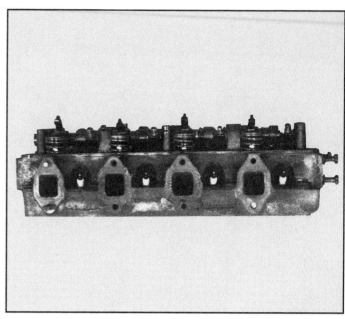

Because the exhaust port configuration of the polyspherical engine is exclusive to this family, exhaust manifolds and headers from any other engine family cannot be used.

1964 through 1967 273, which uses a smaller crank-flange torque converter hub recess.

Since the A engines are internally balanced, a flywheel or torque converter from any of the internally balanced LA engines would work just fine (with the exception of the pre-1968 273 engine, due to the difference in the crankshaft flange). The engine mounting bracket lugs on the sides of the A engine block are the same as on the 273 and 318 LA engines, so bolting the engine into the chassis poses no major hassles.

If you wish to swap between an A engine and a 340 or 360 LA engine, some reworking of the left-side engine mounting bracket will be required. Accessory mounting may require a little creativity, depending on your application. If you encounter a difference in the water pump outlet location, where the A engine has the outlet on the left side and the LA engine has the outlet on the right side (1970 and later), the water pumps can be swapped between these two engines as well, although the ignition timing marks may be difficult to read afterward.

Distributors can also be interchanged between A engines and LA engines, so a dual-point or an electronic-ignition distributor from an LA

engine would work fine on an A engine. The two-barrel carburetors on 273 and 318 engines can also be interchanged with those used on A engines. However, the two-barrel carburetor used on the 360 cubic-inch engine is larger than the one used on the smaller 273 and 318 cubic-inch engines, and will not interchange due to its larger mounting flange and wider mounting-stud spacing. Oil pans can be swapped with 273, 318, and 340 LA engines as long as the correct pick-up tube is used.

The greatest incompatibility you will likely find when swapping between the A engine and LA engine families is the exhaust. As mentioned previously, because of the difference in exhaust port configuration, headers and exhaust manifolds cannot be interchanged between these two engine families.

Internally, the rod bearings on an A engine will interchange with those on any LA engine. Similarly, the main bearings on A engines are the same as those on the 273, 318, and 340 LA engines. The timing chain and gears will interchange as well, as will the oil-pump driveshaft on 1962 and later engines.

Despite the fact that the bore and stroke are the same as the 318 LA engine, the pistons will not inter-

change. Additionally, although the cam journals are the same diameter, camshafts cannot be interchanged, due to a difference in lobe sequencing. In an A engine, the valves are arranged E-I-E-I-E-I-E-I, while in an LA engine the valves are arranged E-I-I-E-E-I-I-E. If you wish to install electronic ignition on an A engine, a Mopar Performance electronic ignition kit for an LA engine will get the job done.

Considering the attributes of the A engine combustion chambers, valve arrangement, and port configuration, one can't help wondering if it is possible to adapt A engine cylinder heads to an LA engine block. After all, LA engines are lighter, more compact, and afford larger displacements than the A engine family. Additionally, parts for LA engines are readily available, and the selection of aftermarket parts like camshafts, pistons, and rings is outstanding.

Unfortunately, the design of the LA engine family was so far removed from that of the A engine family that cylinder head interchangeability was not even a consideration. The differences between the cylinder heads of these two engine families are far from subtle; there is no practical way to interchange them.

CHRYSLER PERFORMANCE ENGINES
Small-Block LA Engines

The Chrysler family of small-block V-8 engines, dating from 1964 through 1992, was actually designated the "LA engine" family. As noted in Chapter 2, many people refer to this family of small-blocks as A engines, but this brings some confusion when the true A engines, dating from 1956 through 1966, are brought into the discussion. For clarity, we will refer to the later family of small blocks by Chrysler's designation, LA engine, instead of the misleading nickname A engine.

Detroit's compact cars of the early 1960s were a great success in the marketplace. Ford's Falcon and Chevrolet's Chevy II and Corvair were doing well, and Chrysler's refinement of the Dodge Dart and Plymouth Valiant for the 1963 model year sent public demand for these cars to stellar levels. The evolution of the compacts and resultant birth of the pony car in 1964 were simply a natural progression. Lee Iaccocca, who was a Ford styling engineer in

those years, designed the Mustang, which was little more than a reskinned Falcon intended to appeal to the younger car buyers of the day.

Meanwhile, however, the engineers at Plymouth were busy doing a little reskinning of their own. The sheet metal of the Valiant was reworked into what became the Barracuda, a fastback with a large wrap-around rear window and a fold-down rear seat. While the Barracuda never reached the sales volume of the Mustang, it did beat the Mustang into the showrooms by a couple of weeks.

The base engine in the Barracuda remained a six cylinder, but early in the planning stages Chrysler realized that in order to appeal to the youthful segment of the car buying public the Barracuda needed a V-8 option. Chrysler's small V-8, the polyspherical 318 cubic-inch A engine, was deemed unsuitable for these new lightweight, agile cars with cramped

engine quarters. A smaller, lighter engine was needed, and so came the birth of the 273 cubic-inch V-8 LA engine in 1964. The bore and stroke of the 273 measure 3.63 inches by 3.31 inches respectively.

Chrysler offered this new engine in both the Dodge Dart and the Plymouth Barracuda, along with the newly introduced A-833 four-speed

Early 273 engines use 5/16-inch diameter intake manifold bolts, while late 273s and all other LA engines use 3/8-inch diameter bolts.

manual transmission. The 273 cubic-inch engine was introduced with two-barrel carburetion, but by 1965 it could be ordered with a Carter AFB in place of the small two barrel. Despite its small displacement, this engine delivered adequate power, and the Dart and Barracuda so equipped quickly gained reputations as well-balanced, fun cars to drive.

Throughout the 1960s Chrysler engineered a number of car packages intended for drag racing. Max Wedge cars and Hemi-powered super-stockers were the best known, but Dodge also offered an interesting package on its 1966 Dart. It seems that Chrysler was interested in having the Dart dominate the drag racing D class, and so designed a car for that purpose. Among other modifications, the 273 received high-compression pistons, a 700 CFM Holley carburetor, steel-tube headers, a radical camshaft, and a 275-horsepower rating. Additionally, the rear axle was fitted with a very steep, numerically high axle ratio. Available with a four-speed transmission only, this package was known as the D-Dart. An obscure package in its day (and despite the findings and writings of Chrysler historians over the last few decades), today it is practically unheard of.

For the 1967 model year Chrysler introduced a sister to the 273, a new version of the LA engine with a displacement of 318 cubic inches. The bore of this new 318 measured 3.91 inches, while the stroke remained the same as the 273 at 3.31 inches. The new 318 LA engine had the same bore and stroke measurements as the 318 A engine it replaced. It was available in two-barrel form only. Nearly every part of the 318 is interchangeable with the 273, and from the outside it is impossible to distinguish one from the other without looking at the numbers on the block. In fact, due to the difference in bore sizes, the blocks, pistons, and rings are just about the only pieces that cannot be interchanged between the 273 and 318 LA engines.

In 1968, Chrysler introduced hydraulic lifters into the LA engines. Up to that time, all had solid lifters with adjustable rocker arms for adjusting valve lash. With the new lifters came new non-adjustable stamped steel rocker arms and new pushrods. Additionally, cast-iron crankshafts were first used in 1968 model 273 and 318 cubic-inch engines. Unlike later cast crank engines of larger displacements, all 273 and 318 engines with cast crankshafts are internally balanced, as are their steel crank counterparts, so the interchangeability of complete engines is not a problem.

The big news for 1968, however, was the birth of the 340 cubic-inch LA engine. This was the first small-block designed as a performance engine from the start. The bore measured 4.04 inches, while the stroke stayed the same as the 273 and 318 engines at 3.31 inches. The 340 was available with the Carter AVS four-barrel carburetor only. The intake runners and intake ports were larger than those of the 273 and 318 engines, and the intake valves measured 2.02 inches in diameter. These valves seem huge when compared to the 1.78-inch intake valves of the 273 and 318 engines.

The same considerations were made on the exhaust side. While the 273 and 318 made do with 1.50-inch exhaust valves, the new 340 received 1.60-inch exhaust valves, larger exhaust ports, and special free-flowing exhaust manifolds. The cam profiles selected for the 340 were aggressive for production passenger cars with automatic transmissions, but the engines destined for cars with manual transmissions received even hotter cams. All of these factors, when coupled with a compression ratio of 10.5:1, resulted in legendary performance on the street and racetrack alike.

The lower end of the 340 was strengthened somewhat over its 273 and 318 cubic-inch sisters. Although the 340 shared the same stroke, main-journal diameter, and rod-journal diameter with its sisters, it received a stronger forged-steel crankshaft, different rods with floating wrist pins, a double-roller timing chain and sprockets, and a windage tray. The left-side engine mounting ears, to which the engine mounting bracket attached, were also reconfigured slightly. For that reason, the new 340 required a

Through 1967, 273 engines used solid-lifter camshafts with adjustable rocker arms.

This is the crankshaft flange of a 1964-1967 273 engine. The flywheel/flex plate centering ring measures 2.15 inches in diameter, the same as on all 1962 and later V-8 engines. The torque converter hub recess measures only 1.57 inches across. In 1968 the 273 torque converter hub recess was enlarged to 1.82 inches in diameter, the same as on all other 1962 and later V-8 engines.

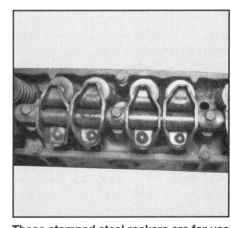

These stamped steel rockers are for use with hydraulic lifters and are the most commonly seen LA engine rockers.

different left-side engine mounting bracket (although it is possible to modify a 273/318 left-side bracket to work with the 340).

Many external pieces can be interchanged between the 340 and 273/318 engines. The oil pan, timing chain cover, water pump, rocker covers, distributor, and all brackets and pulleys (with the exception of the left-side engine mounting bracket) were all carried over to the 340. Also, the rocker arms, rocker shafts, pushrods, oil pump pick-up tube, and lifters are among the internal pieces that can be interchanged.

The only noteworthy change for 1969 was that all 340s, regardless of transmission type, received the camshaft that had been used in the 1968 automatic transmission applications. This camshaft was used in all 340 engines from this point forward.

In 1970, Chrysler made some changes to the entire LA engine family. First, the 273 engine was dropped from the A engine lineup. On the 318 and 340 engines, the cast-iron water pump, which had the lower radiator hose nipple on the driver's side, was superseded by an aluminum pump with a relocated lower radiator hose nipple that moved the hose to the passenger's side of the engine. Obviously, this necessitated that the lower nipple on the radiator be moved to the passenger's side, but it also meant that the timing marks had to be moved as well. Before 1970, the timing marks had been on the passenger's side, but with the lower radiator hose repositioned, the timing marks would be difficult to read. Therefore, a new timing chain cover and crankshaft balancer were needed in order to relocate the timing marks to the driver's side. Furthermore, beginning in 1970 a larger diameter bypass hose was used, which required a larger nipple at the front of the intake manifold.

In 1970 Chrysler came out with the 340 T/A engine, which was used in the Plymouth AAR 'Cuda and Dodge Challenger T/A models only. The T/A engine block can be easily identified by the letters "TA" cast into the side of the block immediately following the numerals "340." These blocks were of a thicker casting than the standard

340, and they had additional material in the main bearing webbing for more strength. Because of this, they weighed approximately 20 pounds more than the standard 340 blocks.

T/A engines also had special cylinder heads in which the pushrod holes for the intake valves were moved slightly. This was done in order to smooth out the dogleg hump in the intake ports that is common to all pro-

duction LA engine heads. Relocating the pushrod holes required special rocker arms because of the different operating angle of the intake pushrods, and although the T/A engines used hydraulic camshafts, they used adjustable rocker arms.

The induction system of the T/A engines consisted of an intake manifold topped with three Holley two-barrel carburetors. The center carburetor

The 340 T/A engine was the only LA engine to use an adjustable valvetrain with a hydraulic lifter camshaft. Though similar to the 273 adjustable pieces, the T/A engines feature special offset intake rockers that work in conjunction with the relocated pushrod holes in the heads. (Photo by Larry Charney)

340 T/A engines were fed by a trio of Holley carburetors. Only the center carburetor was used under normal driving conditions, while the outer carburetors were opened by vacuum as the engine demanded additional volume.

was used during all modes of operation, while the outer carburetors were used only at wide-open throttle, and were actuated by the venturi vacuum signal generated in the center carburetor. Using vacuum to operate the outer carburetors ensured that they would be in operation only when the engine needed the extra volume of fuel/air mixture. This provided for massive flow potential without the threat of overcarburetion, which would likely have occurred had the outer carburetors been actuated by progressive linkage.

For the 1971 model year the 340 T/A engine was dropped, as were the AAR 'Cuda and Challenger T/A models in which it was used. The Carter AVS carburetor, which had been used on all other 340 engines up to that point, was replaced by the Carter Thermo-Quad. The AVS was of a square-bore design, meaning that the primary and secondary throttle bores were nearly identical in diameter. The Thermo-Quad, however, had relatively small primary throttle bores and huge, 2.25-inch secondary throttle bores. The thinking here was that small primaries would offer good air velocity through the venturis and, therefore, a strong vacuum signal for good fuel atomization. This would ensure crisp low-speed throttle response and acceptable emissions, while the huge secondaries would ensure that there was no loss of performance potential at wide-open throttle. In fact, a Thermo-Quad can easily outflow an AVS carburetor. It is ironic that at the same time the Thermo-Quad was introduced, the free-flowing exhaust manifolds that had been used through 1970 were replaced by new manifolds that were somewhat more restrictive.

In 1971, Chrysler also introduced the 360 cubic-inch LA engine. The 360, with a bore and stroke of 4.00 inches by 3.58 inches respectively, is the only production LA engine that does not have a 3.31-inch stroke. All 360 engines came with cast crankshafts, and all were externally balanced, meaning that some of the weight needed to balance the crankshaft was actually moved to the crankshaft balancer and flywheel or torque

Although the 273/318 left-side engine mounting bracket is wider than the 340/360 piece, with a little fabrication it can be made to work.

Depending on the body style of the car and the exhaust system used, many times the factory installed a right-angle oil filter adapter.

The 273/318/340 rear main bearing cap features a large arch against which the oil pan end seal fits.

converter. For this reason, balancers and torque converters cannot be interchanged with other engines unless special consideration is given to engine balance.

The main journal diameter of the 360 was increased from 2.50 inches to 2.81 inches for the sake of reliability and durability with the cast crankshaft. Because of the larger main journals the main bores in the block are larger, so a redesigned rear main cap was needed. As a result, 360 engines require a different oil pan than all other LA engines. The 360 has the same 9.599-inch deck height and uses the same 6.123-inch connecting rod length as all other LA engines. In order to accommodate the longer stroke, the wrist pins are located higher in the pistons.

The cylinder heads used on the new 360 engine were nearly identical to the 340 heads in terms of port size and shape. They used the same 1.60-inch diameter exhaust valve as the 340, but had a smaller 1.88-inch diameter intake valve. The two-barrel intake manifold used on the 360 was different than that used on the 318. Not only were the ports larger, but the carburetor mounting flange was also larger and the carburetor mounting studs were spaced further apart than on the 318, for the 360 used the same size carburetor as found on 361, 383, and 400 cubic-inch big-block engines.

The rear main bearing cap of the 360 was redesigned and has a much smaller arch.

A pre-1972 crankshaft pulley has been placed on a 1972-up damper. Note the mismatched hole.

Because of this difference, the rear portion of a 273/318/340 oil pan looks like this ...

... while the same portion of a 360 pan looks like this.

By 1972, compression ratios were falling and cam profiles were becoming more tame in order to comply with the emission regulations of the Environmental Protection Agency (EPA). It was around this time that odd-looking additions such as exhaust gas recirculation (EGR) valves, air injection systems, and charcoal vapor canisters, and their miles of vacuum hose, began to appear. Oil companies had discovered decades earlier that adding tetraethyl lead to gasoline provided an inexpensive way of increasing the octane rating in order to quell detonation. As an important side benefit, the lead additive also provided lubrication for an engine's exhaust valve faces and seats. Without this lead, the exhaust valves were prone to burning, and the seats

wore out more rapidly, causing the exhaust valve head to recede into the seat.

By 1972, however, the advent of catalytic converters was on the horizon, and given the tendency of lead to coat things, carmakers realized that leaded fuel would not be compatible with catalytic converters. Furthermore, the EPA was warning that lead in gasoline was an unacceptable air pollutant. It was apparent that the days of leaded gasoline were numbered. Starting in 1972, Chrysler began induction-hardening the exhaust valve seats in preparation for the use of low-lead and unleaded fuels. Harder valves made of higher quality material also appeared.

In 1972, the 340 began sharing cylinder heads with the 360, losing not only its high-compression ratio, but also its 2.02-inch intake valves. Although it

seemed that the 340 had been castrated, the new lower compression ratio pistons and hardened exhaust seats of the 360 heads made this version of the 340 more suitable for the no-lead/low-octane fuels to come.

Also in 1972, the bolt pattern of the crankshaft pulley was changed on all V-8 engines. All crank pulleys are retained by six bolts, but through 1971 one of these bolts was offset slightly. For 1972, all six bolts were evenly spaced in a symmetrical pattern. For this reason, 1972 and later pulleys cannot be simply swapped with earlier pulleys. Should you encounter a mismatch between pulley and damper bolt patterns, you can use a rattail file and elongate one hole in the pulley into an oval shape, then weld the unused portion of the hole closed. You must be sure to grind the weld so that the pulley sits flush against the face of the damper and the underside of the bolt head sits flush against the pulley.

In its last year, 1973, the 340 lost its forged-steel crankshaft in favor of a cast crankshaft. The 1973 340 is the only 340 that is externally balanced, but the amount of weight necessary to balance this engine is different than that of any other externally balanced engine. Therefore, the same regard to crankshaft balancers and torque converters applies here as with the 360. They cannot be swapped with other engines unless special consideration is given to this balance.

As the 1970s marched on, the EPA tightened its grip on the automakers, and not much in the way of new car excitement came from Detroit. By the late 1970s the 318 had received a four-barrel carburetor in police applications. This was the first time the 318 LA engine had ever received anything other than a two-barrel carburetor, and the first time since the mid-1960s that a small runner four-barrel LA engine intake manifold had been used at all. At the end of 1978, with the demise of the big-block engines, the LA engine no longer used the large thermostat that it had shared with the B and RB engine families. Beginning in 1979, the LA engine used the same small thermostat as the Slant Six, and had a stamped steel thermostat housing in place of the cast-iron and cast-aluminum housings that had been used up to that point.

Although by the mid-1970s the EPA was cracking down on automobile tailpipe emissions, it hadn't been as strict with light trucks. In 1978, trucks were not yet required to have catalytic converters. Furthermore, once the EPA certified the emissions of a particular engine package for passenger car use, it allowed a number of changes for that same package to be used in light trucks without requiring the manufacturer to run the entire certification cycle.

Chrysler saw this loophole as a window of opportunity, and in 1978 it released the "Li'l Red Express Truck." This truck, which was available in 1978 and 1979 only, was the last hurrah for the high-performance carbureted LA engine. The 1978 Li'l Red Express Truck was powered by a 360 with the old 340 camshaft and a Thermo-Quad carburetor, and the exhaust was passed through functional dual-exhaust stacks on each side of the bed.

Today, nearly all auto manufacturers offer some type of sport truck, and with seemingly endless varieties of Dakota R/Ts, Cyclones, and Lightnings, to name a few, the Li'l Red now seems like a marketing concept that was a few years ahead of its time. In the late 1970s, however, trucks were still largely thought of as utilitarian vehicles. Despite the fact that it was only available for two years, the Li'l Red Express Truck was nevertheless a trend setter. When comparing its quarter-mile

elapsed times with that of other 1978 trucks, Li'l Red crushed the competition, including the Ford 460 and the Chevrolet 454 cubic-inch trucks.

In 1979 Chrysler fitted the Li'l Red Express Truck with a catalytic converter, and the 340 camshaft was dropped in favor of the more emissions-friendly 360 camshaft. Original plans for the Li'l Red called for the use of Direct Connection W-2 cylinder heads. Using these heads on a production vehicle had two positive sides. First, W-2 race heads would enhance the performance of these trucks. Second, the Chrysler racing program strongly pushed for their use because doing so would also legalize them for stock classes in drag racing. The first prototype truck fitted with these heads ran a scorching 13.76 quarter-mile elapsed time at 119 miles per hour! For various reasons, however, the W-2 cylinder heads never made it into production.

The EPA's emission regulations continued to tighten as time passed, and during the 1980s on-board computers began to control more of a vehicle's functions. Carburetors with computer-driven mixture control solenoids appeared, and for 1986 the Carter Thermo-Quad carburetor was replaced by the Rochester Quadra-Jet carburetor on 360 cubic-inch engines. Carburetors were replaced by throttle-body type electronic fuel injection on 318 cubic-inch engines in trucks in 1988, while the last of the rear-wheel-

drive cars retained carburetors. In 1989, the 360 lost its Quadra-Jet in favor of electronic fuel injection. Throttle body fuel injection remained on the 318 LA engine through 1991 and on the 360 through 1992.

It is interesting to note that in the late 1980s, research and development of cylinder head port and combustion chamber configurations led to designs that promoted good fuel atomization and combustion, which not only helped reduce emissions, but also increased performance. In fact, it has been argued that the 1989 through 1991 360 head is at least as good as, if not better than, the early 340 head in terms of port flow and performance potential.

Aside from the evolution of cylinder heads in the 1980s, the only drastic internal change happened in 1988,

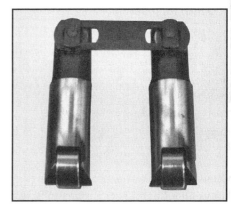

Manufacturers of aftermarket roller lifter camshafts typically link their lifters together to keep them from turning in their bores.

When Chrysler began using roller lifters in the LA engines, they machined flats in the upper portion of the lifter bodies.

Yokes placed over the lifter bodies align with these flats and keep the lifters from turning.

The yokes are held in place by a sheet metal "spider" that attaches to these bosses in the lifter valley.

when roller lifters replaced the flat lifters used up to that point in 318 engines. The 360 engine received roller lifters in 1989. The purpose of roller lifters is to eliminate the friction between the cam lobe and lifter face. Roller lifters must be properly aligned and prevented from turning. Aftermarket manufacturers of roller cams typically link the lifters together in pairs to keep them aligned, but Chrysler chose to accomplish this by using yokes that align with flats on the lifter bodies. The yokes are held in place by a "spider" made of spring steel and bolted to bosses cast into the lifter valley. New cylinder block castings were needed to accommodate all of this new hardware, since non-roller cam blocks will not accept the roller lifter yokes and have no provisions to attach the spider.

Because roller lifters are taller than standard hydraulic lifters, shorter pushrods were also used, but the rocker arms, shafts, and valve hard-

A conventional flat hydraulic lifter and camshaft package can be installed in place of the factory roller set-up. Standard hydraulic lifter pushrods will be needed.

ware all remained the same. It is possible to install a flat-lifter camshaft into a block originally intended for a roller cam and lifters provided the correct pushrods are used and the yokes and spider are omitted. It is not possible, however, to install a production style roller cam and lifters in an engine not originally designed for these pieces.

LA Engine Blocks

Many different LA engine blocks were used between the introduction of the 273 at the beginning of the 1964 model year and the end of 1992, when the Magnum engines replaced the last of the LA engines. From the start, Chrysler employed the newest lightweight casting technology, and the results were strong, compact, relatively light engine blocks.

Because the 273, 318, 340, and 360 all have different bore sizes, they each require a different block. Inside, the 273 and 318 blocks are nearly identical, the only major difference being that the 273 has a 3.63-inch diameter bore, while the bore of the 318 measures 3.91 inches. The 340 is also quite similar, with a 4.040-inch diameter bore size that is larger still, and the different left-side mounting ears. All three of these engines use crankshafts with a 2.50-inch main journal diameter and a 3.31-inch stroke.

Although many of the internal pieces, such as crankshafts and connecting rods, were different between

these engines in production, most can physically be interchanged because they are the same dimensionally. However, they will require proper balancing. The inside of the 360 block is similar to that of the 273, 318, and 340, but with a 4.000-inch bore diameter. The engine mounting ears on the left side of the block are the same as those on the 340, but the webbing at the bottom of the block is different to accommodate the larger 2.81-inch diameter main journals of the new 3.58-inch stroke cast crankshaft. Consequently, no other production crankshaft can be used in a 360 block.

The 1970 T/A block, which was used in the 1970 Plymouth AAR 'Cuda and Dodge Challenger T/A, was at one time the block of choice for those doing serious race engine build-ups. Like all LA engine blocks, the T/A block was originally equipped with two-bolt main caps. The additional material in the webbing of the T/A block not only strengthened the bottom end, but made it easy to add four-bolt main caps. Considering that the T/A block was used in these two cars only, and that it was only a one-year deal, one can easily understand why these blocks were hard to find 30 years ago when they were practically new. Nowadays, these blocks are so scarce and the cars in which they were originally used are so collectible, used T/A blocks trade for serious coin.

It would be foolish to base a performance build-up on a T/A block, assuming you could find one in good condition. The standard blocks are more than adequate for most performance engine builds, and quite acceptable for moderate race engines. If you feel that you need more strength than a standard production block can offer, check the Mopar Performance offerings.

Generally speaking, by the end of the 1970s, cylinder blocks became lighter as the castings became thinner, and some of the material that was shed from the blocks came from the cylinder walls. From the 1960s to the mid-1970s, all 273, 318, and 340 engines had decent castings. The 1971 and 1972 360 engines have blocks that were cast using the 340 water jacket molds. Because the finished bore of a 360 is 0.040 inches smaller than that of a 340, in most cases these early 360 blocks could support up to a 0.100-inch overbore! Before you attempt to bore a block that far, however, have it sonic checked.

From the mid-1970s through 1987 little changed for the 318 and 360 blocks. The 1988 model year saw the introduction of roller lifters, as well as changes in the castings in the areas of the lifter bores and lifter valleys to accommodate the related hardware. Because the roller lifters are much taller than standard mechanical or hydraulic lifters, the lifter bores are taller. Yokes are used to align the lifters, and the tops of the lifter bores are machined to provide seats for these yokes. The yokes are retained by a spring steel "spider" which is bolted to bosses that were added to the middle of the lifter valley. The changes that were incorporated into the LA engine blocks at this time were carried over to the 1992 and later Magnum engines, which also use roller lifters.

LA Engine Cylinder Heads

LA engine cylinder heads can be broken down into two groups: 273/318 heads and 340/360 heads. All heads used on 273 and 318 cubic-inch engines have intake and exhaust valves that measure 1.78 and 1.50 inches in diameter respectively, and combustion chamber volumes typical-

ly measuring in the neighborhood of 60 to 65 cc. Though their intake and exhaust ports are similar to those of the 340 and 360 heads, they are comparatively smaller.

The 1968 through 1971 340 engines use cylinder heads with

For the purpose of comparison, this 340/360 intake manifold gasket has been placed on the intake side of a 360 head.

The difference in port size is obvious when the same gasket is placed on a 318 head.

intake and exhaust valves that measure 2.02 and 1.60 inches in diameter respectively. These heads, with the casting number 2531894, are commonly referred to as "X" heads, because a large X is cast into the heads between two of the spark plug holes. The 1972 and 1973 340 engines received the heads used on the 360 with smaller 1.88-inch diameter intake valves, but the same 1.60-inch exhaust valves. These heads, with casting number 3418915, are known as "J" heads, because a large J is cast into the heads in a manner similar to that of the "X" heads. These 1.88/1.60-inch valve sizes remained in 360 engines through 1992. In addition to the larger valve sizes, 340/360 heads have larger intake and exhaust ports than do the 273/318 heads, and their larger combustion chambers are typically in the 70 to 75 cc range.

The same difference can be seen on the exhaust side when a 340/360 header gasket is placed on the exhaust side of a 273/318 head.

The early 340 "X" head can be identified by the large X cast into the cylinder head next to a spark plug hole. The 340/360 "J" head can be identified by a large letter J in the same location, although it sometimes appears backward.

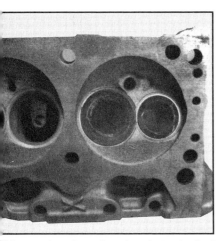

This combustion chamber is typical of the open chambers found in nearly all LA engine heads.

All LA engines use shaft-mounted rocker arms of a 1.5:1 ratio, providing the foundation for a strong, reliable valvetrain. The 1964 through 1967 273 engines use adjustable rocker arms because these engines are equipped with solid-lifter camshafts. The 1970 340 Six Pack/Six Barrel T/A engines also have adjustable rocker arms, although these engines have the standard 340 hydraulic-lifter camshaft. The intake rocker arms in T/A engines have much more offset than those in other engines in order to move the pushrods slightly, providing less encroachment on the intake ports and making room for larger, straighter ports without the "dogleg" inherent in the design of standard LA engine intake ports. All other LA engines share the same stamped steel non-adjustable rocker arms.

There are essentially four different LA engine pushrods. Early 273 engines with solid lifters use pushrods with a ball at the lower end and a cup at the upper end. A ball at the bottom of the rocker arm adjusting screw fits into this cup. The 1970 340 T/A engine uses this same style pushrod, but in a shorter length because the hydraulic lifters are taller than the solid lifters of the 273. In fact, early 273 adjustable rockers can be installed on any LA engine with hydraulic lifters, but custom-length pushrods will be needed due to this difference in the lengths of solid and hydraulic lifters. All other LA engines through 1987 use flat-bottom hydraulic lifters, and all use the same pushrods with a ball at each end. The

1988 through 1991 318 engines and 1989 through 1992 360 engines use hydraulic roller lifters, which are considerably longer than flat-bottom hydraulic lifters. Although the same style pushrods with a ball at each end are used in these engines, they are considerably shorter, again due to the difference in the lengths of the flat-bottom and roller lifters.

In all LA engines, oil is fed to the rocker shafts via a passage in each side of the block. The oil flows from the camshaft bores upward through the block, through the heads, and into the rocker shafts. As oil flows through the rocker shafts it passes through holes in the bottoms of the shafts where it lubricates the rocker arms. Gravity and splash work together to supply oil to the valve tips and stems

and to the pushrods. Proper indexing of the rocker shafts is crucial in order for all of the valvetrain components to receive proper lubrication. Production rocker shafts have a flat – or a "notch" as Chrysler calls it. On the driver's side head, this flat should be positioned downward and toward the front of the engine. On the passenger's side head, it should be positioned downward and toward the rear of the engine.

Because of the difference in port size, 340 and 360 cubic-inch engines have intake manifolds with larger runners than 273 and 318 engines. While it is physically possible to interchange intake manifolds between any LA engines, opinions vary as to whether the large runner 340/360 intake manifolds should be installed on 273 or

LA ENGINES BORE X STROKE

Engine	Bore X Stroke
273	3.630 X 3.31
318	3.910 X 3.31
340	4.040 X 3.31
360	4.000 X 3.58

Year	Engine	Cylinder Head Casting Number
1964-65	273	2465315
1966	273	2536178
1967	273/318	2806213
1968-69	273	2843675
1968-71	318	2843675
1968-71	340	2531894
1970	340-6 T/A	3418915
1971-72	360	3418915
1972-74	318	2843675
1972	340	3481915
1973	340	3671587
1973-74	360	3671587
1975-76	318	3769973
1975	360	3769974
1976	360	3671587-3769974
1977-83	318	4027163-4027593
1977-80	360	4027596-4071051

318 engines because of the mismatch in port size. In theory it is a bad idea, but in practice many hotrodders have achieved good results as long as the larger 340/360 intake manifold gaskets were used.

On the exhaust side, you certainly wouldn't want to mate early 273 or 318 exhaust manifolds, which have small openings, to the larger exhaust ports of 340 or 360 heads. Installing 340 or 360 exhaust manifolds on a 273 or 318 engine, however, creates no problems, despite the fact that the openings in the manifolds are significantly larger than the exhaust ports. In fact, 1968 through 1970 340 exhaust manifolds are about the least restrictive manifolds ever used on LA engines, and they work well on the smaller displacement engines, too. By the mid-1970s, many applications specified the same exhaust manifolds for the 318 and 360 engines. Typical aftermarket headers, most of which have 1-5/8-inch diameter primary tubes, fit all 273, 318, 340, and 360 engines, despite the differences in exhaust port size.

When engineers design an engine, or when an engine is re-engineered by an engine builder, the intended use of the engine is the greatest determining factor in the selection of nearly all parts, and this consideration plays a key role in what machine work should be done. An engine intended for drag racing is built with one type of operation in mind – wide-open throttle. Street engines, on the other hand, see a wide variety of driving conditions. As hotrodders we are always searching for ways to improve wide-open throttle performance, but the fact is that the majority of the time a street engine is in operation it is idling, cruising at low speeds, or maintaining a steady speed at part throttle on open roads. In reality, on the street an engine will spend only a small percentage of its time operating at wide-open throttle. Concessions must be made so that the car will respond in an acceptable manner during all other modes of operation. In street engines there is always a trade-off of some sort – a compromise between all-out power, driveability, economy, cost, and emissions.

As this relates to cylinder heads, valve and port sizes and port shapes are decided with all of these goals in mind. No doubt you have heard the term velocity associated with talk of intake and exhaust ports and intake manifolds. Maintaining the velocity of the fuel/air mixture as it travels from the carburetor to the cylinders is important for even fuel distribution, good throttle response, and good overall driveability. At the risk of over simplification, let's think of an engine as an air pump; it can only pump so much air in a given time at a given engine speed.

Let's compare two engines, one with small intake manifold runners and small port heads, and the other with comparatively large intake manifold runners and large port heads. These two engines are identical in every other aspect. If we operate them at exactly the same speed and load, the air passing through the small intake manifold runners and ports would be doing so at a greater speed, or velocity, than the air passing through the large runners and ports. The engine with large runners and ports might make more power at high speeds at wide open throttle, but the engine with smaller ports and runners would theoretically have better low-speed characteristics and throttle response. (In Chapter 12, "Cylinder Heads and Breathing," we will get into greater depth on this subject and explain velocity more thoroughly.)

Any LA engine cylinder head can be used on any LA engine. With the exception of the 1970 340 T/A heads, which use special rocker arms and pushrods unique to those heads, as long as the same style rocker arms and pushrods of that engine are retained, they will work with whichever cylinder heads are selected. It should be noted that early 273 engines use 5/16-inch diameter intake manifold bolts, while all later engines use 3/8-inch diameter bolts. If we look at the difference in combustion chamber volumes between the 273/318 heads and the 340/360 heads, it is apparent that using a pair of 273/318 heads on a 340 or 360 engine would be an easy way to boost the compression ratio. However, the smaller valve and port

sizes would negate any overall gain i performance. Low-speed throttl response may become a little mor crisp, but midrange and upper RPM horsepower would certainly suffer.

Bolting a pair of 340 or 360 head with 1.88-inch diameter intake valve to a 273 or 318 engine can dramatica ly improve midrange and upper RPM horsepower. However, low-spee throttle response and driveability ma suffer, due largely to the resultant dro in compression ratio, but also becaus the somewhat larger cross sectiona area of the ports doesn't promote quit as much velocity on smaller displace ment engines operating at low speeds Milling 0.060 of an inch from the dec surface of the heads will solve the com pression ratio problem, although it ma then be necessary to mill the intak manifold slightly, too.

If the engine package is complete with a production 340 or 360 four-ba rel intake manifold and carburetor, pair of headers with 1 5/8-inch prima ry tubes, and a mild-performanc camshaft (such as a stock replace ment 340 piece), a 318 can be trans formed into a good all-around stree engine on a shoestring budget. standard low stall speed 273 or 31 torque converter would work, bu using a torque converter with a sta speed in the 2,000 to 2,400 rpm rang would allow the engine to reach it power band more easily and alleviat any poor low-speed driveability symp toms. Reliability, low cost, good drive ability, acceptable economy, and vast ly improved performance are a among the attributes of 273 and 31 engines built this way.

For street engines, you should sta with the 1.88-inch diameter intak valves. Using heads with 2.02-inc diameter intake valves will certainl require bore notches on 273 engines and even the 1.88-inch valves will b tight. You should check for prope valve-to-cylinder wall clearance whe building a 273 using 340/360 heads since the small 3.63-inch bore doesn afford much extra room. The 1.88-inc intake valves and 1.60-inch exhaus valves work fine on 318 engines because they fit easily into the 3.91 inch diameter bore. If you are planning to use 2.02-inch valves, it is a goo

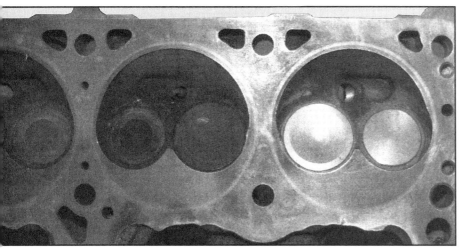

The 1986-1991 318 cylinder head features heart-shaped closed combustion chambers.

These free flowing 1968-1970 340 exhaust manifolds will not cover the air injection holes of later cylinder heads.

In heads intended for use with air injection, a tiny hole beneath each exhaust port runs upward into the port. If headers or non-air injection manifolds are used, these holes must be blocked or eight tiny exhaust leaks will result.

dea to check the valve-to-cylinder clearance on this engine, too. The easiest way to do this is to place the valves into their respective guides, then slip a small piece of vacuum hose over each of the valve stems. Bolt the heads to the empty block, then look up each cylinder from the bottom. Open and close each valve 3/4 of an inch or so while checking the clearance between the head of the valve and the cylinder wall. There should be at least 0.020 or 0.030 inches clearance at all points of valve lift.

The 1964 273 engines use heads with heart-shaped combustion chambers, but all other LA engine cylinder heads through 1985 have open chambers. Heart-shaped chambers reappeared in 1986 on 318 engines and remained through 1991. All 340/360 cylinder heads have open chambers, regardless of the year.

The intake and exhaust port configuration of the LA engine changed very little through 1985, and despite the size difference between 273/318 ports and 340/360 ports, the shape and layout is nearly identical. Although the large 2.02-inch intake valves of the early 340 were replaced by 1.88-inch valves, the configuration of the intake ports remained the same. In fact, it is a common practice to cut larger intake valve seats into a pair of later 340/360 heads so that they will accept 2.02-inch valves. Doing so results in a pair of heads that are essentially the same as the 1968 through 1971 340 "X" heads.

Beginning in 1973, some engines began using heads with provisions for air injection. By 1975 heads of this style

were being used in all applications. In an air injection system, a small amount of air is injected into each exhaust port. This air mixes with the exhaust as it leaves the cylinder and supplies additional oxygen to aid in completing the combustion of the fuel/air mixture. It also helps to ensure that there is adequate oxygen reaching the catalytic converter so that it can do its job and further reduce tailpipe emissions.

The Slant Six, LA engine, and B/RB engine families all route air differently, but ultimately it reaches the exhaust ports. On LA engines, the air is routed from the air injection tubes to the rear of each exhaust manifold. From there, a passage in the manifold runs the length of the manifold, and smaller passages route the air to the cylinder heads,

where small holes located just below the exhaust ports lead the air into the exhaust ports.

You may encounter incompatibilities if you are swapping cylinder heads or exhaust manifolds between engines with and without provisions for air injection, or if you are installing headers on engines with provisions for air injection. When headers or early exhaust manifolds are used with heads that have provisions for air injection, the small holes that lead into the exhaust ports are left uncovered and create eight exhaust leaks. In this situation, the holes must be plugged. If you are mating later manifolds with the additional passages to earlier cylinder heads not intended for air injection, check to be sure that there are no casting bumps that would keep the manifolds from sitting flat against the machined surfaces of the heads. If there are protrusions, you will need to grind them. It certainly wouldn't hurt to plug the four tiny holes in each manifold below the exhaust ports, but the air injection passages inside the manifold are separate from the large passage for the exhaust. Therefore, this should not be necessary unless the manifold is cracked internally or porous.

In the late 1980s and early 1990s, "swirl ports" and "swirl port technology" were the rage. In 1986 a new intake port design was introduced on the 318 engine. This new style cylinder head is the same head on which heart-shaped combustion chambers were re-introduced, but the shape of the combustion chamber has nothing to do with the ability of the intake ports to initiate swirl. Minor changes to the shape of the intake ports, most notably in the ceilings of the ports, causes the fuel/air mixture to swirl like a cyclone as it rushes into the cylinders. This action helps to disperse the fuel evenly in the cylinder, and thoroughly mixes the exhaust gases remaining in the cylinder as well as those from the EGR valve.

With this technology in use, not only were emissions reduced, but performance was also improved. The 360 received this technology in 1988. It has been argued that for street use, the 1988 through 1991 360 heads will outperform even the 1968 through 1971 340 "X" head, despite the difference in intake valve diameter!

Tips For Swapping LA Engines

Engines in Chrysler's LA engine family are largely interchangeable, provided the proper related pieces are used. All LA engines use the same bell housing bolt pattern on the rear face of the block, and all use the same six-bolt staggered pattern for attaching the flywheel or flex plate to the rear of the crankshaft. Through 1967, 273 engines used a flywheel centering ring that was the same size as those used on the other V-8 engines, but a much smaller torque converter hub recess, sized the same as those on the Slant Six engines of that time. The rear crankshaft flanges of all 1968 and later 273 engines were the same as those found on all 318, 340, and 360 engines.

Manual Transmission Pilot Bushing

If your car has a manual transmission, the small pilot hole in the end of the crankshaft of the engine you are swapping in may already have a pilot bushing installed, even if the engine was originally in a car with an automatic transmission. If not, you will need to install one, and it is here that things can get interesting.

Some crankshafts have the pilot bushing hole drilled and finished to the proper size for a standard pilot bushing. This is the case on mos engines with forged-steel crankshafts Some crankshafts have the hole drilled but not properly finished to size. A standard pilot bushing won't fi in the hole no matter how hard you try to persuade it. This typically occurs or engines with cast crankshafts. Here you have a few different options. The textbook methods would be to disas semble your engine and replace the crankshaft with one that has already been finished to size, or take the exist ing crankshaft to a machinist who would finish the hole to the proper size for the correct interference fit of the pilot bushing.

The second alternative would be to modify the pilot bushing, and I've seer some really creative attempts at this involving files, grinders, and even hacksaws! Like the circus announce says, kids, don't try this at home! O course, a competent machinist could turn the bushing and reduce its oute diameter, but he would want to fit the bushing to the crankshaft, so you would need to supply him with eithe the crankshaft or the complete engine if you didn't want to disassemble it.

Fortunately, the folks at NAPA have recognized this as a common trouble spot when swapping Chrysle engines, and they offer a special pilo bushing with a reduced outer diame ter that will fit the unfinished pilot hole of the crankshaft. Because the pilot hole is not finished, however, its sur face is often somewhat rough. A few dabs of thread locking compound wil

If your car has a manual transmission, you will need to install a pilot bushing in your crankshaft.

This 1990s era production pilot bearing fits into the torque converter hub recess of the crankshaft.

Some crankshafts were never drilled for a pilot bushing.

help ensure that the bushing stays out once driven into place.

Another alternative would be to use the roller pilot bearing from a mid- to late-1990s truck with a five-speed manual transmission. This style of pilot bearing uses a roller bearing pressed into the center of an aluminum disc, which is then pressed into the portion of the crankshaft flange where the automatic transmission torque-converter hub would rest if the car was so equipped. When this type of bearing is used, the tip of the input shaft of the transmission still occupies the pilot hole in the end of the crankshaft, but there is no contact, for it rides in the bearing. This bearing is also available from Mopar Performance.

Another possibility would be that there is no pilot hole at all. Although this pitfall is normally encountered only with big-block engines (most notably the 400), it is mentioned here because it has been rumored that there are LA engine crankshafts in existence that have no pilot holes. Although the odds of encountering one are highly unlikely, should you run across such an engine, you have three options. First, you could remove the crankshaft and have it drilled for a pilot bushing. Second, you could replace the crankshaft with one that has already been drilled for a pilot bushing. Third (although this is a cheap and dirty fix), you could use the aforementioned pilot bearing from a late truck and simply lop off the unused portion of the input shaft from your transmission, which would be the

last 1 1/4 inch or so. Of course, if you choose this method, that transmission will only work with that style pilot bearing, no matter what engine you decide to mate it to later.

Engine Mounting

The configuration of the engine mounting ears from the polyspherical A engine was carried over to the 273 cubic-inch LA engine, and later to the 318 LA engine, making swaps between these engines straightforward. The driver's side mounting ears are slightly different on the 340 and 360 cubic-inch engines, so they require a somewhat narrower mounting bracket on that side, while the passenger's side mounting ears are spaced the same on all LA engines.

Oil Pans

Oil pans and pick-up tubes vary from vehicle chassis to chassis, with trucks typically requiring front sump pans on models through 1971 and rear sump pans from 1972 on. Passenger cars typically require center sump pans, but there are slight variations among these pans for steering linkage and K-frame clearance. Oil pans from 273, 318, and 340 engines are completely interchangeable. All of these engines have the same 2.50-inch main journal diameter, the same rear main bearing cap design, and the same oil pan gasket package. On 360 engines, however, you must use oil pans that are exclusive to the 360. Due to the larger 2.81-inch diameter main journals, the rear main bearing cap had to be redesigned. The 360 engine rear main bearing cap uses a smaller diameter grooved arch for the rear oil pan seal and, consequently, an oil pan that was reshaped in this area.

Water Pumps and Timing Marks

As mentioned previously, the cast-iron water pump used through 1969 was replaced by an aluminum water pump in 1970, at which time the lower radiator hose was moved from the driver's side to the passenger's side of the engine. Because of this, the timing chain cover and crank damper were

changed so that the timing marks were moved from the passenger's side to the driver's side of the engine, since the lower hose would have made it difficult to read the marks otherwise. There have been a number of variations of the aluminum water pump, and in terms of fit they are completely interchangeable.

When interchanging between the cast-iron and aluminum pumps, the obvious difference you will encounter is that the radiator will have to be changed, too, due to the relocation of the lower hose. In addition, accessory mounting can be difficult, since the cast-iron pump has ears that are often used for mounting the alternator and power steering pump. None of the aluminum pumps have these ears. If you have a pre-1970 car and wish to install a later engine, you could bolt your water pump to the later timing chain cover and retain your radiator and accessory mountings, but the timing marks would be difficult to read. A better solution would be to use a 1970 or later timing chain cover and crankshaft damper. Any LA engine timing chain cover can be bolted to any LA engine, so interchangeability between different size engines is not a problem. (For tips on selecting the correct crankshaft damper, see Chapter 10, "Crankshafts and Balancing.")

Balancing

When contemplating an engine swap, it is important for you to know which engines are externally balanced. All 273 and 318 engines are internally balanced, regardless of whether they have forged-steel or cast crankshafts. The 1968 through 1972 340, which was equipped with a forged-steel crankshaft, is also internally balanced. Therefore, flywheels and torque converters are interchangeable between them. The only exception is the 1964 through 1967 273 engine, not due to its balance requirements, but because of its small crankshaft flange opening. Early 273 flywheels can be interchanged with other engines, but torque converters cannot.

The recess in the outer ring of this external balance crankshaft damper extends nearly half way around. This is a late 360 piece.

The three large holes in this flywheel were drilled to weight it properly for use behind a 360.

The large weight on each side of the drain plug indicates that this torque converter is for an externally balanced engine.

All 360 engines are externally balanced, but thankfully the amount of external weight necessary to adequately balance the engine remained the same from 1971 through 1992. It was not until the introduction of the Magnum engines in 1993 that the external weight of the 360 was changed. If you wish to install a 360 in place of any other A or LA engine, you will need to use a flywheel or torque converter that is properly weighted for a 360. If your car has an automatic transmission and you wish to reuse your existing torque converter, you will need to use a specially weighted B&M flex plate, or properly position and weld the necessary weight from a Mopar Performance torque converter weight package.

The same considerations apply to the 1973 340 engine, which uses an externally balanced cast crankshaft. Short of swapping in an earlier internally balanced forged crankshaft and damper, your options are the same as those listed for the 360. Because the amount of external weight needed to properly balance a cast crank 340 is different from that of the 360, specially weighted pieces cannot be interchanged between them. (See Chapter 10 for more information.)

Pulleys. As mentioned previously, the crankshaft pulley bolt pattern was changed for the 1972 model year. Although this does not cause a big

problem, it is an issue that must be addressed when it arises.

Intake Manifolds. A number of different intake manifolds have been used on LA engines, and it sometimes happens that the subtle differences between them cause real headaches during engine swaps. A few things to keep in mind are that intake manifolds of differing heights can cause misalignments in carburetor and kickdown linkage, and the kickdown linkage is different between two-barrel and four-barrel engines. The kickdown linkage *MUST be connected and working properly* or transmission damage will occur!

Another trouble spot is that all 1978 and earlier V-8 engines use a much larger thermostat and housing than is found in the 1979 and later engines. The smaller thermostat opening was moved slightly toward the driver's side, making room for the axial air conditioning compressors that appeared around that time and replaced the V-2 compressors that had been used up to that point.

Another intake manifold related nuisance is the differences in choke coil wells that have taken place over the years. This problem can usually be overcome through scrounging pieces and/or fabricating linkage. Also, the bypass hose nipple diameter was enlarged in 1970, because the new aluminum water pump required a larger bypass hose. Since the later nipple will not fit the earlier manifolds, it is necessary to use the later bypass hose and cut a short piece of hose to use as a bushing over the smaller nipple. With this small piece of hose in place, the bypass hose can be installed.

Air Injection. Incompatibilities can also be encountered when swapping LA engines with and without provisions for air injection. This same problem arises when headers are installed on an engine with provisions for air injection. Just because an engine doesn't actually have air injection doesn't mean that it does not have provisions for air injection. If you discover that your engine has small holes below the exhaust ports that will be left open, you must plug them in order to eliminate exhaust leaks.

CHRYSLER PERFORMANCE ENGINES
Magnum Small-Block Engines

The Magnum series of engines was introduced in Dodge trucks at the beginning of the 1992 model year. The Magnum name was actually borrowed from the Dodge's line of high-performance engines of the late 1960s and early '70s. To further confuse things, there was a car called the Dodge Magnum in the late 1970s, which was a sister to the Dodge Charger and Chrysler Cordoba. Today the Magnum name is most commonly associated with 1992 and later Dodge truck engines and the crate engines that are based on these production truck engines.

The Magnum family of engines includes the 3.9-liter V-6, the 5.2-liter (318 cubic-inch) V-8, and the 5.9-liter (360 cubic-inch) V-8 engines. Following their introduction, they were the only engines available in trucks, since the big-blocks had been dropped at the end of the 1978 model year and the Slant Six had been phased out of production in domestic trucks during the 1987 model year.

In 1992, only the 3.9-liter V-6 and the 5.2-liter V-8 were available as Magnums, while the 5.9-liter engine remained a throttle body injected LA engine. The 5.9-liter Magnum did not appear until 1993. The 5.2-liter Magnum was available across the board in Dodge trucks, as well as in the Jeep Grand Cherokee, through 1998, but in the Grand Cherokee it was replaced by an all new 4.7-liter overhead cam engine for the 1999 model year. The 4.7-liter engine shares nothing with any of the earlier Magnum or LA engines.

For the 2000 model year, the 4.7-liter engine replaced the 5.2-liter Magnum in both the Dodge Durango and Dakota trucks. The 5.9-liter Magnum was still available in the Dakota R/T, and both the 5.2- and 5.9-liter Magnums lived into the 2000 model year beneath the hoods of full-sized Dodge trucks. This chapter focuses on the 5.2- and 5.9-liter Magnum engines only. There is certainly some information that applies to the 3.9-liter Magnum engine, but

because that engine is not a popular candidate for engine swaps, it is not covered in detail here. The 4.7-liter V-8 is also excluded from this chapter.

The Magnum V-8 engines are very closely related to the LA engine family of small-blocks, and are actually an outgrowth of that family. As such, there is a great deal of compatibility and interchangeability between them. The major similarities and differences between the LA engine family and Magnum engine family are highlighted in this chapter.

Externally, Magnum engines look quite different than their LA engine cousins. The large, round beer-barrel shaped intake manifold, ribbed steel rectangular rocker covers, and strange looking timing chain cover and water pump are all departures from the familiar pieces of the LA engines. In fact, due to the serpentine drive belt system, Magnum engine water pumps and cooling fans are designed to rotate counter clockwise, backward from the rotation of the engine.

The serpentine drive belt system used on production Magnum engines is quite different from the V-belt system used on LA engines. Beneath all the pulleys, brackets, and accessories lurks a 360 Magnum engine!

Through 1987, all LA engines were fed a fuel/air mixture via a carburetor or carburetors. Beginning in 1988, 318 engines were fitted with throttle-body fuel injection, and 360 engines followed in 1989. In a throttle-body fuel injection system, fuel injectors located inside the throttle body spray fuel into the incoming air. With the fuel atomized into the air, the fuel/air mixture is carried through the intake manifold plenum into the intake manifold runners, through the intake ports, and into the cylinders. Throttle-body fuel injection systems are much like carbureted

systems in that they use wet intake manifolds – that is to say, both fuel and air are distributed and delivered to the cylinders by the intake manifold.

Magnum engines were designed for port fuel injection from the start. (Chrysler calls it MPI, which stands for multi-point injection.) The new, shorter throttle body is still connected to the driver's right foot via a cable, but it only regulates air flow into the intake manifold. As on the throttle-body injection systems, the throttle body also provides a convenient place to mount the throttle position

sensor (TPS), which tells the computer how far the throttle blades are opened, and the idle air control (IAC) motor, which regulates the engine idle speed.

Air flows through the throttle body into a large plenum inside the barrel-shaped intake manifold. From there long runners carry the air from the bottom of the plenum, loop around the top of the plenum, and deliver it to the intake ports of the cylinder heads. Just before passing into the intake ports, the fuel injectors spray a carefully controlled amount of fuel into the incoming air. The intake manifold runners measure 14 1/2 inches in length, and when added to the four inches of port length in the cylinder heads, there is an astonishing 18 1/2 inches of total length. Because the intake runners of a port fuel-injection system carry only air, port fuel-injected engines are said to have *dry* intake manifolds.

When designing a wet intake manifold, engineers must be concerned with the delivery of both air and fuel to all of the cylinders. Inside the manifold, air and fuel do not respond the same way to curves. Fuel tends to collect – or "hang" – on the outside wall of a curve in an intake runner and to puddle on the floor, especially during cold operation. Nearly all carbureted and throttle-body injected engines have some means of supplying heat to the intake manifold to help alleviate

The tall, rounded intake manifold provides long runners and a large plenum in a small package.

With the manifold upside down and the plenum cover removed, the runners are visible. (Note: Plenum gasket failure is common and results in oil consumption, rough idle, and detonation.)

these conditions and aid in fuel vaporization. Even so, the basic manifold design must be such that the fuel stays suspended in the air.

When a dry intake manifold is designed, fuel delivery and distribution are not a concern, since that task is handled individually by the fuel injectors. Therefore, large plenums and long, sweeping runners of unconventional shapes can be employed without the drawbacks of fuel puddling or unequal fuel distribution. Magnum intake manifolds are designed to deliver air only, and no attempt should be made to adapt them for use with carburetors or throttle-body fuel injection.

In both throttle-body and port fuel-injection systems, the length of time that the fuel injectors stay open each time they are energized is called pulse width, and is expressed in milliseconds. The longer the pulse width, the more fuel that will pass through the injectors, and the richer the fuel mixture.

In a throttle-body injection system, the fuel is sprayed into the throttle body bores just above the throttle blades, and the air carries the fuel to the cylinders. Since the intake manifold distributes the air and fuel to the cylinders, the timing of the injector pulses in relation to the engine is not a factor, and the injectors typically fire with a frequency of ten times per second.

On a port fuel-injected engine, however, since the fuel is administered to each cylinder individually, the timing

of the injector openings must be coordinated with the openings of the intake valves for optimum fuel atomization and proper combustion. Furthermore, for peak combustion efficiency, the ignition timing must be controlled accurately.

Before the introduction of the Magnum engines, the on-board computer received the necessary engine reference signal from the distributor pick-up, for it was an easy place to obtain this signal. Considering the fact that the distributor is driven by a gear, and that gear is meshed with another gear on the camshaft, and the camshaft is driven by a chain that becomes increasingly loose with accumulated mileage, it becomes apparent that the distributor cannot provide the computer with the accurate, stable information about the crankshaft position that is critical to a port fuel-injection system.

For this reason, Magnum engines have used crank sensors from the beginning. Mounted behind the right side cylinder head, the crank sensor bolts to a special boss on the engine block and protrudes through a notch in the transmission bell housing where it "reads" notches or windows in the manual transmission flywheel or automatic transmission flex plate. By taking the signal directly from the crankshaft, the computer knows the exact position of the crankshaft and pistons and can more accurately control the firing of the fuel injectors

and ignition coil. The distributor pick-up is now used to tell the computer which stroke the pistons are on.

For example, since cylinders number one and number six are companion cylinders in Chrysler V-8 engines, their pistons will reach top dead center at the same time. However, the computer needs to know which one is coming up on the compression stroke and which one is coming up on the exhaust stroke. Because the distributor rotates only half a turn for each crankshaft revolution, by reading both the crank sensor and distributor pick-up the computer knows which piston is on which stroke.

The heart of the Magnum engines is its upper end. In addition to the newly designed intake manifold and port fuel injection, the top end consists of new cylinder heads that breathe extremely well when compared to production LA engine cylinder heads. They feature 1.925-inch diameter intake valves and 1.625-inch diameter exhaust valves, and valve stems which measure 5/16 inches in diameter. These cylinder heads are constructed of cast iron and have no exhaust crossover passages, for the dry intake manifold of the Magnum engines does not require heat since it carries no fuel.

The valves are actuated by new stamped-steel rocker arms that are anchored to the cylinder head castings by individual pedestals. These new rocker arms are of a 1.6:1 ratio. Like the last of the LA engines, Magnum engines use roller lifter

The multi-point injection system used on Magnum engines requires a flex plate or flywheel that incorporates a special ring with holes ...

... which are read by a crankshaft position sensor.

The sensor is bolted to the two bosses that were added just behind the right-side cylinder head.

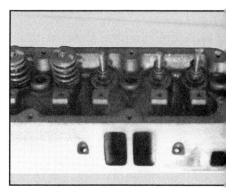

The redesigned Magnum hardware includes 5/16-inch diameter valve stems with steel-clad seals ...

The crankshaft sensor extends through a notch in the bell housing in order to "read" the flex plate.

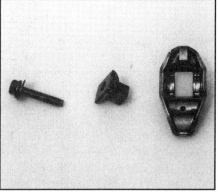

Instead of using rocker shafts, the rockers are mounted via individual pedestals.

... and valve springs that are slightly conical and use smaller, lighter retainers.

camshafts, with the lifters held in alignment by yokes that are retained by a spring steel "spider." Hollow pushrods span the distance between the lifters and the rocker arms. The conical valve springs found on Magnum engines are of a variable rate, and therefore help to keep spring oscillation in check.

Swirl port technology was first used in 318 LA engines in 1986 and 360 LA engines in 1989, and remained through the end of production of the LA engines. The term "swirl port" refers to the tendency of the intake ports causing the incoming fuel/air mixture to "swirl" like a cyclone as it enters the cylinders. This helps to evenly disperse the fuel, air, and exhaust gases that are left in the cylinders, as well as those exhaust gases that are metered by the EGR valve as the cylinder is filled. Normally, the ability of an intake port to induce "swirl" is achieved by the shape of the roof of the port. Magnum cylinder heads are designed to swirl. They also have closed combustion chambers, which has nothing to do with their abil-

Magnum cylinder heads feature ten-bolt rocker cover retention, as compared with five-bolt retention on LA engines.

ty to swirl. Unlike the LA engine family, where the 318 and 360 engines use different cylinder heads, valve sizes, and intake manifold runner sizes, the 5.2- and 5.9-liter Magnum engines share the same cylinder head castings, valve sizes, and intake manifolds.

All other popular Chrysler V-8 engines have oiling systems that pump oil from the camshaft bearings through passages in the block and heads to the rocker shafts, from which the rocker arms, pushrods, and valve stems receive oil. Because there are no rocker shafts in Magnum engines, the oiling system is somewhat different. Magnum engine blocks have no oil passages leading upward from the camshaft bores, and the cylinder heads are not drilled for oil passages, either. Instead, oil flows from the hydraulic lifters upward through the pushrods to the rocker arms, where it lubricates the rockers, pedestals, and valve stems.

Although the external appearance, cylinder heads, and valvetrain of the Magnum engines are quite different than that of the LA engines, the lower ends of the Magnum and LA engines are quite similar. The 5.2-liter Magnum has a 3.91-inch bore diameter and a 3.31-inch stroke. These dimensions look familiar, for they are the same bore and stroke as both the 318 polyspherical A-engine and the 318 LA engine. Like its predecessors, the crankshaft of the 5.2-liter Magnum has rod and main journal diameters of 2.125 inches and 2.500 inches respectively. The 5.9-liter Magnum has a bore diameter of 4.00 inches and a stroke of 3.58 inches, the same bore and stroke measurements as the 360 cubic-inch LA engine. The main and rod journal diameters of its crankshaft measure 2.125 and 2.810 inches respectively, the same as the 360 LA engine.

Unlike the LA engine family, however, in which the 360 cubic-inch engine uses an oil pan that is exclusive to that engine, the 5.2-liter and 5.9 liter engines share the same oil pan, although each calls for the use of a different oil-pan gasket. In fact, a 360 LA engine oil pan can be used on either the 5.2-liter or 5.9-liter Magnum engine, provided the proper oil pan gasket is used.

In a Magnum engine, oil flows from the lifters, upward through the hollow pushrods, to the rocker arms.

The 5.2- and 5.9-liter engines share the same oil pan, which is essentially the same as the 360 LA engine pan. If a 360 LA engine pan is used on a 5.9-liter Magnum, the LA engine pan gasket should be used.

The 5.9-liter Magnum oil-pan gasket has a small tab on each side of the rear main bearing cap, while the 5.2-liter Magnum pan gasket does not.

Production Magnum engines use roller lifters that are nearly identical to those in late LA engines. Flats on the upper portion of the lifter bodies …

… align with the yokes.

The yokes are retained by a spring steel "spider" ...

... that attaches to these holes in the center of the lifter valley

Although the engine in this photo is a 360 LA engine, it illustrates the fact that the left-side mounting ears of the 340 and 360 LA engines and 5.9-liter Magnum engine are positioned closer together than those on the 273 and 318 LA engines and 5.2-liter Magnum, which is what this bracket fits.

The LA engine roller lifter camshaft (top) is nearly identical to the Magnum engine camshaft (bottom). It has a slightly longer snout and oil feed holes for the cylinder heads in journals number two and four.

Because the Magnum engines use roller lifters, they have the same tall lifter bores as appear on the last of the LA engines, and like the LA engines the tops of these bores are machined to accept yokes that keep the rollers on the bottoms of the lifters aligned with the camshaft. A spring steel "spider" holds the yokes in position atop the lifter bores, and in the center of the lifter valley are bosses which are drilled and tapped for the bolts that hold the spider in place.

Internally, the biggest difference between the Magnum and LA engine cylinder blocks is that the LA engines have drilled oil passages running from the cam bore to the cylinder head deck surface in order to supply oil to the cylinder heads and rocker shafts. Because Magnum engines oil the rock-er arms through the pushrods, these oil passages are not drilled. If a Magnum cylinder block was to be used with pre-Magnum cylinder heads, these oil feed holes would have to be drilled. This is possible, for the Magnum blocks are cast with the necessary material in place for this passage.

Externally, the cylinder blocks of the 5.2- and 5.9-liter Magnum engines are nearly identical to those of the 318 and 360 cubic-inch LA engines. The bell housing bolt pattern and crank-shaft flange bolt pattern are exactly the same. All four engines use the same engine mounting ears on the right side of the block, but the left-side mounting ears of the 5.2-liter Magnum are the same as those of the 273 and 318 cubic-inch LA engines, while the left-side mounting ears of the 5.9-liter Magnum engines are the same as those found on 340 and 360 cubic-inch LA engines.

In many 1994 and later truck applications, the engine is mounted by brackets that attach near the middle of the block on each side, but the earlier mounting ears are still provided. The timing chain cover attaching bolts are drilled on the same pattern for all engines, so it is possible to bolt an LA engine timing chain cover to a Magnum engine block. Additionally, timing chains can be interchanged between LA engines and Magnum engines. Camshafts, however, are another story.

Carbureted LA engines have mechanical fuel pumps which are bolted to the side of the timing chain cover. Inside the timing chain cover an eccentric operates the fuel pump lever. This eccentric is bolted to the camshaft and sits against the front side of the camshaft sprocket. The nose of the camshaft protrudes from the front of the camshaft sprocket, properly locating the eccentric. When the LA engines were fitted with throt-tle-body fuel injection, the mechanical fuel pump was replaced by an electric fuel pump located in the fuel tank. The fuel pump eccentric was simply omitted from the camshaft sprocket and a cupped washer was installed in its place. A block-off plate was attached to the timing chain cover to cover the hole left by the absence of the mechanical fuel pump.

From the start, Magnum engines were designed for fuel injection.

The snout of an LA engine camshaft must protrude beyond the face of the camshaft sprocket in order to locate the fuel pump eccentric.

In a Magnum engine, however, the camshaft snout ends just short of the face of the cam shaft sprocket.

Once again, there was no need for a mechanical fuel pump. Therefore, the nose of a camshaft for a Magnum engine is somewhat short-er than that of the LA engines. A fuel pump eccentric cannot be properly attached to a Magnum camshaft. It is possible to use an LA engine camshaft in a Magnum engine, but the folks at Mopar Performance warn that an LA engine timing chain cover must be used. They claim that due to the longer nose of the LA engine camshaft, the Magnum tim-ing chain cover will not fit over the camshaft sprocket bolt. Although I have never encountered clearance trouble, this is one area that war-rants extra attention.

Automatic Transmission Considerations

All Magnum engines have cast-iron crankshafts. Like the 318 cubic-inch LA engine, the 5.2-liter Magnum

Although this is a late LA engine, the lifter valley is identical to that in a Magnum engine. A flat lifter hydraulic camshaft and lifters can be used in a Magnum block as long as Jeep-style lifters and custom hollow pushrods are used.

engine is internally balanced. The 360 LA engine is externally balanced, and so is the 5.9-liter Magnum, although the amount of weight necessary to properly balance the 5.9-liter Magnum is less than that of the 360 LA engine. For this reason, crank dampers and weighted flywheels, flex plates, and torque converters should never be swapped between 360 LA engines and 5.9-liter Magnum engines. All Magnum engines have a crank sensor that "reads" an exciter ring which is integral with either the flywheel in manual transmission applications or the flex plate in automatic transmis-sion applications.

Through about 1995, the selective four-bolt pattern used to join the torque converter and flex plate was the same that had been used with all A-904, A-500, and A-518 transmis-sions, and A-727 transmissions with 11-inch torque converters for decades. Therefore, it is possible to use most zero-balanced torque con-verters behind a 5.2-liter Magnum, as long as the early Magnum flex plate is used. During this time, the 5.9-liter engines used the same flex plate as the 5.2-liter engines, but the neces-sary balance weight was welded to the torque converter.

Around 1996 things changed. The unevenly spaced flex plate/torque converter bolt pattern was dropped in

This torque converter is weighted for use with a 360 LA engine. Note the large weight on each side of the drain plug, which is positioned at six o'clock.

Through 1995, the 5.9-liter Magnum engine used this style torque converter weight. It weighs less than the weights of the 360 LA engine.

In 1996 the weight moved to the flex plate.

1996 and later torque converters with evenly spaced bolt holes can be identified by this 90-degree stamping.

When a torque converter and flex plate in a pre-1996 truck have been replaced with later style pieces (perhaps during a warranty repair), this sticker on the flex plate identifies it as the later style piece.

favor of a four-bolt evenly spaced bolt pattern. Torque converters with the evenly spaced bolt pattern are identified by a 90-degree stamp on the face of the torque converter, and a sticker on the flex plate warns of this new style bolt pattern. At this time, the balance weight needed on 5.9-liter engines was moved from the torque converter to the flex plate. From this point forward it is possible to swap torque converters between 5.2- and 5.9-liter Magnum engines, but the flex plates are not interchangeable due to the balance weight. Early torque converters cannot be used with the later flex plates because of the difference in bolt patterns.

Chrysler then superseded the early Magnum torque converters and flex plates in some applications with the later "90 degree" style units, and this is where things can become really confusing. For example, suppose you wanted to use a 5.2-liter Magnum engine from a 1994 Dodge truck. The flex plate originally used in that truck would be compatible with most earlier torque converters. Yet, if the torque converter in that truck had been replaced at some point (perhaps during a transmission repair while the truck was under warranty), it is possible that it now has the later style torque converter and flex plate with the evenly spaced bolt pattern. Therefore, that flex plate would not work with any earlier torque converter.

What all of this boils down to is that in order for the fuel injection system on a Magnum engine to work, it must have a crankshaft sensor and exciter ring. Whether you use a flex plate with unevenly spaced torque converter bolt holes or a later one with evenly spaced converter bolt holes, you must use a torque converter with matching, evenly or unevenly spaced, bolt holes. Since aftermarket high stall-speed torque converters for Chrysler applications are of the unevenly spaced variety using one of these converters would require the use of an early flex plate.

In the case of the 5.9-liter Magnum, because it is an externally balanced engine, it must have a balance weight either on the torque converter (early style, unevenly spaced torque converter bolt holes) or on the flex plate (late style, evenly spaced torque converter bolt holes). If you wish to use an aftermarket high stall-speed torque converter behind a 5.9-liter Magnum, you will need an early style (unevenly spaced) flex plate and a Mopar Performance torque converter weight package. This package includes the weights that are necessary to properly balance the engine, and instructions on how to position the weights on the torque converter so that they can be welded in place.

Manual Transmission Considerations

In manual transmission applications, in order for the port fuel injection to work, the exciter ring, which is read by the crankshaft sensor, must be present, which means that a Magnum flywheel must be used. Be sure not to interchange flywheels for 5.2-liter and 5.9-liter engines due to the internal balance of the 5.2-liter engine and the external balance of the 5.9-liter engine. Most Magnum crankshafts are drilled for a manual transmission pilot bushing, but not all are finished to the proper size. If yours is drilled, try to test-fit a pilot bushing. If it can be driven into the crankshaft, you're all set. If it can't, you have a couple of options. (See Chapter Three, "Manual Transmission Pilot Bushing" for more details on these options.)

Although most Magnum crankshafts were drilled for pilot bushings ...

This roller-style pilot bearing resides in the recess normally occupied by the torque converter hub in automatic transmission applications.

Why a Magnum?

There are many reasons to consider Magnum engines or engine pieces. First is their availability. At one time it was nearly impossible to find a used Magnum in a junkyard, and as of this writing they are still pricey compared to LA engines. As each year goes by, there are more and more of them around, and the older they get, the more obtainable they become.

There is also the issue of the crate engines, for the only small-block crate engines available from Mopar Performance are based on the 5.9-liter Magnum. The real advantage of the Magnum engines, however, is in the cylinder heads. With their generous valve sizes and well designed ports, in stock form Magnum cylinder heads breathe more freely than any of the recent LA engine heads.

... some were not.

Someone with an older, pre-Magnum era vehicle who is interested in a Magnum engine usually wants to do one of three things:

- install a complete Magnum engine in place of an LA engine, and retrofit the fuel injection system to the vehicle;
- install a Magnum engine in place of an LA engine, but feed it with a four-barrel carburetor and ignite it with conventional electronic ignition; or,
- swap Magnum engine pieces onto an existing LA engine.

Physically bolting a Magnum engine in place of an LA engine is fairly straightforward. The right side engine mounting bracket from your existing LA engine will bolt to the Magnum block regardless of which LA engine you are removing or which Magnum you are installing. The left-side mounting ears of the 5.2-liter Magnum are configured the same as the 273 and 318 cubic-inch LA engines, while the ears of the 5.9-liter Magnum are configured the same as the 340 and 360 cubic-inch LA engines. Depending on which Magnum engine you wish to install, you will need either a 273/318 left-side mounting bracket or a 340/360 left-side bracket for your vehicle.

Passenger cars typically use center-sump oil pans, pickup trucks through 1971 use front-sump oil pans, and trucks from 1972 to present use rear-sump oil pans. Each style oil pan has a matching pick-up tube. Since Magnum engines were installed from the factory in trucks only, they have rear-sump pans that will not fit into the chassis of a passenger car. Bolting a 360 LA engine oil pan and pick-up tube designed for your particular vehicle to the Magnum engine will allow it to fit into the chassis. Be sure to use the correct oil-pan gasket for your particular Magnum engine, since the 5.2-liter and 5.9-liter Magnum engines call for different oil-pan gaskets.

Magnum exhaust ports are shaped much like those of LA engines, and the exhaust mounting area of the head is nearly identical to that of an early LA engine head without provisions for air injection. Therefore, it is possible to use headers for LA engines on Magnum engines. Early LA engine exhaust manifolds without provisions for air injection will work fine, too. Later exhaust manifolds with air injection passages may need to be ground slightly in order to sit flush against the cylinder heads. The passages within the exhaust manifold used to route the air from the air injection system to the exhaust ports are separate from the large passage that routes the exhaust from the ports to the exhaust pipe. Although they will be left open when the manifold is bolted to a Magnum cylinder head, they shouldn't need to be plugged, since they will not leak exhaust unless the manifold is cracked internally.

Magnum exhaust manifolds are said to breathe extremely well, with the 1968 through 1970 340 exhaust manifolds being the only production small-block manifolds capable of outflowing them. Unfortunately, the exhaust outlets of the Magnum manifolds are located so far rearward that they will not clear the firewall in many passenger car applications.

The timing chain cover, water pump, accessory mounting, and serpentine drive belt system of the Magnum engines are much different than those of the LA engines, but these components can be removed from an LA engine and installed on a Magnum. You should consider this an all or nothing choice. Mixing and matching Magnum and LA engine pieces will be quite difficult, and the difficulty will be compounded by the fact that the Magnum water pump and fan turn counterclockwise.

Another point to consider here is that the nose of the Magnum camshaft is slightly shorter than that of the LA engines. A Magnum camshaft will fit behind an LA engine timing chain cover, but as mentioned earlier, an LA engine camshaft may not fit beneath a Magnum timing chain cover. Furthermore, if you plan to use a carburetor fed by a mechanical fuel pump you must use an LA style timing chain cover, because the Magnum timing chain cover will not accept a mechanical fuel pump. Using an LA engine timing chain cover will afford a greater selection of camshafts.

Using an LA engine camshaft and flat hydraulic lifters in a Magnum engine is possible as long as a few extra measures are taken. First, because flat-bottom hydraulic lifters are shorter than roller lifters, and because Magnum rocker arms are lubricated by oil that is pumped through the pushrods, a set of custom length hollow pushrods will be needed. In addition, because Chrysler original equipment hydraulic lifters are not designed to deliver oil to the remainder of the valvetrain, they have no oil feed hole to push oil up the pushrod. Lifters for older Jeep engines are dimensionally the same as Chrysler lifters, and have the necessary oil feed hole. In many cases, aftermarket companies supply Jeep style lifters in Chrysler camshaft and lifter packages, so you may luck into a set of the right lifters with your new cam and lifter package. If you do this, simply omit the yokes and spider that are necessary to maintain the alignment of the roller lifters.

Be advised, though, that the Magnum engines have a 1.6:1 rocker arm ratio, while the LA engines have a 1.5:1 rocker arm ratio. In fact, most V-8 engines have a 1.5:1 rocker arm ratio. If the camshaft lobes are 0.300 inches tall, then by multiplying the numbers together the actual valve lift can be determined as follows:

0.300 inches lobe lift X 1.5 rocker arm ratio = 0.450 inches valve lift

Actually, this has already been done by the camshaft manufacturer. When the valve lift of a camshaft is indicated, the actual lobe lift has already been multiplied by the stock rocker arm ratio of that engine. As we can see from the example, an LA engine camshaft that is said to produce 0.450 inches of valve lift only has 0.300 inches of lobe lift. In the case of Magnum engines, however, the rocker arm ratio is 1.6:1. Plugging *this* rocker arm ratio into the equation goes like this:

0.300 inches lobe lift X 1.6 rocker arm ratio = 0.480 inches valve lift

By switching from the 1.5:1 rocker arm ratio to a 1.6:1 ratio, the 0.450-inch lift camshaft effectively grows to a 0.480-inch lift camshaft! A greater rocker arm ratio not only increases maximum valve lift, but also opens the valves more quickly. Many engine builders select a camshaft not by its advertised duration, but by its duration at 0.050 inches lift, for it is generally accepted that below 0.050 inches there is not enough valve lift to have a significant impact on the operation of the engine. Combining an LA engine camshaft with Magnum heads, and thereby increasing the anticipated rocker arm ratio from 1.5:1 to 1.6:1, will cause the valves to reach 0.050 inches of lift sooner than they would with the 1.5:1 rocker arm ratio of the LA engine. This will increase the effec-

This crankshaft damper is of a conventional design and is weighted for 5.9-liter Magnum engines.

If you wish to install a pre-1972 LA engine crankshaft pulley on a Magnum damper, one hole will not line up properly.

Beginning in the 2000 model year, the serpentine belt crank pulley and damper hub are cast as one piece. Installing an LA engine crankshaft pulley would require the use of an earlier Magnum damper.

tive duration of the camshaft and could alter the personality of the engine somewhat.

Adapting a Magnum engine to work with a solid-lifter camshaft would not be a simple feat for a couple of reasons. First, original equipment style solid lifters have no passages to supply oil to the pushrods in order to feed the upper end of the engine. Special lifters with the appropriate oil feed hole would be needed. Second, production Magnum rocker arms are not adjustable. Should you decide to use a solid-lifter camshaft anyway, you will be glad to know that Mopar Performance now offers adjustable rocker arms in the standard 1.6:1 ratio for Magnum engines.

If you wish to use all of the hardware from the front of an LA engine, depending on the year of the engine from which you remove the pieces, you may encounter a difference in the crankshaft pulley bolt pattern. On LA engines used through the 1971 model year, the crankshaft pulley was attached to the crankshaft damper by six bolts, one of which was offset slightly. Beginning in 1972, the offending bolt was moved, resulting in a symmetrical bolt pattern. Should you

encounter a mismatch between the Magnum crankshaft damper and your LA engine pulleys, the affected hole in the pulley can be widened into an oval shape, then the unused portion of the hole welded shut. Be sure to grind the weld flat on both sides of the pulley so that the pulley sits flush against the damper and the bottom side of the bolt head sits flush against the pulley.

Installing a Fuel Injected Magnum Into an Older Vehicle

If you are planning to install a Magnum engine assembly complete with the computer controlled port fuel-injection system into an older vehicle, you will need to cut a notch in the transmission bell housing for the crankshaft position sensor to pass through. It will also be necessary to use the Magnum style flex plate that matches your torque converter and to address whatever external balancing issues may arise, all of which were discussed earlier.

In addition, it will be necessary to install a suitable electric fuel pump. Chrysler vehicles with electronic fuel injection all use electric fuel pumps located inside the fuel tank for a cou-

ple of reasons. First, when the pump is on operation, atmospheric pressure acting on the fuel in the tank is the only force that pushes fuel from the fuel pick-up to the pump. The further from the pick-up the pump is located, the harder it will have to work and the less effective it will be. Second, the fuel in the tank helps to cool the pump, thereby increasing its life expectancy. Adapting an in-tank electric fuel pump to work in a tank not originally designed for such a pump can be a challenge. An aftermarket externally mounted fuel pump could handle the chore as long as it meets or exceeds the specifications of the factory pump.

There are essentially two variations of the Magnum fuel injection system. Early systems require a fuel return line that carries fuel back to the tank, while later "returnless" systems do not require a fuel return line. Be sure to choose an aftermarket pump that is compatible with whichever system you have, and run a return line if needed.

You will need to mount an oxygen sensor in the exhaust system. If your vehicle has single exhaust, an oxygen sensor bung can be welded into the pipe just downstream of the

This Dodge Custom Royal has been tastefully fitted with a Magnum engine and the electronics necessary for it to operate.

If you go this route, an oxygen sensor will have to be added. Heated units (three- or four-wire) work best, especially if the sensor is several inches or more away from the exhaust manifold.

The pre-OBD II data link connector looks like this and is located in the engine compartment wire harness.

"Y" where the pipes are joined. It must be located ahead of any catalytic converter(s). If your vehicle has dual exhaust, a cross pipe can be added, and the oxygen sensor bung can be welded into this pipe. From this location the sensor can sample the exhaust from both cylinder banks and provide the computer with more accurate overall fuel mixture information.

In addition, you will need a wiring harness and computer, or PCM (powertrain control module) for the Magnum engine. For best results with easier hook-up and fewer hassles, stay with the earliest system you can find. The older systems were more simple than later systems, and fuel control systems evolved rapidly in the 1990s. By the

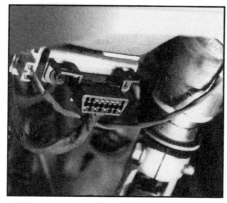

The OBD II data link connector looks like this and is mounted rigidly under the dash.

mid-1990s, the hydraulic governor in the transmissions of nearly all Dodge and Jeep trucks had been replaced by an output shaft speed sensor and a governor pressure solenoid in the valve body. The PCM cycles the governor pressure solenoid based on information it receives from the output shaft speed sensor. For fewer headaches you should avoid this system, and you certainly won't want to use a computer system from a 1997 or later truck with OBDII (On Board Diagnostics II).

OBDII was mandated by the federal government as a means of standardizing terminology and diagnostic scan tools between all of the vehicle manufacturers. With these mandates came several new computer monitors, and in many cases, additional related hardware. Vehicles with OBDII are characterized by a trapezoid shaped diagnostic connector located under the dashboard inside the truck. Earlier non-OBDII systems use a nearly square connector located under the hood in the engine compartment wiring harness.

Whatever year wiring harness and computer you choose, be sure to have the appropriate service manual on hand. Unless you are experienced in automotive wiring, this is a job best left to an automotive electrical expert. It would also be helpful to enlist the expertise of somebody well versed in Chrysler computer systems.

Installing a Carbureted Magnum Into an Older Vehicle

If you plan to use a Magnum engine in an older vehicle but don't want the

hassles of retrofitting the vehicle with all of the necessary plumbing and wiring, it is possible to use a carburetor and Chrysler electronic ignition. If the vehicle already has electronic ignition, then installing it on the Magnum engine is as simple as installing the electronic ignition coil and dropping the electronic ignition distributor into the hole in place of the Magnum distributor.

A pre-Magnum set of spark plug wires will also be needed, as will a distributor cap and rotor. Because there will be no need for a crankshaft position sensor, it is not necessary to notch the bell housing. Furthermore, it will not be necessary to use a Magnum style flex plate. If you are using a 5.2-liter Magnum, a standard flex plate and "zero" balance torque converter will work just fine in vehicles with automatic transmissions, and a "zero" balance flywheel will get the job done in vehicles with manual transmissions. If you are using a 5.9-liter Magnum in a vehicle with an automatic transmission, a standard flex plate and "zero" balance torque converter can be used provided the Mopar Performance torque converter weight package is used and the proper weight is added to the torque converter as discussed earlier. If you are installing a 5.9-liter Magnum into a vehicle with a manual transmission, a flywheel for a 5.9-liter Magnum should be used in order to obtain the proper balance.

Installing a carburetor on a Magnum engine is not as simple as it might first appear. As discussed earlier, the Magnum engines use a dry intake manifold that does not deliver fuel to the cylinders. Because there is no fuel in the intake manifold, there is no reason to heat the manifold with exhaust gas. Consequently, the cylinder heads have no exhaust crossover passages. For all-out performance this is a good thing, since eliminating the exhaust crossover will keep the intake manifold cooler, providing a denser fuel/air charge to the cylinders.

In fact, blocking the crossover passage is a trick commonly employed on LA engines used for racing. In day to day driving, however, especially in cold climates, heating the intake manifold promotes better fuel vaporization and helps to keep the fuel from puddling in the intake manifold during low-speed operation. Eliminating the exhaust heat from the intake manifold of a carbureted engine can create some poor cold weather driveability symptoms. Furthermore, without an exhaust crossover, a production style automatic choke will not operate, because the choke well will not receive the heat necessary to cause the bi-metallic spring inside to relax its tension on the choke blade. This leaves a manually operated choke, an electric choke, or no choke as your options.

Although the large runners in an intake manifold from a 340 or 360 cubic-inch LA engine match up to the intake ports in the Magnum heads, the manifold attaching bolts are not compatible. Magnum intake manifold bolts pass vertically through the manifold into the heads, while LA engine intake manifold bolts run at an angle through the intake manifold into the heads. Early attempts at mating an LA engine intake manifold to Magnum cylinder heads required that the intake manifold bolt holes be welded and drilled so that the bolts could pass vertically through the manifold into the heads. Since then, Mopar Performance has released both an aluminum single-plane and an aluminum dual-plane intake manifold that will allow the use of a single four-barrel carburetor on Magnum engines.

If you wish to supply fuel to the carburetor with a mechanical fuel pump, you will have to use an LA engine timing chain cover and camshaft, as discussed earlier. The Magnum timing chain cover has no provisions for a mechanical fuel pump, and the comparatively short nose of the Magnum camshaft affords no means to properly center a fuel pump eccentric.

Magnum Heads Onto LA Engines

Before getting into the specific hardware required to adapt a pair of Magnum engine cylinder heads to an LA engine, let's examine how the characteristics of the engine will change. We already know that the Magnum cylinder heads breathe extremely well in stock form. Better breathing means that they have the potential to make more horsepower, and more horsepower is certainly reason enough to perform this swap. There are some other characteristics of the engine that will change, too. Depending on your intended use of the engine and how you view the changes in these other characteristics, they could be considered additional benefits or drawbacks.

First, the Magnum engines have cylinder heads with closed combustion chambers which are smaller than those of the LA engines. Pistons with a positive deck height (meaning that they protrude from the tops of the cylinders at top dead center) cannot be used. Furthermore, replacing the cylinder heads on an LA engine with Magnum cylinder heads will typically increase the compression ratio by a couple tenths of a point. On an engine with a relatively low compression ratio, this would be a good thing. If the subject engine already has a high compression ratio, however, switching to Magnum heads will drive it even higher.

All LA engines use rocker arms which pivot on a common rocker shaft. This makes for a sturdy, rigid valvetrain. Instead of rocker shafts, Magnum engines have individual pivots, or pedestals, for each of the rocker arms. In applications using high-lift camshafts with stiff valve springs, if the integrity of the valvetrain becomes questionable, fabricating and installing bridges or a girdle to tie the pedestals together would certainly help to stiffen the valvetrain.

As mentioned earlier, LA engines have a rocker arm ratio of 1.5:1, while Magnum engines have a rocker arm ratio of 1.6:1. Swapping a pair of Magnum cylinder heads onto an LA engine, which will automatically increase the rocker arm ratio from 1.5:1 to 1.6:1, will increase both the maximum lift of the camshaft and its effective duration. If the engine has a stock or very mild performance camshaft, the 1.6:1 rocker arm ratio of the Magnum cylinder heads would offer a performance benefit. If the engine has a camshaft with an aggressive profile, and the idle quality and vacuum are marginal, the 1.6:1 rocker arm ratio could make the situation even worse. Additionally, if the engine has high-compression pistons and a "big" camshaft, the 1.6:1 rocker arm ratio could contribute to insufficient valve-to-piston clearance.

One final aspect of the Magnum cylinder head to LA engine swap, mentioned earlier, should be reemphasized. Because Magnum engines were not originally intended to have any induction system other than port fuel injection, there was no reason to incorporate exhaust heat crossover passages into the cylinder heads. In a race engine the absence of the exhaust crossover is a benefit, for the cooler the intake manifold remains, the denser the fuel/air charge will be when it reaches the cylinders, and the more power the engine will produce. In a carbureted street engine, however, operating without a heated intake manifold can cause it to be cantankerous, especially in cold weather. In addition, a conventional factory style automatic choke will be useless.

Because the Magnum family of engines is based so closely on the LA engine family, the Magnum cylinder heads can be readily adapted to the LA engine cylinder blocks. The exhaust poses no major hassles, because, as mentioned previously, the Magnum and LA engine heads are nearly identical in this area. Using headers is recommended, for they are less restrictive than cast-iron manifolds, but if you decide to use exhaust manifolds that are compatible with air injection, be sure that they sit flush against the heads. If they don't, grind away the offending material as necessary. Headers and early non-air injection manifolds bolt up with no problems.

As mentioned previously, although the intake ports of the Magnum cylinder heads and the runners of the LA engine intake manifolds line up, the Magnum heads are drilled and tapped for vertical intake manifold bolts, while the LA engine intake manifolds are drilled for angled bolts. Here you have a couple of choices. You could weld closed the bolt holes of a production LA engine intake manifold, then drill them vertically for use with the

Magnum heads. Or you could simply purchase a Mopar Performance intake manifold meant for such a situation. Mopar Performance offers both a single-plane and a dual-plane intake manifold that will fit either Magnum engines or LA engines with Magnum cylinder heads and accept a four-barrel carburetor. The single-plane manifold would be a good choice for a high-RPM race engine, but the dual-plane manifold would be the better bet for a street engine.

The biggest difference between the Magnum and LA engines that must be addressed in such a swap is the method by which the rocker arms, pushrods, and valve stems receive oil. As we have already discussed, LA engine cylinder heads are fed oil through passages that run upward from the cam bores, and the oil then flows through the rocker shafts to the rocker arms, pushrods, and valve stems. Magnum engines feed oil from the lifters, through the pushrods, to the rocker arms and valve stems.

In order to adapt Magnum heads to an LA engine, this method of supplying lubrication to the upper portion of the valvetrain must also be employed. The key is the lifters. Because oil reaching the lifters in an LA engine is not expected to lubricate anything beyond that point, Chrysler engineers saw no need to put an oil feed hole in the center of the pushrod pocket of their hydraulic lifters. In a Magnum valvetrain, however, oil must pass beyond this point in order to reach the rocker arms. Therefore, original-equipment Chrysler LA engine lifters are not suited for use with Magnum cylinder heads.

Three types of lifters were used in LA engines: solid, hydraulic flat-bottom, and hydraulic roller. Because of the one-piece construction of a solid lifter, the fact that there is no pushrod oil-feed hole, and the fact that production Magnum rocker arms are not adjustable, special hardware is needed in order to use solid lifters with Magnum cylinder heads. If you wish to use a solid-lifter camshaft with Magnum heads, Mopar Performance offers an adjustable rocker arm package for the Magnum engines. Special lifters will also be needed.

If you wish to adapt a pair of Magnum cylinder heads to an LA engine with hydraulic roller lifters, simply substitute a set of Magnum roller lifters and pushrods, then proceed with bolting the engine together. Because Magnum lifters are dimensionally the same as LA engine roller lifters, they are a drop-in replacement.

The vast majority of LA engines were built with hydraulic flat-bottom lifters. In order to complete the Magnum head swap, you will need a set of lifters with pushrod oil feed holes. Fortunately, the lifters used in older Jeep V-8 engines (pre-Magnum) are of the same dimensions as those used by Chrysler in the LA engines, except that they have the pushrod oil feed hole. Jeep lifters will get the job done.

Before you rush to order a set of Jeep lifters, it would be a good idea to check your current lifters. Although original-equipment hydraulic lifters for LA engines have no pushrod oil feed hole, many aftermarket lifters do have this hole. In the relentless effort of many aftermarket companies to consolidate part numbers and applications, the same replacement hydraulic lifters are often specified for older Jeep engines and Chrysler LA engines, although the original equipment lifters for these engines are different. If the lifters in your engine have ever been replaced by aftermarket pieces, you may already have lifters that are compatible with the Magnum valvetrain.

A word of caution is in order here. Flat-bottom lifters and their cam lobes wear-mate together, and this process begins the moment an engine with a new cam and lifter package is first started. This wearing together, or seating, of parts occurs rapidly during the first few minutes of operation, and continues at a slower rate for the first hour or so. For this reason, NEVER install a used lifter on ANY cam lobe other than the one it was originally mated to. When the lifters are removed from an engine, they must be kept in order if they are to be reused so that they are placed on their respective cam lobes.

It is an acceptable practice, however, to install new lifters on a used camshaft provided there is no abnormal or extreme wear. Because it is difficult to inspect the camshaft when it is in the engine, you can get an idea of its condition by inspecting the wear on the faces of the lifters. After removing your old lifters, inspect them closely for dished or galled faces. When new, the face of a flat-bottom lifter actually has a very slight radius. Holding the face of a lifter against a straight edge or against the body of another lifter will make it easy to see how badly it is dished, if at all. If the lifters are excessively worn, replace the camshaft, too.

When installing the Magnum cylinder heads on the LA engine block, don't worry about the oil passages from the cam bores to each of the deck surfaces. It is not necessary to block these passages, since the Magnum cylinder heads will cap them off adequately.

With the heads and lifters in place, a set of custom-length hollow pushrods will be needed. These pushrods must be open at each end so that oil can flow through them. Because Chevrolet engines use the same type of valvetrain oiling, custom pushrods should be available from just about any speed shop.

Intake manifold choices were discussed earlier. Whether you choose to modify a production LA engine intake manifold to work with the Magnum cylinder heads or simply bolt on one of the Mopar Performance intake manifolds, a Magnum intake manifold gasket package will seal it up. Be sure to use a high quality gasket package. Early production Magnum intake manifold gaskets are prone to failure.

Finally, because the Magnum engines have rocker covers that are retained by ten bolts each, whereas the LA engine rocker covers are held in place by only five, you will need a pair of Magnum engine rocker covers.

CHRYSLER PERFORMANCE ENGINES
Big-Block B and RB Engines

By the late 1950s Chrysler realized it needed to design an engine that was powerful, reliable, and less expensive to manufacture than its current offerings. Chrysler's early Hemi engines had earned the well-deserved reputation of being strong-running and more than up to the task of powering the cars of the day. During the 1950s, carmakers realized that horsepower sells cars, and the Hemi certainly made it possible for Chrysler to climb to the top of the horsepower charts. The biggest drawback in the design of the Hemi engines was that they were expensive to manufacture. Chrysler needed an engine that would make acceptable horsepower, yet be less expensive to manufacture than the Hemi.

Wedge head engines are more simple by design than hemispherical head engines. With all of the valves operating at the same angle, the valvetrain is less complicated, the cylinder heads can be made narrower, and, because all of the valve guides

and seats are inline, they are much more straightforward to machine. With this type of thinking in Chrysler's engineering department, the death knell eventually sounded for the early Hemi, and in 1958 Chrysler introduced the B engine in both 350 and 361 cubic-inch versions.

When the B engine was introduced, it was unlike any engine that preceded it. Some people mistakenly believe that it was based on the early Hemi block, but it was not. The new B engine used a deep-skirt block, meaning that the sides of the block extend well below the centerline of the crank-

Hydraulic lifters, stamped steel rocker arms, and a single rocker shaft make for a less expensive valvetrain than that of a Hemi.

A pair of early long-cross ram intake manifolds has been fitted to this engine.

shaft. This design offers greater rigidity to the bottom end of the engine. The block of the early Hemi is more like that of the A-engine, where the skirts of the block end at the parting line of the mains, right at the centerline of the crankshaft. It is true that the 426 Hemi, which spanned from 1964 through 1971, is a close cousin of the B engine, but the early Hemi is not. Furthermore, the rocker arms are constructed of stamped steel and attached to the heads via a common shaft. This is a simple, inexpensive, yet effective layout, but it is also unlike any valvetrain that Chrysler produced up to that point.

Throughout the two decades of big-block engine production, Chrysler used two different deck heights. In measuring the distance between the crankshaft centerline and block deck surface, low-deck engines measure 9.980 inches and are classified as "B engines." Tall-deck engines measure 10.725 inches and are classified as "RB engines," with the "R" standing for raised deck. The 350 and 361 cubic-inch engines are both low-

deck engines. The 350 has a 4.06-inch diameter bore, and the 361 has a 4.12-inch diameter bore. Both engines have the 3.38-inch stroke that is common to all B engines.

A year after Chrysler introduced the first two B engines, it also came out with the first RB engine. This largely forgotten engine has a bore size of 4.03 inches and a 3.75-inch stroke, netting a displacement of 383 cubic inches. While just about everybody is familiar with the 383, the popular version of the 383 is the 1961 and later B engine. This is a tall-deck 383, which was available in 1959 and 1960 only, and many Chrysler fans are not even aware of its existence. It uses the same 3.75-inch stroke as all other RB engines that would follow.

Due to of the difference in deck heights, RB engines are slightly taller and slightly wider than B engines. Because of this, the cylinder heads of an RB engine are slightly further apart than those on a B engine, so intake manifolds will not interchange between them.

By 1960 the bore size of the RB engine was increased to 4.18 inches and the 413 was born. The performance pinnacle of that year was realized when the 413 was fitted with two four-barrel carburetors mounted to dual long-ram intake manifolds. These manifolds, with runners that measure approximately 30 inches, placed the carburetors outboard of the valve covers, which resulted in extra long sweeping runners and engines that produced unbelievable torque. The factory rated these engines at 380 horsepower and an astounding 450 lbs./ft. of torque.

In 1961 Chrysler introduced the low-deck version of the 383. It had a 4.25-inch diameter bore, the same 3.38-inch stroke as the 350 and 361 engines, and it retained the same 1.95-inch intake valves and 1.60-inch exhaust valves as all other B and RB engines up to that point.

The following year the intake valve diameter was increased on all B and RB engines to 2.08 inches, but the small 1.60-inch exhaust valves remained in all cylinder

This 1962 Dodge is equipped with the dual four-barrel 383 engine.

Through 1961 all V-8 engines used this style eight-bolt crankshaft flange. In 1962 the switch was made to the common six-bolt flange.

Max Wedge engines use two four-barrel carburetors mounted diagonally across from each other atop a short-cross ram intake manifold.

heads except those designed for the Chrysler 300-J. There was a special package offered on the 383 that year that included two Carter AFB four-barrel carburetors mounted inline and the special 300-J cylinder heads. In this form the 383 was rated at 343 horsepower. Also in 1962 a new RB engine was introduced with a bore diameter of 4.25 inches. When coupled with the 3.75-inch stroke RB crankshaft, the

resulting displacement was 426 cubic inches. With the exception of the block, pistons, and rings, all other major aspects of the new 426 wedge head engine are the same as the 413.

Also in 1962, the rear flange area of the crankshaft was changed from a flat flange with an eight-bolt pattern to the contemporary style which is familiar to most of us and

incorporates the flex plate/flywheel centering ring and a staggered six-bolt pattern.

The big news for 1962, however, was the introduction of the 413 Max Wedge. This engine package was designed primarily for racing, although many Max Wedge cars found their way onto the street. The 426 cubic-inch Max Wedge Stage II and Stage III engines were carried

Despite the punishment they were destined to endure, Max Wedge blocks came equipped with two-bolt main caps, though they were fortified with additional material in the main webbing.

These wild looking cast-iron manifolds certainly contributed to the breathing capability of the Max Wedge engines.

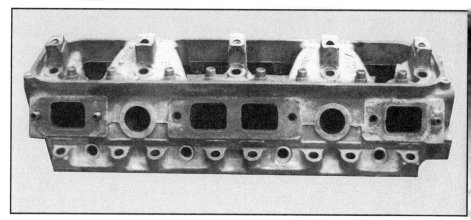

Larger-than-standard exhaust ports ...

... and intake ports were among the performance enhancements of the cylinder heads. Note the absence of an exhaust crossover passage.

Like all B and RB engine heads of the period, Max Wedge cylinder heads have closed chambers. Due to their large exhaust valves, bore notches were required.

over to the 1963 and 1964 model years respectively. These engines have two Carter AFB carburetors mounted diagonally slightly above and just inboard of the rocker covers on a short-ram intake manifold. The total runner length of this one-piece, short-ram intake manifold is 16 inches, making it more effective at midrange and high RPMs than the long-runner manifolds. Special cast-iron exhaust "headers" round out the external deviations from the standard passenger car engines.

Internally, these engines share little with standard production engines. The blocks, crankshafts, rods, and pistons were all designed to endure the rigors of racing. Compression ratios range from 11.0:1 to 13.5:1, and camshafts with as much as .520 inches of lift, were used in these engines. Special large-port cylinder heads were also part of the Max Wedge package, and the tops of the cylin-

der bores had to be notched to accommodate the large 1 7/8-inch exhaust valves. The actual intake and exhaust valve sizes are 2.08 inches and 1.88 inches respectively. Today, nearly 40 years after these engines were produced, many still compete. Original pieces for these engines have become very difficult to find and quite costly.

While it is true that the Max Wedge engines were extremely competitive in drag racing, Chrysler realized in

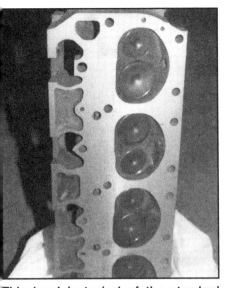

This head is typical of the standard cylinder heads used through 1967 with closed chambers, 2.08-inch diameter intake valves, and 1.60-inch diameter exhaust valves.

From 1968 on, all B and RB engines breathed through cylinder heads with open chambers, 2.08-inch diameter intake valves, and 1.74-inch diameter exhaust valves.

the early 1960s that it was lacking the competitive edge to dominate the high banks. The fact is that while the wedge head engines were (and still are) good engines for drag racing, they simply couldn't breathe freely enough at high RPMs to be competitive in NASCAR. During the 1964 racing season the Race Hemi made its debut and stole the spotlight from the wedge engines. At that point

most racers switched to Hemi power.

Through 1962, the rocker shafts were supported by stands that were bolted to the heads with the rocker shafts. These early heads also used rocker covers that were retained by only four bolts. Beginning in 1963, cast-in rocker shaft stands appeared, and the rocker covers were retained by six bolts.

In 1966 a new RB engine was introduced with a 4.32-inch diameter

bore. It used the same 3.75 stroke as the previous RB engines and displaced 440 cubic inches. Although it replaced the 413 in passenger cars at that point, the 413 lived on for several more years in trucks, motor homes, and industrial applications. In 1966 the new 440 saw duty in large passenger cars only. The following year, 1967, Chrysler produced a performance version of the

The 1969 1/2 through 1971 440 Six Barrel/Six Pack engines were the performance pinnacle of the 440.

The 1970-1971 440 "Six Pack Rods," as they are commonly called, are beefier forgings than the standard rods. Note the difference in the widths of the beams between the 440-6 rod and a 383 rod, which is representative of all other B and RB engine rod beams.

External balancing became common at the dawn of the 1970s. The large hole was drilled into this flywheel at the factory in order to externally balance it for use behind a 440-6 engine.

440 which was standard in the new Dodge Coronet R/T and the Plymouth Belvedere GTX. These engines featured cylinder heads that were very similar to the 300-J heads from a few years earlier, with 2.08-inch intake valves and 1.74-inch exhaust valves. All other B and RB engines that year retained the smaller 1.60-inch exhaust valves.

All B and RB engines up to this point had closed combustion chambers, but in 1968 new open-chamber heads replaced the closed-chamber heads. These heads used 2.08-inch diameter intake valves and 1.74-inch diameter exhaust valves. They were designed primarily for use on the 440 and high-performance version of the

383, but also found their way onto 383 two-barrel engines as well.

The Plymouth Road Runner and Dodge Super Bee also hit the streets in 1968, and the base engine in these cars was a high-performance 383. These engines, rated at 335 horsepower, were fitted with the aforementioned new heads, 440 camshaft, a new high-rise four-barrel intake manifold, and new free-flowing exhaust manifolds. Similarly equipped 440 HP engines that year were rated at 375 horsepower.

While combined sales of Road Runners and Super Bees were well on their way to reaching astounding levels in 1969, in mid-year the Dodge 440 Six Pack and Plymouth 440 Six Barrel engines became available in these models. From the outside, 440-6 powered Road Runners and Super Bees differed from their brethren in that they wore plain steel wheels and matte black fiberglass lift-off style hoods, each with a large scoop molded into the middle. Drivetrain improvements were consistent with those of Hemi-powered cars. Transmission choices consisted of either a heavy-duty Torqueflite automatic transmission or an 18-spline input shaft "Hemi box" four-speed manual transmission, and Dana 60 rear axles were standard equipment in four-speed cars. Instead of the standard Carter AVS four-barrel carburetor, these monsters were fed by a trio of Holley two-barrel carburetors mounted atop a special intake manifold. Their 390 horsepower rating is thought by many to be a bit on the conservative side.

In a Chrysler Six Pack/Six Barrel induction system, during normal operation only the center carburetor is in use. When maximum power is demanded, the center carburetor is opened all the way at first. As engine RPM increases, the volume of air flowing through the carburetor increases, creating a stronger venturi vacuum signal. This venturi vacuum is used to operate a vacuum chamber on each of the outboard carburetors. With the outboard carburetors activated by vacuum, it is possible to have both acceptable

low-speed driveability and maximum wide-open-throttle performance since the throttle plates in the outboard carburetors open only as the engine requires additional fuel/air mixture.

In theory, if the system is operating correctly, it is impossible to "overcarburete" the engine. The 426 Hemi was conservatively rated at 425 horsepower, but its strength is in its free-breathing cylinder heads. Consequently, its peak power occurs at high RPMs. Despite the fact that the 440-6 engines were rated at 35 horsepower less, they develop more low-end torque than the Hemi, and their power comes on strong in the midrange – both desirable qualities for a street engine. In some boulevard brawls, 440-6 engines have been known to best even the Hemi!

In the spring of 1969, *Super Stock* magazine performed a test of the new 1969 1/2 440 Six Barrel Road Runner at Cecil County Dragway in Rising Sun, Maryland. The legendary "Mr. Four Speed," Ronnie Sox, took the helm. With 4.10 rear gears and on-street tires he clicked off a 13.09-second elapsed time at 110.75 mph. With some external fiddling and tweaking, these numbers improved to a best of 12.92 at 111.66 mph! Over the last 30 years there has been much speculation on the origin of the car Mr. Sox drove that day. Some believe that this car was a "ringer," specially modified by the factory for use as a press car. Legend has it that this car was plucked from the inventory of a Chrysler Plymouth dealership in nearby Wilmington, Delaware and borrowed for the day.

In 1970 the 440 Six Pack/Six Barrel engines were equipped with beefier connecting rods that had wider beams than the standard 440 rods. This additional girth equaled additional weight, and it was no longer possible to properly balance the engine with the counterweights on the crankshaft. At this point, Chrysler created its first externally balanced engine. Some of the weight necessary to balance the

As the 1970s got underway, dished pistons were commonly used to lower compression ratios.

When mixing pre-1972 and post-1971 crankshaft dampers and pulleys, there is often a mismatch at one of the bolt holes.

engine was moved to the flywheel and crank damper. This caused an intentional static imbalance in those components that, when mated to the crankshaft, would offset the imbalance in the engine. These "Six Pack" rods, and requisite external balancing, were used in 1970 and 1971 model year 440-6 engines and found their way into a number of 440 HP engines, too. This is important to know when you are swapping engines, dampers, flywheels, or torque converters.

As the 1971 model year neared, the Environmental Protection Agency began to impose tighter emissions standards. One of the first steps in this direction, which occurred late in the 1971 model year, was that the coveted "906" cylinder heads were replaced by new castings with flatter intake ports designed for better emissions. The valve sizes, chamber volume, and exhaust port configuration remained.

At the end of the 1971 model year, shortly before the demise of the 383, some of the last 383 two-barrel engines were fitted with cast-iron crankshafts in place of the forged-steel units that had been used up to that point. Because cast-iron is not as dense as forged steel, the counterweights on a cast-iron crankshaft are not as heavy as similarly sized counterweights of a forged-steel crankshaft. In the case of the 383 they could not adequate-

ly offset the weight of the rods, pistons, and crankshaft rod journal throws. It was again necessary to add some additional balancing weight to the crankshaft damper and torque converter or flywheel, creating yet another externally balanced engine.

For the 1972 model year, Chrysler dropped the 440 Six Pack/Six Barrel engines, as well as the Hemi. The 383 was replaced by the new 400 cubic-inch B engine. This new engine used a bore size of 4.34 inches, the largest standard bore size of any B or RB engine. It used the same 3.38-inch stroke that is common to all low-deck B engines. Unfortunately, from its beginning the 400 earned a bad reputation as a smog motor, regarded by many as a low-performance pig. A low-compression ratio, tame camshaft profile, and somewhat more restrictive exhaust manifolds were largely responsible for the fact that even with an additional 17 cubic inches, the 400 couldn't begin to compare with the performance level of the 335 horsepower 383. The fact that it had a new "pollution" carburetor, the Carter Thermo-Quad, and was laden with a maze of vacuum hose did nothing for its visual appeal. Consequently, for many years the 400 was overlooked by performance enthusiasts.

The 400 engine has a cast-iron crankshaft that is externally bal-

anced. Although early 400s used in manual transmission applications are said to have forged-steel crankshafts, they are extremely rare. Typically, the cast crankshafts used in 400s are not drilled for a pilot bushing, so adapting one for use with a manual transmission is not exactly a straightforward swap. This is covered in greater detail at the end of this chapter in the section on engine swap considerations.

Also in 1972 the crankshaft pulley bolt pattern was changed on all Chrysler V-8 engines. Engines used in cars through the 1971 model year have crankshaft pulleys that are retained to the crank damper by six bolts, one of which is offset slightly. Engines from 1972 and later use six evenly spaced bolts.

By the time the 1972 model year rolled around, the heyday of the muscle car had passed. Emissions regulations had begun to strangle the power levels, and "pollution controls" such as EGR valves, charcoal vapor recovery canisters, and air pumps (along with their associated miles of vacuum hoses) were beginning to appear. For decades, tetraethyl lead had been added to gasoline as a cheap but effective way of increasing the fuel's octane rating. As an additional benefit, this lead acted as a lubricant, greatly extending the life of the exhaust valves and seats. By 1972, however, catalytic converters were on the horizon, and given the tendency of

This torque converter is weighted for use behind an externally balanced engine. Be sure to use the proper torque converter for your engine.

B and RB engine cast crankshafts have the engine displacement cast into the shaft. Note the sharp, well-defined edges on the counterweights.

lead to coat things, it was clear that leaded fuel was not compatible with catalytic converters. Furthermore, the EPA had begun to realize that pumping toxic lead into the air might not be a good idea after all. It was clear that the days of leaded fuel were numbered.

With the 1972 model year, Chrysler began hardening the exhaust valve seats in all of its engines for longer life in the absence of tetraethyl lead. Although fully induction-hardened exhaust valve seats did not appear until 1976, the exhaust seats in any B or RB engine head from 1972 through 1978 should hold up fine with unleaded fuel.

Around this time cast crankshafts began appearing in 440 engines, and by the end of the 1973 model year all big-block engines used cast crankshafts. As is the case with the cast crankshaft in the 400 engine, the cast crankshaft in the 440 has counterweights that cannot sufficiently offset the weight of the related components in the engine. For this reason, the cast-crankshaft 440 is externally balanced. The amount of external weight necessary to properly balance the cast crankshaft 440 is different from that of the 440 Six Pack/Six Barrel engines, and is also different from the amount of weight used to balance the 400 engines. Consequently, crankshaft dampers are exclusive to each of these engines, as are torque converters and flywheels unless the external balance issue is addressed.

Note that since all B engines use the same 3.38-inch stroke, 2.625-inch diameter main journals, and 2.38-inch diameter rod journals, any B engine crankshaft will physically fit into any B engine and will work fine as long as it is properly balanced. The same is true of RB engines, for all have the same 3.75-inch stroke, 2.75-inch diameter main journals, and 2.38-inch diameter rod journals.

In 1975, catalytic converters appeared on cars meeting federal emissions standards, and in 1976 fully induction-hardened exhaust valve seats came about, making the cylinder heads even more durable when used with unleaded fuel. Also in 1976, both the 400 and 440 cylinder block castings were made significantly thinner than they had been in previous years. Finally, the 440 was dropped from production at the end of the 1977 model year. The 400 was canceled a year later.

Cylinder Blocks

The cylinder blocks of Chrysler's B and RB engines were designed as rugged, durable pieces. They are of a deep-skirt design, meaning that the sides of the block extend downward well below the crankshaft centerline. This design affords a rigid bottom end, a shallow, flat oil pan, and lends itself well to the adaptation of cross-bolted main caps. The bell-housing bolt

The counterweights of this forged 440 crankshaft have edges that are much more rounded, and with a grainy appearance in some places.

By peering into the crankcase of this 383, you can see that the skirts of the block extend well past the centerline of the crankshaft.

The 1965 C-bodies and 1967-1969 A body Darts and Barracudas with B or RB engines use this special left-side mounting bracket. Not all blocks have the bosses necessary to attach the bracket.

pattern on the rear of the block is the same on all B and RB engine blocks. This bolt pattern is shared with the 426 Hemi, but is different from any other family of engines.

External bosses and mounting ears are the same in most cases, with the biggest difference being on a boss located on the front side of the block just ahead of number one cylinder. This boss was used for engine mounting on the 1965 C-body cars and on the 1967 through 1969 383 and 440-powered Dodge Dart and Plymouth Barracuda, all of which use the same left-side engine mounting bracket. In some applications this boss is also used for accessory mounting. On some blocks this boss has been drilled and tapped, and on some there is simply a blank boss that can be drilled and tapped if needed. Some blocks do not have this boss at all.

Blocks of two different deck heights were used in Chrysler's family of big-block engines. The B engines, which consist of the 350, 361, short-deck 383, and 400, all measure 9.980 inches from the crankshaft centerline to the top of the deck surface. The RB engines, which consist of the early tall-deck 383, 413, 426 wedge, and 440, all measure 10.725 inches from the crankshaft centerline to the deck surface. Within the B engine or RB

engine groups, various displacements were achieved by using various bore sizes. Therefore, no two engines with different displacements share the same block.

If you have a 383 with a damaged block, for example, and you wish to use a 400 block in its place, it is possible as long as you use pistons and rings of the proper size for the 400 bores. Be sure to check the weights of the pistons in your original engine and those for the replacement block. If they are different (and they probably are), the engine will need to be rebalanced.

There have been some cases where engines of two different displacements have actually used the same casting and therefore shared casting numbers, but the cylinders were actually finished to different sizes. Most notably, this occurred on industrial 413 and 426 wedge engines. Although these engines may share casting numbers, the actual part numbers are different because of the difference in bore sizes.

Through the two decades of big-block evolution, the cylinder blocks gradually became thinner and lighter. Generally this is not a problem on pre-1976 blocks, for most will easily accept a 0.040- or even 0.060-inch overbore. Blocks from 1976 through 1978 have cylinder walls that are significantly thinner,

and Chrysler recommends no more than a 0.020-inch overbore for racing purposes. If you wish to bore a late block beyond 0.020 inches, you should have it sonic checked to be sure that the cylinders can safely support such an overbore.

In comparing different blocks, some standard passenger car blocks have external ribs, and these are thought to be more rigid than non-ribbed blocks. All production blocks have two-bolt main caps, and all but the Max Wedge blocks have standard webbing throughout the main saddles. In fact, the webbing in the B engines is nearly identical to that in the RB engines, despite the difference in crankshaft main journal diameter. Only the Max Wedge blocks have additional girth in the main webbing for increased durability in the harsh racing environment.

Cylinder Heads

With the exception of Max Wedge cylinder heads, any production B or RB engine cylinder head can be installed on any B or RB engine. Through the 1962 model year, all big-block cylinder heads use rocker shafts mounted to the head via aluminum pedestals, and rocker covers retained by only four bolts. This changed in 1963, when the rocker shaft pedestals were first cast as part of the cylinder head. Integral rocker pedestals were used for the rest of B and RB engine production. Also in 1963, the rocker covers were attached by six bolts, which helps to reduce the chance of oil leaks. This, too, was carried through the end of production.

The Max Wedge engines are known as Stage I, Stage II, and Stage III for model years 1962, 1963, and 1964 respectively. The cylinder heads used on these engines are easy to identify, for there is no exhaust heat crossover passage. Their huge ports are approximately 25 percent larger than the ports in standard passenger car cylinder heads, so production intake manifolds will not work with these heads. Consequently, there is no intake manifold available that would work with Max Wedge heads on a B engine. Max Wedge heads use 2.08-inch diameter intake valves and 1.88-inch exhaust valves.

From the inception of the B engine in 1958, through 1961 all engines used cylinder heads with 1.95-inch diameter intake valves and 1.60-inch diameter exhaust valves. In 1962 the intake valve was increased to 2.08-inches diameter, but the small 1.60-inch exhaust valve remained. High-performance cylinder heads used on the Chrysler 300-J have 2.08-inch intake valves and larger 1.74-inch diameter exhaust valves, but all other engines through 1966 made do with the 2.08-inch intake and 1.60-inch exhaust valves that were standard from 1962 up to that point. In 1967, with the introduction of the Plymouth Belvedere GTX and Dodge Coronet R/T, a high-performance version of the 440 was used as the standard engine in those cars. The heads on this engine have 2.08-inch intake valves and 1.74-inch exhaust valves. Identified by casting number 2780915, these heads are commonly referred to simply as "915" heads and were used by Chrysler for one year only.

Through the 1967 model year, all B and RB engine cylinder heads were of a closed chamber design. For the 1968 model year a new cylinder head, identified by casting number 2843906, was introduced. It features open chambers with 2.08-inch intake and 1.74-inch exhaust valve diameters. This head is undoubtedly the most popular of all B and RB engine cylinder heads because it has excellent flow potential, and its open chambers promote good flame propagation. Additionally, because it was used in nearly all applications well into the 1971 model year, it is not a difficult head to find.

Late in the 1971 model year a new "emissions" head replaced the "906" head. This head is similar to the "906," except that it uses flatter intake ports. This head was used through 1972, but was replaced by a revised head in 1973 that has additional cooling passages around the spark plugs which helps to keep the spark plugs cooler and increase their durability. From 1973 through 1978, the basic cylinder head castings remained virtually unchanged. It is true that the 1972 and later heads have hardened exhaust valve seats, but not until 1976 were the seats fully induction-hardened. Even so, any cylinder head from 1972 through 1978 should live happily on a diet of unleaded fuel.

With the exception of some Max Wedge engines, all B and RB engines have non-adjustable valvetrains consisting of stamped steel rocker arms and hydraulic lifters. Although the early aluminum rocker shaft pedestals were susceptible to cracking, all 1963 and later engines with integral rocker shaft pedestals have strong, rigid valvetrains. Rocker arms and shafts can be interchanged between any of the big-block engines, and pushrods can be interchanged between any of

B-ENGINE BORE X STROKE

Low Deck

Engine	Bore X Stroke
361	4.125 X 3.375
383	4.250 X 3.375
400	4.340 X 3.375

RB ENGINE BORE X STROKE

Raised Deck

Engine	Bore X Stroke
413	4.180 X 3.750
426	4.250 X 3.750
440	4.320 X 3.750

CYLINDER HEAD CASTING NUMBERS

Year	Engine	Cylinder Head Casting Number
1960-62	361, 383, 413	2206324
1962	413 Max Wedge	2402286
1963	361, 383, 413	2463200
1963	426 Max Wedge	2463209
1964-67	361, 383	2406516
1966-67	440 Std.	2406516
1967	440 High Perf.	2780915
1968-early 71	383, 440	2843906
Late 1971-72	383, 400, 440	3462346
1973	400, 440 Std.	3462346
1973	400, 440 Motor Home	3751213
1974	400, 440	3769902
1975	400, 440	3769975
1976-78	400, 440	4006452

The timing marks of the B and RB engines are typically located on the right side of the engine, but different engine/body/accessory combinations could cause them to be located elsewhere.

the B engines or RB engines, but not between B and RB engines, for the different deck heights of these engines require the use of different length pushrods. Early pushrods are of a stepped design, where one end is somewhat smaller in diameter than the other. The small end should be installed in the lifter, and the large end in the cup of the rocker arm.

Oil is fed to the upper portion of the valvetrain from the cam bearings. Oil flows upward through a passage in each bank of the block, into the cylinder heads, and into the rocker shafts. As oil flows through the shafts it exits to the rocker arms through holes in the shaft, lubricating the shaft and rocker arms. Oil flowing along the tops of the rocker arms lubricates the pushrods and valve tips and stems. The rocker shafts will physically bolt to the heads in any of four different positions, but the proper position is with the oil holes facing as close as possible to straight down toward the ground.

Engine Swap Considerations

Because all of the B and RB engines are so similar, a great deal of interchangeability exists between them. It is possible to install virtually any 1962 or later B or RB engine into

an engine bay formerly occupied by any 1962 or later B or RB engine. Before 1962, eight-bolt crankshaft flanges with no centering ring were the norm, but all crankshaft flanges from that point on have a common six-bolt pattern. All engines use the same bell-housing bolt pattern on the rear of the block, and all use the same engine mounting attaching ears on the sides of the block.

The only exceptions are the 1965 C-body and 1967 through 1969 383 and 440-powered A-bodies, which use a special left-side mounting bracket which positions the mount ahead of the steering box. One of the bolts for this special bracket must be attached to a boss in the front of the block, and this boss is not present on all blocks.

External components such as oil pans, water pump housings, accessory mounting brackets, and exhaust manifolds can all be interchanged between the various engines. In fact, about the only external pieces that cannot be interchanged between B and RB engines are the intake manifold and distributor. Furthermore, if the car you are working on has extremely tight exhaust clearance, or if it has a single exhaust system with a Y-pipe, you could encounter trouble with the exhaust when swapping between

a B and an RB engine. The difference in deck height causes a difference in the overall height and width of these engines.

Depending on what year of car you are working on, the lower radiator hose could be located on either the driver's side or the passenger's side of the vehicle. On vehicles through the 1971 model year, the lower hose is typically located on the driver's side of the engine. Vehicles from 1974 and later typically have the lower hose on the passenger's side. On 1972 and 1973 vehicles, the hose could be on either side. If your replacement engine has the lower hose outlet located on the wrong side, the water pump housing can be switched from the original engine, but in some cases this can make the timing marks difficult to read. It might be possible to swap the crankshaft damper and timing chain cover, but be sure that what you are installing is compatible with the balance of your engine.

Another problem related to the crankshaft damper which often occurs when swapping engines is the attaching bolt pattern of the crankshaft pulleys. Through 1971 the crankshaft pulleys on all Chrysler V-8 engines were attached with six bolts, one of which was staggered. Beginning in 1972, all six bolts were evenly spaced. If you encounter a mismatch here, you can use a rattail file to open up the bolt hole into the shape of an oval, then the unused portion of the hole can be welded closed. The weld must then be ground flat so that the pulley sits flush against the face of the damper and so that the bolt head sits flush against the pulley.

When you are planning an engine swap, it is important to know how both the existing engine and replacement engine are balanced. Swapping internally balanced engines is straightforward, for the balance of the engines really isn't a consideration. All pre-1970 B and RB engines are internally balanced. However, 1970 and 1971 440 Six Pack/Six

Barrel engines, with their heavier rods, require external balancing, as do some 440 HP engines that use the same rods. Cast-crank 440s are also externally balanced, but with a different amount of weight than the 440-6 engines. The cast crankshafts used in 400 engines also require external weight, but in a different amount than either of the externally balanced 440 engines.

None of the crankshaft dampers can be interchanged between these different engines or between any of the internally balanced engines. Furthermore, flywheels and torque converters cannot be interchanged unless steps are taken to assure proper engine balancing. B&M offers flex plates that are specially balanced so that zero-balanced torque converters for any of the internally balanced engines can be used behind an externally balanced engine. Another approach would be to use a Mopar Performance torque-converter weight package and weld the necessary weight to a zero-balanced torque converter. The third option would be to disassemble the engine and have it balanced using Mallory metal to move the external weight to the counterweights of the crankshaft.

If the vehicle has a manual transmission, your choices are more limited. Short of obtaining a flywheel with the proper balance for the engine you are using, you are stuck with one of two choices. You could disassemble the engine and have it internally balanced, then use a zero-balanced flywheel. Your second choice would be to have a zero-balanced flywheel properly balanced for your engine. The *Mopar Performance Chassis* book has instructions and diagrams showing how and where to drill a flywheel for use behind any of the externally balanced engines, but this is a critical operation that should be performed by a qualified machinist. It is certainly not for the faint of heart.

Another problem frequently arises when swapping engines in vehicles with manual transmissions,

Not all crankshafts were drilled to accept a pilot bushing. This is typical of 400 crankshafts.

This mid-1990s pilot bearing fits tightly into the recess of the crank flange normally occupied by the torque converter hub.

since not all engines were originally intended for use with manual transmissions. The input shaft of a manual transmission is supported by a bushing that is pressed into a hole in the end of the crankshaft. If you look into the end of a crankshaft, you will find one of three scenarios. First, the hole could be properly sized for a pilot bushing, and may even have a bushing already in place, even if the engine came from a car with an automatic transmission. Second, it could have what appears to be the proper hole, but it might not be finished to the correct size for a pilot bushing. Third, it might have no pilot hole at all.

If you find a pilot bushing present in your crankshaft, simply replace it if it is worn and proceed with your swap. If you find an empty pilot hole, attempt to install a pilot bushing. If it fits, drive it flush and proceed. If it won't go, your crankshaft pilot hole was not properly sized for a pilot bushing. Here you have a couple of choices. First, you could remove the crankshaft and replace it with one that has been properly finished for a pilot bushing. Second, you could have a machine shop finish it to size.

Either of these methods would be a textbook correct solution to the situation, but a third and much more simple solution exists. NAPA has recognized this as a common problem and offers a thin-walled

pilot bushing that will fit the unfinished pilot holes in Chrysler crankshafts. A few dabs of thread locking compound will help to hold it in place. Don't attempt to modify a stock pilot bushing. I've seen a number of creative attempts at this involving everything from bench grinders to hacksaws, and none of them worked well.

The other possibility with your crankshaft is that there is no pilot hole at all. If this is the case, you have three choices. First, you could obtain a crankshaft with a pilot hole. Second, you could remove your crankshaft and have it drilled for a pilot bushing. The third possibility (the down and dirty method) would be to use a production style pilot bearing for a mid to late 1990s truck. This pilot bearing is also available from Mopar Performance. Instead of fitting into a hole deep in the crankshaft, the large aluminum disc that contains the bearing fits tightly into the large hole normally occupied by the torque converter hub. The input shaft of the transmission would then have to be shortened by approximately 1 1/4 inches. Cutting the input shaft of an otherwise perfectly good transmission is certainly not the preferred method around this problem, for once the input shaft has been cut, this style pilot bearing must be used no matter what engine you decide to use the transmission behind later.

CHRYSLER PERFORMANCE ENGINES

Hemi Engines

For a car fanatic, there is no mistaking a Chrysler Hemi engine. It is paradise to peer into an engine bay and find a pair of the distinctive wide rocker covers with large rubber boots through which the spark plug wires pass. These engines look *mean!* Aside from the visual appeal, what makes a Hemi a Hemi?

The term Hemi is actually short for hemispherical, which describes the half-round shape of the combustion chamber. So what makes a Hemi head "better" than a conventional wedge head? In an engine with a wedge-shaped combustion chamber, the intake and exhaust valves sit next to each other and operate on the same plane. With the intake ports and exhaust ports located on opposite sides of the head, the fuel/air mixture entering through an intake port must curve sharply downward as it approaches the intake valve. Once the fuel/air mixture has entered the engine and has been burned, as

the piston reaches the end of its power stroke the exhaust valve opens. The exhaust gasses rush past the exhaust valve, but must

round a fairly sharp curve in the exhaust port immediately after passing the exhaust valve before leaving the head.

What makes a Hemi a Hemi: These are the combustion chambers of a 426 Hemi head.

In a hemispherical combustion chamber, the valves are canted. Because they oppose each other to a large degree, the ports leading to the valves do not need to curve nearly as sharply as they do in a wedge head. Straighter ports translate into better flow and more power potential. (You've probably read about "trick" wedge heads from various manufacturers who boast that they have raised ports. Raising the ports helps to make the curve in the port more gradual, which promotes better flow through the port.) Furthermore, since the valves are not positioned side by side, there is room in the combustion chamber for much larger valves than in a wedge head.

Near the end of the exhaust stroke, before the exhaust valve fully closes, the intake valve begins

Because the intake and exhaust valves oppose each other to a large degree, the Hemi combustion chamber lends itself well to scavenging during overlap.

to open to allow for cylinder scavenging. The period of time that both valves are open is called *overlap*, and is measured in the number of degrees of crankshaft rotation that occurs while both valves are open. Generally speaking, the more radical the camshaft, the more overlap it has, and the choppier the idle quality of the engine.

Cylinder scavenging refers to the cylinder ridding itself of spent exhaust gasses so that on the intake stroke it will fill more completely with a fresh fuel/air charge. Burned gasses left in the cylinder would displace some of the incoming fuel/air mixture, so for maximum power it is important to rid the cylinder of spent gasses.

As the exhaust gasses leave the cylinder, they have a certain amount of inertia. At the end of the exhaust stroke, as the piston reaches top dead center, the inertia of the exhaust gasses leaving the cylinder creates a low-pressure area in the cylinder, which helps to initiate the flow of the fuel/air charge into the cylinder. As the incoming mixture enters the cylinder, it pushes the last of the exhaust gasses out, thus completing the scavenging process. (This is more thoroughly discussed in Chapter 12, "Cylinder Heads and Breathing.")

Because the intake and exhaust valves in a Hemi combustion chamber face each other, you can probably visualize that before the exhaust valve fully closes, the

incoming mixture flows past th opening intake valve and sweep across the cylinder, pushing th exhaust gasses past the exhaus valve. In a wedge head engine, it i easy to visualize how it would b possible that as both valves are o their seats, the incoming mixtur could simply flow straight past th exhaust valve, leaving some of th exhaust still in the cylinder.

Chrysler's research and develop ment of the hemispherical combus tion chamber dates back to th 1930s. It continued well into th 1940s, but ceased at the end o World War II when the production o hemi-powered tanks and aircra was stopped. A short while late Chrysler engineers were intereste in extracting more horsepower fror Chrysler automobile engines, an their interest in the hemispherica combustion chamber was renewec Experimenting with in-line six-cylin der engines, Chrysler engineers se out to develop a hemispherica style cylinder head with a mor straightforward valvetrain, and me with success. These new engine proved to be both powerful and reli able. Soon this technology wa applied to V-8 engines, with th same success.

Through the 1950s there wer several variations of the early Herr V-8 engine. At that time, engine were not shared between the divi sions of Chrysler Corporation th way they were in the 1960s an beyond. This resulted in a variety o "divisional" engines, since many o

Due to this arrangement, the intake ports …

… and exhaust ports of a Hemi head can be curved less thar those of a wedge head.

Although the hemispherical cylinder heads of the early Hemi engine lent themselves well to free breathing, small displacement versions were often fitted with two-barrel carburetors and restrictive manifolds.

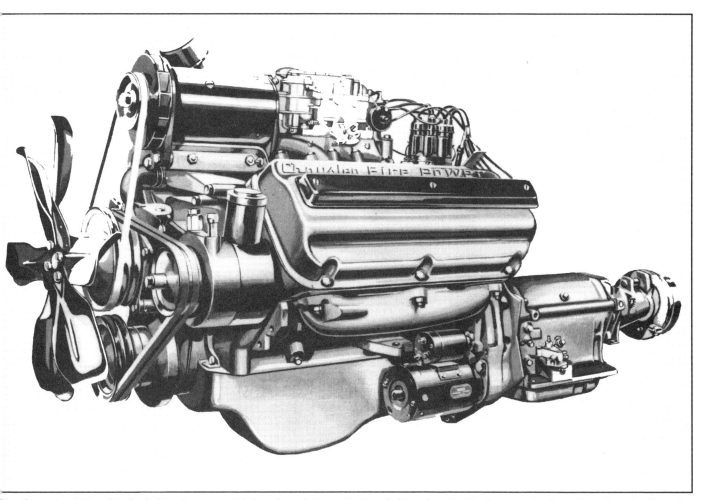

The Chrysler 392 cubic-inch Hemi was the high point of the early Hemi. (Reprinted with the permission of the DaimlerChrysler Corporate Historical Collection)

these early engines were used in only one division of the corporation. Furthermore, each division of Chrysler Corporation that received a Hemi engine had a different name for it.

In 1951 the Chrysler Firepower, which displaced 331 cubic inches and developed a whopping (for that time) 180 horsepower, was launched. DeSoto followed in 1952 with the introduction of the FireDome engine, which displaced 276 cubic inches. The next year, Dodge began offering the 241 cubic-inch RedRam engine. There were a number of variations of Hemi engines over the next few years, and by 1954 the 331 cubic-inch FirePower could be had with a rating of 235 horsepower when ordered with a four-barrel carburetor.

In 1955 Chrysler Corporation launched the Chrysler 300. This was arguably the first true American muscle car. It was powered by a 331 cubic-inch Hemi, and a pair of in-line four-barrel carburetors gave it far more "hair" than any of the earlier versions. The 1955 Chrysler 300 was aptly named for the 300-horsepower rating of this engine. In 1956, the standard engine in the 300B was a 331 cubic-inch Hemi with high compression and a hotter camshaft. It now boasted 340 horsepower in standard form, with a 355-horsepower version offered as an option.

The following year, the 300C featured a new 392 cubic-inch Firepower Hemi, which was rated at 375 horsepower. This engine, which was exclusive to the 300C, was also fed by a duo of four-barrel carburetors, while 392 engines in other Chrysler cars were topped with a single four-barrel carburetor. In 1958 the 300D was again equipped with two four-barrel carburetors, unless the optional Bendix Electrojector electronic fuel injection system was selected. Only a handful of cars were fitted with the Bendix system. Because these systems were trouble prone, cars with this system were eventually recalled and fitted

with the same dual four-barrel set-up that was standard equipment that year.

With Chrysler Corporation's four divisions – Dodge, Plymouth, Chrysler, and DeSoto – each having its own engines, it became apparent that the corporation as a whole had far more engines than it needed. Chrysler executives realized that by consolidating engines and sharing "corporate" engines between divisions, the cost of manufacturing would decrease and the parts system would have fewer part numbers to track and keep in inventory. Overall, significant savings could be realized.

The first step was taken in the 1956 model year with the introduction of the A-engine, and by the 1959 model year there were no more divisional engines. As Chrysler scrutinized its various engines, it realized that by replacing the Hemi engines wholly with wedge engines, it could further reduce manufacturing costs, since a wedge engine could be designed with a less intricate valvetrain that used fewer parts than the Hemi. Chrysler engineers also knew that if the intake and exhaust valves were arranged so that they operated on the same plane, wedge style cylinder heads required far less complicated machining than the Hemi heads. Work began on the new B engine, and the Hemi engines were dropped completely at the end of the 1958 model year.

Early Hemis in Racing

Because of the power potential of the Hemi engines, they dominated many types of racing. The Grand National Series got its start in 1949, later becoming the National Association of Stock Car Auto Racing (NASCAR). The timing was right for NASCAR and the legacy of the Hemi to grow together. Many of NASCAR's early stars – including such legends as Lee Petty, Tim Flock, Herb Thomas, Buck Baker, Frank "Rebel" Mundy, Speedy Thompson, and Norm Nelson (to

name a few) – piloted Hemi-powered stock cars in the days whe the tracks were dirt and a stock ca was just that – a *stock* car.

Carl Keikhaefer, owner of th Mercury Marine outboard engin company, was neither a racer nor fan, but was a successful business man looking for a new way to pro mote his company's products. Hi market research had identified fan of stock car racing as potential con sumers for his wares, so h believed that by assembling a win ning team he could draw attentio to his company. His entrance int Grand National racing coincide with the introduction of the Chrysle 300 in 1955.

Because of Keikhaefer's carefu planning and preparation, and th fact that he had brought togethe the best drivers and most competi tive cars, the Mercury Outboard team was rewarded with the Gran National championship for the 195 season. In 1956 Chrysler uppe the ante with an even hotter Herr in the Chrysler 300B, an Keikhaefer did likewise by expand ing his team. That year the Mercur Outboards team won 30 of the 5 events they entered, and agai took the series championship.

The dominance of the Mercur Outboards team over the rest of th teams dismayed NASCAR official track owners, and even race fans Race officials began tearing dow Keikhaefer's cars regularly in a attempt to disqualify them. Some fans threw bottles and such at th cars while others boycotted th races altogether. What had been whole-hearted attempt at advertis ing for Mercury Marine actuall became negative publicity, anc Keikhaefer pulled out of NASCAF after the 1956 season.

During the late 1950s and earl 1960s, NASCAR was in a period o rapid growth and change. Dir tracks began to give way to paved high-banked super speedways as several new tracks were opened Darlington, Daytona, and Charlotte were among the first, and with these new tracks came much high er speeds. Manufacturers were

lso turning up the heat with facto-
y sponsorships and more competi-
ve packages, such as Chevrolet's
uel-injected small block and Ford's
upercharged 312. During this time
Chrysler was making do with
he wedge-head engines. Through
960, the 361-powered Plymouths
riven by Lee Petty and son,
Richard, were tearing up the tracks,
ut it was a Chevrolet that bested
Richard Petty in the points race
hat year. The following year
hey began using 383s, but the
competition had become even
ougher, and none of the Chrysler
eams came anywhere near to cap-
uring the championship.

The year 1962 saw the introduc-
ion of the Chrysler 413 Max
Wedge, and the following year its
displacement grew to 426 cubic
nches. The Stage I, II, and III Max
Wedges of 1962, 1963, and 1964
espectively were extremely successful in NHRA drag racing. These
engines were capable of producing
astounding torque, which is essen-
ial in accelerating a car from a
standing start, but the new super
speedways of NASCAR, with their
ong straights and sweeping
panked turns were conducive to
sustained high speeds. To be competitive, an engine had to be capa-
ole of breathing well and producing
horsepower at high RPMs. In this
environment, even the Max Wedge
engines could not dominate the
new Pontiac 421, the Ford 427, or
he Chevrolet 427.

Birth of the 426 Hemi

Chrysler executives realized that
n order to become competitive
again in NASCAR, they would have
o take drastic measures. During
he winter of 1962-63, a team of
Chrysler engineers took on the task
of designing an engine capable of
dominating the high banks. These
designers turned once again to the
nemispherical combustion chamber
design. Their goal was to have the
engine completed in time to race in
the 1964 Daytona 500.

Given such a tight time schedule,
t was necessary to use as many

Because the skirts of an early Hemi block end at the centerline of the crankshaft, it is not of a deep-skirt design. Early Hemi engines more closely resemble the early A engines than the B and RB engines that would follow.

pre-existing pieces as possible. Consequently, the 426 Hemi was based closely on the 426 Wedge. The block is of the same deep-skirt design as the B and RB engines, it has the same 4.25-inch diameter bore and 3.75-inch stroke as the 426 Wedge, and uses the same 4.80-inch bore center spacing. The bell-housing bolt pattern on the face of the block is the same as that used for the B and RB engine family, and the water pump housings and oil pans can be interchanged between the 426 Hemi and the B and RB engines, provided the proper pick-up is used.

Hemi engines use a 1/2-inch diameter pick-up tube. Oil pumps can be interchanged between Hemi and big-block engines, but the Hemi pumps typically have a stiffer spring on the pressure relief valve in order to increase the oil pressure. Distributors can be physically interchanged between RB engines and Hemis, although Hemi engines typically need less spark advance than wedge engines.

In a wedge-shaped combustion chamber, the spark plug is located

at one side of the chamber. When it ignites the fuel/air mixture, the flame front must travel from that point all the way across the combustion chamber as the mixture burns. Because the spark plug in a Hemi engine is centrally located, the flame starts at the center and travels outward to the edges of the combustion chamber. Since the distance from the center of the chamber to the outer edge is half the distance of the entire width of the chamber, you can think of the flame front in a hemispherical combustion chamber as having to travel only about half the distance of the flame front in a wedge-shaped combustion chamber. (In actuality it isn't quite that simple, but you get the idea.) Because the flame front in a Hemi doesn't have as far to travel as the flame front in a wedge, the total burn takes place in less time. Therefore, less timing advance is needed with a hemispherical combustion chamber.

Because the 426 Hemi was based on the 426 RB engine, it shares virtually nothing with its early Hemi cousins. Early Hemi

The skirts of the 426 Hemi block (and all B and RB engines, for that matter) extend well below the crankshaft centerline.

blocks are not of a deep-skirt design, and these engines are actually more closely related to the A-engine family. There is really nothing that can be interchanged between any of the early Hemi engines and the 426 Hemi.

In designing the "new" Hemi, Chrysler engineers had to overcome several obstacles. Due to the shape of the combustion chambers and ports, the exhaust valves are situated such that the tips of the valves are angled toward the outer extremity of the cylinder heads. The real challenge was designing a valvetrain that could effectively and reliably actuate the exhaust valves at 7,000-plus rpm, but that didn't add monstrous inertia loads for the valve springs to overcome. Some experimenting was done with an articulated valvetrain in which a pushrod ran from the lifter to a bell crank located at the inside of the head near the intake rocker arms. A second pushrod ran from the bell crank to another rocker arm located at the outside of the cylinder head. This rocker arm then acted on the valve tip. Although this arrange-

ment was effective, it was thought to be unreliable during sustained high-RPM operation.

At the same time, another challenge presented itself. Because Hemi-powered Dodge and Plymouth vehicles were to be built on the normal production assembly line, the techniques used to assemble these cars must be the same as for all other cars coming down those lines. During assembly, the engine, transmission, and K-frame were bolted together as a large assembly, then mated to the body of the car from the bottom. Because Hemi cylinder heads are so much wider than those of the B and RB engines, the overall width of the 426 Hemi would be significantly greater than that of the 426 Wedge, perhaps so wide that the engine could not be installed easily from the bottom.

Although he is quick to give credit to the other members of the engineering team for their contributions, it was Tom Hoover who came up with the idea that solved both of these problems. As he modestly explained, by tipping the combustion chambers inboard toward the center of the engine, the overall width of the engine would be decreased. Additionally, the actuation of the exhaust valves could be accomplished with conventional (albeit long) rocker arms similar to those that had proven their reliability in the 392 Hemi several years earlier. For this innovation, Hoover has often been called "Father of the Hemi." Rolling the combustion chambers inward did alter the port shapes somewhat, favoring the intake ports by straightening them slightly while compromising the exhaust ports. In fact, some argue that the early Hemi engines have true hemispherical combustion chambers, while the 426 Hemi does not.

The 426 Hemi was ready for the 1964 Daytona 500 and propelled Dodge and Plymouth cars to a 1-2-3-4 finish. The entire 1964 NASCAR racing season was dominated by Hemi power, and it goes without saying that the competition didn't care to see that happen. The

NASCAR rule book essentially stated that a certain number of units must be produced, implying that the manufacturers were not to produce race-only engines. Just before the beginning of the 1965 season Bill France, president of NASCAR, handed down the edict that banned the Hemi from competition. That decision was later reversed, but not until late in the season.

Chrysler-sponsored teams were back in full force for the 1966 racing season (with de-stroked Hemis used on long tracks), but something very important happened outside the racing program first. In complying with NASCAR regulations that engines used in Grand National racing be available for production automobiles, Chrysler released the Street Hemi option in 1966. Had it not been for this need to homologate the Hemi for racing purposes, it is likely that the Street Hemi would never have seen the light of day!

Street Hemi engines differed from their full-race brethren in that the 12.5:1 compression ratio was lowered to a more streetable 10.25:1 so that it could ingest premium pump gas instead of race fuel. Somewhat tamer camshafts were used, although solid lifters were retained for the first few years of the Street Hemi. NASCAR versions of the Race Hemi were fitted with one large four-barrel carburetor while those used in drag racing received two four-barrel carburetors mounted atop a short-ram intake manifold similar to that of the Max Wedge engines. Street Hemi engines were also the recipients of two four-barrel carburetors, but they were positioned in-line. All in all, Street Hemis weren't too far removed from their full-race brethren. Soon they were dubbed "elephant engines," most likely due to their massive appearance.

426 Hemis Go Drag Racing

The 426 Hemi replaced the Max Wedge engines in NASCAR at the beginning of the 1964 race season and later that year many drag racing teams began to use Hemi engines, too. In addition to the birth

Fitting the 426 Hemi into the narrow A body engine bay is difficult at best.

of the 426 Hemi, 1964 also marked the first year of Chrysler's A-833 four-speed manual transmission. Prior to the introduction of the A-833, all Max Wedge engines had been backed by a Warner T-85 three-speed manual transmission. Many General Motors cars of that era were equipped with the Warner T-10 four-speed manual transmission, but the folks at Chrysler believed that the T-10 lacked the strength necessary to live behind the Max Wedge engines.

Although the Max Wedge engines had proven to be quite successful in drag racing, the Hemi offered even more horsepower potential. Altered wheelbase funny cars appeared the following year and competed in the A/FX class, intended for factory experimental cars. Also in 1965, the first drag race-only package cars were released. Commonly referred to by the A-990 designation, this batch of Dodge Coronets and Plymouth Belvederes, destined to do battle a quarter mile at a time, were fitted with lightweight aluminum body panels, the awesome Race Hemi, and not much else.

Following the restyling of these Dodge and Plymouth B body intermediates, another batch of Hemi-powered Super Stock Dodges and Plymouths was unleashed in 1967. These cars are often called by the first two characters in their Vehicle Identification Numbers. "WO" indicates a 1967 Super Stock Dodge Coronet, while "RO" indicates a 1967 Super Stock Plymouth Belvedere.

In 1968, Chrysler teamed up with Hurst Industries to build the ultimate Super Stock package cars. A number of A-body Dodge Dart and Plymouth Barracuda compacts were plucked from the assembly lines and shipped to Hurst, where they were fitted with fiberglass fenders and hoods and received the modifications necessary to cram a Hemi into the comparatively narrow engine bay.

Due to the confines of the A-body engine compartment, the massive Hemi could not be installed in the traditional assembly line method

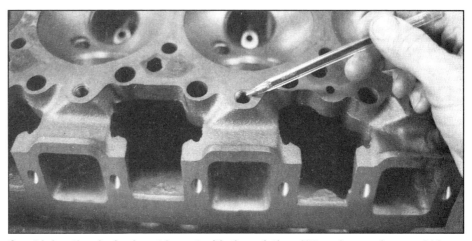

Combining the desired port layout with the existing 426 wedge engine would have caused the upper row of head bolts to pass through the intake ports. To get around this, engineers used studs in place of the upper row of head bolts.

Hemi blocks then had to be designed to accommodate these studs.

The center three main caps of a 426 Hemi are cross-bolted through the skirts of the block.

The engine mounting brackets bolt flush against pads on the block.

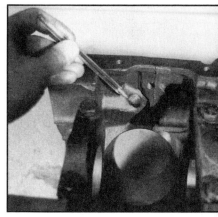

Because Hemi engines use a 1/2-inch diameter oil pick-up tube, the pick-up tube hole was enlarged.

The crank flange of a 426 Hemi accepts eight bolts instead of the usual six.

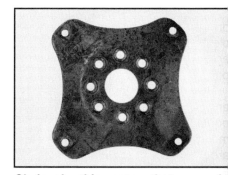

Obviously, this means that a special flex plate or flywheel must be used.

from beneath the body. The master cylinder had to be relocated in order to clear the left-side rocker cover, and the right-side fender apron was crudely reworked, most likely with a sledge hammer. Lightweight glass and the absence of non-essentials such as a radio, heater, window regulators, and sound deadener were characteristic of these cars. The cars were delivered in gel coat and primer, for racers would, no doubt, wish to paint the cars in their own color schemes. Straight out of the box, these cars were capable of running mid-ten second elapsed times. Many of these cars still compete today, now running times well into the eight-second range.

Production of the 426 Street Hemi lasted through the 1971 model year, but due to pressures from rising insurance costs and difficulty in meeting the emissions regulations of the Environmental Protection Agency, the death knell sounded for the Hemi at the end of that year.

Design of the 426 Hemi

When the 426 Hemi was designed, the team of engineers essentially started with a 426 Wedge short block, then added a pair of cylinder heads with hemispherical combustion chambers. In order to achieve the desired port layout, however, it was necessary to rearrange the cylinder head-bolt configuration, for attaching the heads in the same manner as the B and RB engines would have placed head bolts in the desired location of the intake ports. To get around this obstacle, engineers replaced the upper row of head bolts with studs that screw into the deck surface of the heads, then pass through the block. Nuts are threaded onto the studs from inside the lifter valley. Because of this difference in cylinder head attachment, production Hemi heads cannot be interchanged with B or RB engine cylinder heads.

Unlike the Max Wedge engines, which were based on production engines used in passenger cars and trucks, then adapted for use in racing, the 426 Hemi was designed as a race engine. It wasn't until two years after its introduction that it appeared as an option on new car order forms. Because it was bred for racing, only later becoming a production engine, many of the features designed into the Hemi for racing purposes were carried over to the production Street Hemi engines.

For example, the blocks were cast from material with a high nickel content for improved strength, and the center three crankshaft main caps were cross-bolted through the skirts of the block for strength and increased rigidity at high RPMs. Instead of having ears cast into the sides of the block to which the engine mounting brackets would be attached, 426 Hemi engines have holes that are

When shopping for a used Hemi crankshaft, don't be tricked into buying a pre-1962 B or RB engine crankshaft. Though it has an eight-bolt flange, it is of a different configuration than later engines.

Like other production engines, Street Hemi engines use crankshafts with undercut fillets at the ends of the journals.

drilled and tapped in the sides of the block. The mounting brackets sit flush against the sides of the block, and the bolts pass directly into the block.

This deviation from the B and RB engine family means that vehicles equipped with Hemi engines use mounting brackets and K-frames that are exclusive to the Hemi engine. In addition, the oil pick-up tube was enlarged to 1/2-inch in diameter, which means that the threaded hole in the block into which the pick-up tube fits was enlarged, also.

Crankshafts used in Hemi engines are made of forged steel and have the same 2.38-inch diameter rod journal and 2.75-inch diameter main journals as those found in RB engines. Although it is physically possible to interchange Hemi and RB engine crankshafts, the differences in piston and connecting rod weights are reflected in the balancing of the crankshafts. Swapping crankshafts would require that the engine be balanced.

Street Hemi crankshaft dampers are much thicker than those used on other engines.

Installing a four-speed manual transmission behind a Hemi that was originally backed by an automatic transmission should be straightforward, since the crankshafts are all drilled and finished to the proper size to accept a pilot bushing. Due to the Hemi's racing heritage, the rear flange of its crankshaft is drilled for eight bolts, and the center of the flange has the large recess used to center the torque converter hub and the centering ring for the flex plate and flywheel as found on the crankshaft flanges of all 1962 and later V-8 engines.

If you are shopping for a Hemi crankshaft, don't be tricked into purchasing a pre-1962 RB engine crankshaft. This crankshaft also has an eight-bolt flange, but there is no centering ring for the flex plate or flywheel and the hole in the center is not nearly large enough to accommodate the hub of a torque converter.

Hemi crankshafts were treated to tuff-triding, which is a surface-hardening process applied to the journals for improved wear resistance. Consequently, it is not recommended that the journals be machined undersize. Like the crankshafts in all other production V-8 engines, Street Hemis have undercut fillets at the ends of the journals in order to reduce stress and the possibility of cracking at these points. Although these crankshafts are fine for light racing, if the expected output of the engine is over 600 horsepower, the crankshaft should be replaced with a full radius fillet crankshaft.

Unlike some of the engines in other families, all Hemi engines are internally balanced. Two different crankshaft vibration dampers were used, depending on application. Race Hemis from 1964 and 1965 use a thin damper, while 1966 through 1971 Street Hemis use a thick damper. Because of the difference in timing mark locations on the dampers, they cannot be simply interchanged. If you wish to use a Race Hemi damper on a Street Hemi engine or vice-versa, after installing the damper you will have to go through the process of finding absolute top dead center, then make a new mark on the damper to indicate top dead center. The crankshaft pulley is attached to the damper with six evenly spaced bolts, but because the Street Hemi damper is thicker than that of the B and RB engines, different crankshaft pulleys are required.

The connecting rods used in Street Hemi engines are stout, forged-steel pieces that are fitted with 7/16-inch diameter bolts in lieu of the 3/8-inch diameter rod bolts typical of wedge engines. These rods measure 6.861 inches from center to center and are bushed for 1.03-inch diameter floating wrist pins. For NASCAR use, connecting rods with 1/2-inch diameter bolts and pressed 1.094-inch diameter wrist pins are standard fare.

Two different oil pans were used on Street Hemi engines. Engines from 1966 through 1969 were equipped with a five-quart oil pan, while 1970 and 1971 engines were fitted with a deeper six-quart oil pan. The pans can be interchanged as long as the correct pick-up tube is used. Obviously, a five-quart pan will not fit with a pick-up tube intended for a six-quart pan, but a six-quart pan will easily fit over a pick-up tube meant for a five-quart pan. If this happens, the foot of the pick-up tube will be positioned more than an inch from the bottom of the pan. Although it may be covered with oil when the engine is at rest, when the engine is running and oil is circulating it is possible for the oil in the pan to vortex, allowing a spiral of air to reach the pick-up. Check to be sure that the foot of the pick-up tube is 1/4-inch from the bottom of the pan. (See Chapter 8, "Oiling Systems," for

Due to the shape and volume of a Hemi combustion chamber, pistons with large domes that extend well above the deck surface of the block are needed.

Super Stock Hemi engines were originally fitted with short ram intake manifolds that positioned two four-barrel carburetors diagonally across the engine from each other

more information on this subject.)

Due to the shape of the hemispherical combustion chamber, high-dome pistons are required. These pistons can be considered Hemi-only pieces, for they will not interchange with any pistons used in wedge engines. Many engine builders have experimented with modifying the shape of the piston domes to improve flame front propagation and especially to enhance combustion chamber crossflow during valve overlap, but the basic shape of the combustion chamber still requires a sizeable dome on the piston to achieve a desirable compression ratio. The combustion chamber volumes of 1966 and later Hemi engines are quite large compared to a wedge engine, typically around 175cc.

There were three different styles of intake manifolds used on 426 Hemi engines, depending on the intended application of the engine. Hemis destined to conquer the high-banked NASCAR tracks were fitted with intake manifolds that would accept a large single four-barrel carburetor as mandated by the NASCAR rule book. Hemis that were installed in cars as part of a Super Stock package received single-piece short cross-ram intake manifolds which accepted two diagonally opposed four-barrel carburetors. The intake manifolds used on Street Hemi engines also accepted two four-barrel carburetors, but they were mounted in-line, one behind the other.

Street Hemi engines also use two four-barrel carburetors, but with one mounted behind the other.

Because 426 Hemi engines were originally designed for racing, there are no passages in the cylinder heads to supply exhaust heat to the intake manifold. The engineers were aware that with no heat reaching the intake manifold, the cold weather driveability of the Street Hemi would have been extremely poor. In order to combat cold weather ills, a manifold heat package was adapted to the Street Hemi engines. A thermally controlled manifold heat valve, or heat riser, was installed at the outlet of the right side exhaust manifold, similar to those used in other engines.

Just ahead of the manifold heat valve a steel tube routes exhaust from the exhaust manifold to the rear of the intake manifold and connects it to an opening in the manifold. This opening leads to a passage in the intake manifold below the plenum. Exhaust circulates beneath the plenum, then exits through another opening at the rear of the intake manifold. From there, a second steel tube carries the exhaust back to the exhaust pipe just downstream of the manifold heat valve. As is the case with a conventional manifold heat valve, as the engine warms up, the heat in the vicinity of the exhaust manifold causes the heat sensing bi-metallic coil to relax its tension on the valve and open the flapper inside. This allows the

On the back side of this manifold are two homemade plates that cap the passages where the exhaust heat tubes were once connected.

exhaust to take its normal path from the manifold straight to the exhaust pipe. After a few years of daily operation, these pipes usually rusted away and were often disconnected and eliminated.

The cylinder heads used on 426 Hemi engines evolved little during the production span of the engine, but during the first couple of years the material from which they were cast did change. Cast-iron cylinder heads were used on 1964 Race Hemis, but 1965 Super Stock engines received aluminum heads. Street Hemi engines from 1966 through 1971 use cast-iron cylinder heads, and these were also used for the 1968 Super Stock (Dodge Dart and Plymouth Barracuda) engines. All cast-iron cylinder heads were fitted with 2.25-inch intake valves, while the aluminum heads of 1965 use intake valves with a 2.23-inch diameter. The intake valves of the early 426 Hemi engines seem enormous when compared to the 2.08-inch diameter intake valves of the 1968 and later B and RB engines.

All production Hemi cylinder heads use 1.94-inch diameter exhaust valves. The valve stems of both the intake and exhaust valves in all engines measure 5/16-inch in diameter, but the valves used in the aluminum heads are slightly longer than those used in cast-iron heads. Because aluminum is much softer than cast iron, steel valve seat inserts were installed in the aluminum cylinder heads, while the valve seats in the cast-iron heads were machined into the iron of the cylinder head. Rocker covers from 1964 and 1965 can be

interchanged, but the cylinder heads and covers were changed in 1966. Engines from 1966 through 1971 share the same rocker cover shape, so they can all be interchanged. Virtually all replacement cylinder heads available today are based on the 1966 through 1971 castings, so using them would necessitate the use of the appropriate rocker covers.

Like all Chrysler V-8 engines (with the exception of the Magnum small-block engines), the 426 Hemi engines oil the rocker arms through the rocker shafts. Oil passages from the cam bores run upward through the block to the cylinder heads. Passages in the heads route the oil to the rocker shafts. Oil flows through the hollow rocker shafts to the rocker arms, where it also lubricates the valve stems and pushrods.

The rocker arms used in Hemi engines are said to be of a 1.5:1 ratio, but they are not true 1.5:1 rockers. Actually, the intake rocker arms have a 1.56:1 ratio, while the exhaust rocker arms have a 1.52:1 ratio. Through 1969, all Hemi engines were equipped with solid lifter camshafts. The specifications of the 1968 and

The Street Hemi intake manifold is of a dual-plane design.

Atop a Hemi head, long rocker arms are mounted on a pair of rocker shafts.

1969 Street Hemi camshafts are slightly hotter than those used in 1966 and 1967 Street Hemis. Because the solid lifter valvetrains required frequent attention, 1970 and 1971 Street Hemis were equipped with hydraulic lifter camshafts, but the adjustable rocker arms were retained. Because hydraulic lifters are taller than solid lifters, shorter pushrods were used in engines with hydraulic lifters.

It is possible to install a solid lifter camshaft and lifter package in an engine originally equipped with hydraulic lifters as long as the pushrods are replaced with longer solid lifter pushrods. The reverse is true: a hydraulic camshaft and lifter package can be installed in place of a solid lifter camshaft as long as shorter hydraulic lifter pushrods are used. Even for street use, stiff valve springs were selected based on the expected 6500-rpm redline. In some cases the tension of these valve springs was blamed for accelerated camshaft wear, but that was a necessary trade-

off to achieve the high-RPM potential. In comparison, the maximum expected engine speed of wedge engines was 5500 rpm.

On the subject of maintenance, Street Hemi engines earned the reputation of being finicky and temperamental, for generally they are much more sensitive to proper tuning than wedge engines. In fact, it sometimes happened that a Hemi that hadn't received recent attention was bested in street competition by a strong running wedge engine. In all fairness, however, when examining the sensitive nature of the Hemi, one must also consider the racing origin of the engine and the fact that high-performance components – such as a dual-point distributor, solid-lifter valvetrain, and an induction system that consists of dual four-barrel carburetors with mechanically actuated secondaries – all add not only to the raw performance potential of the engine, but to the need for frequent attention as well. Sadly, the nature of the upkeep the

Hemi requires has often been beyond the mechanical ability of the owner of the car.

Chrysler dropped production of the 426 Hemi at the end of the 1971 model year. The EPA had begun to tighten its stranglehold on automakers by imposing tighter standards for emission levels, and the Hemi simply could not comply with these standards. Although the introduction of catalytic converters and unleaded gasoline were on the horizon, induction-hardened exhaust valve seats did not appear in Chrysler engines until 1972, after the demise of the Hemi. Therefore, there were no cast-iron production Hemi cylinder heads with hardened valve seats.

If you are rebuilding a Hemi engine that will see any appreciable street use, spend the extra money to have hardened exhaust valve seat inserts installed in the cylinder heads. The extra expense is not substantial when figured into the total cost of an engine rebuild, and you will have no worries about the durability of the valves operating in the absence of tetraethyl lead. Nothing is worse than completing an engine build-up only to discover a short while later that you must go back into the engine to correct a problem that you could have avoided in the first place. It is even more aggravating if the car has been restored and the engine has been detailed, for all the parts such as the block, cylinder heads, and intake manifold that were assembled before the engine was painted will now have to be disturbed.

Another fuel-related issue must be considered when rebuilding a Hemi that will see street use. When new, the 10.25:1 compression ratio of the Street Hemi engines dictated a diet of premium fuel. Unfortunately, what passes for premium fuel today is nothing like the premium fuel of 30 years ago. The compression ratio should be lowered to somewhere around 9:1. Doing so will allow you to run the proper amount of spark advance without detonation, even with today's low-octane and oxygenated fuels. Perhaps best of all, no longer will you have to worry about pouring octane booster down the side of your car every time you fill the tank!

CHRYSLER PERFORMANCE ENGINES
Mopar Performance Crate Engines

Mopar Performance crate engines are nearly complete engines shipped, as the name implies, in a large crate. A crate engine includes everything from the intake manifold down to the oil pan drain plug, from the timing chain cover to the crankshaft flange. The 300- and 380-horsepower Magnum 360 cubic-inch crate engines also include the crankshaft damper. These engines offer several advantages when compared to rebuilding an engine or building an engine from scratch.

When building an engine from scratch, depending on what type of engine you wish to build, locating useable pieces such as a block, crankshaft, cylinder heads, and rods can be quite an ordeal, as well as costly. Furthermore, the cost of machining must be figured in, for some machine work will certainly be necessary to bring these pieces up to snuff. Because crate engines are virtually complete assemblies, using one means that you won't have to do any of the parts scrounging that

is often necessary when building an engine from scratch.

All of the pieces in a Mopar Performance crate engine are new. This means that all of the dimensions and tolerances are right where the factory intended them to be. When you purchase a used engine or an engine built from used parts, until you tear it down to inspect and measure its components, you can't be sure of what you have. Have the cylinders been bored? How far? Have the rods been reconditioned, and do their lengths now vary? Have the crankshaft journals been turned, and if so, how far? Have the heads been milled? How much? Have they accumulated so many miles and/or valve jobs that the valves are sunk into the cylinder head castings? These are but a few of the concerns regarding the condition of the major components of the engine, and we haven't even mentioned topics such as parts fatigue, clearances, or proper assembly techniques! Because

Mopar Performance crate engines are built from new pieces, none of the potential headaches of purchasing a used engine enter the picture.

When you build an engine, choosing a good combination of parts that work well together for the intended application of the engine is of utmost importance. Selecting the pieces that will give you that combination is tricky at best. With a crate engine, however, there is no guesswork. The decisions of which pieces will work together the best have already been made for you. The combination of parts in each of the crate engines was chosen by Chrysler engineers who have the luxuries of unlimited time for dynomometer testing and the ability to try different combinations of parts. When building an engine, most of us have to wait until it is in the car and running to see if it lives up to our expectations. From that point forward, trying different combinations is costly and time consuming.

The Mopar Performance Commando crate engines featured flat-bottom hydraulic lifters in place of the roller lifters.

Although the cylinder heads used on these engines had the holes drilled for air injection, they were blocked off before the engines were shipped.

While the crate engine concept is certainly nothing new, the folks at Mopar Performance believe that it is an idea whose time has finally arrived. According to Larry Shepard, chief engineer and spokesman for Mopar Performance, 25 complete 426 Hemi engines were put into inventory near the end of the production of the Hemi engine. Chrysler itself later used one of these engines, which left 24 engines in inventory. Five years later, all 24 engines were still sitting in inventory!

It was not until the late 1980s that the need for crate engines was recognized, and Mopar Performance responded by offering 300-horsepower and 360-horsepower versions of Chrysler's then-current 360 cubic-

As on production Magnum Engines, guide plates keep the pushrods and rocker arms aligned on Magnum crate engines.

inch LA truck engine. These engines were called Commandos, borrowing their name from the 1960s Plymouth line of high-performance engines. They were built through 1994, and were eventually replaced by the Magnum crate engines.

300 and 380 Horsepower Magnums

These engines are based on the current 360 cubic-inch Magnum truck engine, but are designed to replace LA engines. They each include an LA engine style timing chain cover and a Mopar Performance M-1 intake manifold that accepts a four-barrel carburetor.

Internally, the 300-horsepower version is not too far removed from its production roots. The standard compression ratio and stock production

360 Magnum crate engines use production style rocker arms and pedestals.

cylinder heads are used, as are the pistons and other internals. The intake and exhaust valve sizes are 1.925 and 1.625 inches diameter respectively. The hydraulic roller lifter camshaft in this engine is quite mild, having 0.385-inch intake valve lift and 0.401-inch exhaust valve lift, with 250 degrees intake duration and 264 degrees exhaust duration. These figures take into account the 1.6:1 rocker arm ratio of the Magnum engines. The intake manifold used on the 300-horsepower version is a dual-plane manifold.

The 380-horsepower Magnum has a 9.0:1 compression ratio and uses the same cylinder heads and other internals as the 300-horsepower version, with the exception of the camshaft. The camshaft specifications are 0.501-inch intake valve lift and 0.513-inch exhaust valve lift with

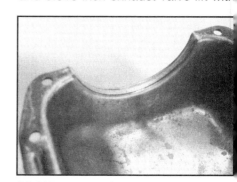

All 360 crate engines can accept a production style 360 LA engine oil pan, but a 360 LA engine oil-pan gasket should be used.

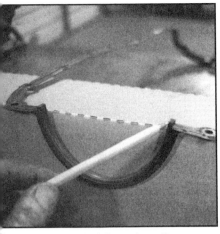

The standard 360 LA engine oil-pan gasket fits the crate engines as well. This gasket is for a production 360 Magnum and shouldn't be used with a 360 LA engine pan because of the strengthening dimples between the bolt holes.

Production roller lifter camshafts used in Magnum truck engines have a short snout that does not protrude past the face of the camshaft sprocket.

Magnum crate engines use special roller camshafts with a longer snout. The additional length of the snout is necessary to locate the fuel pump eccentric.

All Commando and Magnum crate engines accept the standard 340/360 left-side engine mounting bracket.

If you install a pre-1972 crankshaft pulley on any of the crate engines, expect to find a slight mismatch with one of the bolt holes.

This torque converter has been weighted for use behind a 360 Magnum.

All Commando and Magnum crate engines are externally balanced the same as their production counterparts. This damper is on a 360 Commando …

… while this damper fits a 360 Magnum.

288 degrees intake duration and 292 degrees exhaust duration. Again, these specs take into consideration the 1.6:1 rocker arm ratio of these engines. The valve springs are upgraded for use with this hotter camshaft, and the camshaft is driven by a double roller timing chain. The 380-horsepower Magnum is topped by a single plane intake manifold.

The camshafts used in Magnum crate engines are exclusive to these engines. They are designed for use with hydraulic roller lifters, like production Magnum engines. The snout on the camshaft, however, is longer than the snout on a production Magnum engine camshaft, and is actually the same length as the snout on an LA engine camshaft. This is because the extra length of the camshaft snout is intended to protrude from the camshaft sprocket and drive the fuel pump eccentric. According to Mopar Performance, the longer snout on the camshaft of a Magnum crate engine will not fit inside the timing chain cover of a standard Magnum engine, and the camshaft snout of a standard Magnum engine will not properly center the fuel pump eccentric used on LA engines or Magnum crate engines.

Either of these engines will bolt in place of an LA engine using the 340/360 style left-side engine mounting bracket. The exhaust manifolds or headers from the LA engine will bolt up, as will the accessories on the front of the engine. A 1972 or later LA engine crankshaft pulley with a symmetrical

This is a 360 Magnum crate engine. (Photo courtesy of Mopar Performance)

six-bolt pattern will attach to the damper. A 1971 or earlier pulley with one staggered bolt hole will work if the offending bolt hole is elongated and the unused portion is welded shut and ground flat. If the vehicle has air conditioning, mounting the compressor might require some fabrication, since the intake manifolds used on these engines may not allow the compressor to mount as it did on the LA engine.

The only real pitfall in using either of the 360 cubic-inch Magnum crate engines is in their external balancing. Some of the weight necessary to balance the crankshaft is located on the damper and flywheel or torque converter. External balancing is also used on all 360 cubic-inch LA engines and the 1973 cast crankshaft 340 engine, but the 360 Magnum engine, 360 LA engine, and cast-crank 340 engines all require a different amount of external weight for proper balancing. The damper poses no problems, for the crate engines are shipped with the proper damper already installed.

At the other end of the engine, things are not quite so simple. If the Magnum crate engine is being installed into a car with a manual transmission, a flywheel that is properly weighted for a Magnum 360 will have to be used. If the car has an automatic transmission, you will need to start with a "zero"-balance torque converter, then weld the necessary weight to the face of the torque converter. This weight, as well as instructions, are included with the engine.

All crate engines have pilot bushings installed.

The 440-based 500 cubic-inch crate engines are available in either 505 or 545 horsepower form. (Photo courtesy of Mopar Performance)

505 and 545 Horsepower 500 C.I.D. Stroker 440s

Like the Magnum crate engines, these two new 440 engines are assembled from all new parts. The block castings have more material in critical areas, like the cylinder walls and decks, than production blocks, and the numbers two, three, and four main caps are cross-bolted into the skirts of the block, like the production Hemi engines, for additional strength and rigidity. The 500 cubic-inch displacement of these engines is derived from the 4.380-inch bores, 0.060 inches larger than the standard 4.320-inch 440 bores, and the long 4.15-inch stroke crankshaft, as opposed to the 3.75-inch stroke of the 440. Both engines are internally balanced and include everything from the timing chain cover to the rear of the engine, from the single plane M-1 aluminum intake manifold to the oil pan.

The 505 horsepower version has a compression ratio of 9.0:1 and uses the Mopar Performance cast-iron Stage V wedge heads. The intake and exhaust valves measure 2.14 inches and 1.81 inches in diameter respectively. The hydraulic cam specs are 0.509 inches lift with 292 degrees duration. Due to this engine's conservative compression ratio, high-octane pump gas is sufficient fuel for it.

The 545-horsepower version has a higher compression ratio of 10.25:1. This engine uses the Mopar Performance cast-aluminum Stage VI cylinder heads, with the same 2.14-inch diameter intake and 1.81-inch diameter exhaust valves as the 505 horsepower engine. This engine also uses the same hydraulic camshaft, with 0.509 inches valve lift and 292 degrees duration. Compression ratios in engines with aluminum cylinder heads can typically be pushed higher than static compression ratios in engines with cast-iron heads before detonation occurs. For this reason, high-octane pump gas is recommended for use in this engine, despite its high-compression ratio.

Hemi Crate Engines

Three different Hemi crate engines are now available from Mopar Performance: a 426 cubic-inch, 465-horsepower Hemi; a 472 cubic-inch, 525-horsepower Hemi; and a 528 cubic-inch, 610-horsepower Hemi. All three of these engines have a cast-iron cylinder block with cross-bolted numbers two, three, and four main caps, and all include six-quart center sump oil pans. All three of these engines are topped with a single four-

Hemi crate engines can be had in 426, 472, or 528 cubic-inch displacements with 465, 525, or 610 horsepower ratings respectively. (Photo courtesy of Mopar Performance)

barrel, dual plane M-1 aluminum intake manifold, and all have forged aluminum pistons. Like all other crate engines, they are assembled from new parts and are complete from the intake manifold to the oil pan, and include everything from the timing chain cover back to the eight-bolt crankshaft flange.

The 426 cubic-inch version uses the same 4.25-inch bore and 3.75-inch stroke measurements as the production 426 Hemi. It has a 9.0:1 compression ratio, and it uses 2.25-inch diameter intake and 1.94-inch diameter exhaust valves, just like the Street Hemi and cast-iron head Race Hemi engines. The camshaft specs call for 0.495-inch intake valve lift and 0.480-inch exhaust valve lift with 278 degrees duration.

The 472 cubic-inch Hemi is quite similar to the 426 cubic-inch version. The main difference between these two engines is the 4.15-inch stroke crankshaft found in the 472 cubic-inch version. In order to allow this stroker Hemi to breathe as deeply as it wants to, a hotter hydraulic camshaft is used. This camshaft has 0.524-inch intake valve lift and 0.543-inch exhaust valve lift with 292 degrees duration. Upgraded valve springs round out the package.

The 528 cubic-inch Hemi also uses a 4.15-inch stroke crankshaft, but its additional displacement comes from its larger 4.50-inch diameter bore size. It uses the same camshaft as the 472 cubic-inch Hemi, but a higher 10.25:1 compression ratio. The cylinder heads used on the 528 cubic-inch Hemi are cast aluminum, while the standard 2.25-inch diameter intake and 1.94-inch diameter exhaust valve sizes are retained.

Premium pump gas is recommended for use in all Hemi crate engines. The aluminum heads of the 528 engine permit the use of a higher static compression ratio than is possible with cast-iron heads without experiencing detonation.

Mopar Performance 360 C.I.D. Short Blocks

Mopar Performance now offers four different 360 engine short blocks. There are two LA engine versions,

Mopar Performance remanufactured short blocks can be ordered in any of four flavors. (Photo courtesy of Mopar Performance)

one with pistons of a 1.58-inch compression height (the distance from the centerline of the wrist pin to the top of the piston), and one with pistons of a 1.63-inch compression height. These pistons afford advertised compression ratios of 9.0:1 and 10.0:1, although cylinder head and head gasket choices can significantly alter the actual compression ratio of the engine. Two different Magnum versions are available as well, with the same available pistons as the LA engine versions.

While the crate engines can sure make life easy, especially when compared to the headaches often associated with building an engine from scratch, they certainly don't offer the versatility that is possible when building an engine from scratch. Mopar Performance short blocks combine some of the best of both worlds, while keeping costs well within reason.

Unlike the crate engines, the build-up of a Mopar Performance short block does not start with a fresh, new block casting. Instead, "seasoned" (read: "used") blocks are selected. The crankshaft centerline dimension of an LA engine is 9.60 inches, while the same dimension of a Magnum is 9.58 inches. The short blocks are all machined to a 9.56-inch deck height, then bored 0.020 inches oversize to a 4.020-inch

diameter. The pistons used in all short blocks are hypereutectic, with a low-friction coating on the skirts, and all have valve reliefs.

These short blocks come complete with camshafts, double roller timing chains, and LA engine style timing chain covers, but no lifters.

The Magnum short blocks have camshafts with 0.512 inches of valve lift and 280 degrees duration, as computed with the 1.6:1 rocker arm ratio used in Magnum engines, and they are intended for use with hydraulic roller lifters. There are no oil-feed passages to the cylinder heads in the Magnum short blocks, though these holes could be drilled if non-Magnum heads were to be used.

LA engine-style short blocks have camshafts with 0.509 inches of valve lift and 292 degrees duration, as computed with the standard 1.5:1 rocker arm ratio. They are intended for use with flat-bottom hydraulic lifters. These short blocks have the cylinder head oil feed passages that are necessary with all pre-Magnum cylinder heads.

All of these short blocks, both in Magnum and LA engine form, are externally balanced to 360 LA engine specifications, or pre-Magnum specs. A crankshaft damper and flywheel or torque converter balanced for a 360 LA engine will be needed.

CHRYSLER PERFORMANCE ENGINES
Oiling Systems

The motor oil used in any engine performs several vital functions. We always think of it as the "slippery stuff" that provides a protective barrier between moving parts, preventing metal-to-metal contact between these parts. The fact is, motor oil must be up to the task of lubricating all of the pieces inside the engine.

It must be able to circulate upon start-up in sub-zero temperatures and reach all of the parts in the engine quickly in order to protect them. It must be able to lubricate the crankshaft and bearings by establishing a hydraulic wedge between the surfaces of the crankshaft journals and bearing surfaces. Some of the oil slung from the spinning crankshaft will next contact the cylinder walls, where it must be able to provide a thin barrier between the piston skirts and the cylinder walls to prevent scuffing. At the same time it must also lubricate the rings. It must work its way into the wrist-pin bores to protect the piston and wrist pin from galling together.

Some of the oil thrown from the crankshaft will reach the camshaft, where it must provide a protective film between the cam lobes and faces of the lifters. This is an area of extremely high pressure, and these parts are susceptible to rapid wear and galling if the oil is not up to the task of providing proper lubrication. Oil reaching the top end of the engine must provide lubrication for the rocker shafts and rocker arms, as well as the pushrods and valve tips.

The area where the rocker arms meet the valve tips is another area of extremely high pressure which is susceptible to galling if the quality of the oil is poor, or the quantity of oil reaching these parts is insufficient. Lifter and valve tip wear and galling become more of a problem when high-lift camshafts and stiff valve springs are used, and that is why roller lifters and roller tip rockers are often employed in race engines. Some of the oil from the valve tips will run down the valve stems, and a

little bit will get past the valve stem seals and enter the valve guides, where it lubricates the guides and valve stems. Again, this is an area where abnormally rapid wear and scuffing are possible if the oil reaching these parts is of poor quality, or of too little quantity.

While it is true that the primary job of motor oil is to lubricate, it also performs a couple of other vital functions in the engine. A thin film of oil on the cylinder walls, pistons, and rings aids in sealing the rings to the piston ring lands and to the cylinder walls. Additionally, a thin film of oil on the crankshaft helps the materials of the front and rear crankshaft seals to do their jobs of forming a seal against the crankshaft surfaces. The tendency of the oil's molecules to cling together allows this to happen.

A film of oil helps to cushion parts of the engine that are suddenly and violently thrust together. When the fuel/air mixture in a cylinder is fired and the power stroke is initiated, the piston is driven downward against the wrist pin, the rod drives the upper shell of the rod bearing against the crankshaft journal, and the crankshaft is thrust downward against the lower shell of the main bearings. At the same time, the major thrust face of the piston is slammed against the cylinder wall. The film of oil between all of these components cushions these movements.

Oil flowing through an engine cools many of the components in the engine. A piston, for example, gives off heat to the cylinder walls and is also cooled somewhat by the cool fuel/air mixture that enters the engine during the intake stroke. However, a large portion of its heat is absorbed and carried away by the oil that is thrown from the crankshaft to the underside of the piston head. The upper portions of the valve stems and valve springs are also cooled by the oil flowing over them. Ideally, the oil film on the crankshaft journals and bearings, as well as on the camshaft, lifters, and cam bearings, prevents metal-to-metal contact between these pieces. There is still heat generated at these points by the viscous friction of the oil as these pieces move in close proximity to each other under high loads. A constant supply of oil to these points helps to reduce temperatures.

Finally, the oil must keep the components inside the engine clean. As the pieces inside the engine wear, the oil must flush away the particles. Furthermore, although engine builders strive to achieve the best possible ring seal, all engines have some degree of blow-by past the piston rings. Each time a cylinder is fired, there is some water, gasoline, carbon, and other byproducts of combustion that are forced past the piston rings. This is the reason the oil in an engine turns black. In a well-maintained engine with good ring seal, the oil will take longer to turn black than in a similarly maintained engine with poor ring seal that is operated in the same manner. One of the oil's functions is to suspend the impurities and carry them away so that the larger particles can be filtered out of the system. In addition, the raw fuel that gets past the rings dilutes the oil.

So motor oil actually performs five jobs: it lubricates, seals, cushions, cools, and cleans the components inside the engine. When you stop to consider the conditions under which motor oil must operate, you begin to realize how complicated its job in the engine becomes. Oil must overcome extreme variances in temperature, from sub-zero degree cold start-ups to high temperature operation of a few hundred degrees in an engine that is heavily loaded and working hard.

In a street engine, the oil must continue to do its job whether idling in traffic or cruising down the interstate, through numerous heat cycles over thousands of miles. The chemists who formulate motor oil, and the additives to be used in it, are concerned with all of these things. Viscosity improvers must be added to give the oil its proper hot and cold viscosities, and detergents must be added to control the natural tendency of mineral-based motor oil to form sludge and wax deposits. Anti-scuff agents are added to reduce the chances of parts scuffing together (such as the pistons scuffing the cylinder walls), and extreme pressure additives must be included to help prevent galling in areas of high unit pressure, such as the camshaft lobes and lifter faces.

Additives are also included that help the oil resist foaming, oxidation, and varnishing, and others that help to prevent rust and corrosion. It is little wonder that the properties of conventional mineral-based motor oil begin to break down within the first thousand miles that the oil is in the crankcase.

Mineral-based motor oil is by far the most commonly used oil in automobiles today. It is refined from crude oil and it has been in continuous evolution since before the birth of the automobile. The American Petroleum Institute has set standards to classify how "good" a particular oil is. When you see ratings like SF, SG, and SH on a bottle of oil, the first letter, S, indicates that the oil is intended for use in automotive gasoline engines. The second letter indicates the quality of the oil, and the later that letter appears in the alphabet, the better the oil is. Oil rated SH, for example, has to meet tougher criteria than oil rated SF. Oils with ratings like CC, CD, and CE are intended for use in diesel applications, the first letter, C, indicating that the oil is for diesel use.

Some oils are labeled with both gasoline and diesel ratings. That simply means that the oil meets the criteria for both types of engines, but this may not be an entirely good thing. Diesel engines don't generate as much heat during the combustion process as gasoline engines, so the oil in a diesel is typically subjected to lower temperatures than the oil in a gasoline engine. It is plausible that the majority of the additives package in oil rated for diesel engines may be intended to work at lower peak temperatures than those found in oils rated for gasoline engines. Furthermore, the oil formulated for diesel engines often has

One of the functions of motor oil is to prevent scuffing, as seen on this piston face.

This Mopar 15W-40 motor oil has been formulated for use in diesel engines, though its CF-4/SH rating indicates that it has met the criteria for both diesel and gasoline applications.

much more aggressive detergents than oil formulated strictly for gasoline engines.

More than once I have witnessed the effects of a poorly maintained, high mileage gasoline engine after it has been run a short while on oil rated for both gasoline and diesel engines. Typically, the aggressive detergents in the oil attack the sludge that has accumulated in the upper portions of the engine. This may not sound like a bad thing, but instead of slowly dissolving the sludge and melting it away, it breaks up into clumps that work their way down the oil returns to the pan, where they eventually block the pickup and starve the engine for lubrication. For reasons such as this, you should always try, if at all possible, to stay with oil that is intended solely for gasoline engines.

The Society of Automotive Engineers has devised a universally accepted system for rating the viscosity – or thickness – of motor oil. In the early days of the automobile, oils were assigned a single viscosity rating, typically 20, 30, 40, or 50 weight. These numbers referred to the viscosity of the oil when hot (210 degrees Fahrenheit). The higher the number, the thicker the oil. Oils intended for use in cold climates were rated not by their hot viscosity, but by their cold viscosity, and this was evident by their "W" suffix. Tested at temperatures as cold as -31 degrees Fahrenheit, they were rated 0W, 5W, 10W, 15W, 20W, and 25W. Nearly all oils sold today are intended for both hot and cold weather use. Called multi-viscosity oils, they include both cold and hot viscosity ratings, such as 10W-30 or 20W-50.

Synthetic Oils versus Mineral-Based Oils

A number of years ago, high-priced synthetic oils became the rage in automotive circles. There was a lot of advertising hype as the manufacturers of synthetic oils made bold claims about the capabilities of their products. Dismissed by many skeptics as just another passing fad, widespread use of synthetic oil has been slow to catch on, and the comparatively high price of synthetic oil certainly hasn't

Mobil 1 is the most widely recognized name in synthetic oil.

helped matters. Many people question if there is even a need for synthetic oil, considering the fact that mineral-based oils have become so good in recent years.

During its life in an engine, mineral-based oil protects parts moving against each other, but its molecules are sheared in the process. This leads to viscosity breakdown. At extremely cold temperatures it is difficult to circulate through an engine, and it can take quite some time to reach the upper portions of the engine after start-up. The film strength of many mineral-based oils becomes severely weakened at temperatures slightly over 220 degrees Fahrenheit, and even the best begin to oxidize between 250 and 300 degrees. This can spell disaster in any engine, but many race engines place higher demands on an oil than even the best mineral-based oil can provide.

Synthetic oils have been in existence for over a half-century, having been used in some aircraft as far back as the early 1940s. When synthetic oil is formulated, chemists actually "build" the oil molecules through several chemical processes. The results are oil molecules that are larger and much stronger than those of conventional mineral-based oil. These stronger molecules provide more "slipperiness" than mineral-based oil molecules, thus promoting better lubrication. The strength of these molecules provides greater resistance to shear, so the viscosity of the oil is much more stable and not as prone to breakdown.

Unlike mineral-based oils, synthetic oils can be pumped freely through an

engine at temperatures as low as -50 degrees Fahrenheit, and remain stable while operating at temperatures of 450 to 500 degrees Fahrenheit for extended periods of time, and 700 degrees for short periods. Some will even withstand brief temperature spikes of over 800 degrees. Because synthetic oils remain stable at such high temperatures, they are less likely to boil off, and they don't coke or decompose into sludge the way mineral-based oils can.

The manufacturers of synthetic oil boast about better fuel mileage and increased oil change intervals as a way to offset the higher cost of synthetic oil. In actuality, the improvement in fuel mileage will most likely be negligible, and although synthetic oil doesn't break down as quickly as mineral-based oil, it still becomes contaminated with the byproducts of combustion that leak past the piston rings. Although the oil molecules may be capable of lasting the 25,000 or even 50,000 miles that the manufacturers claim, the oil will become contaminated long before then. Some experts in the field recommend doubling the oil change interval if synthetic oil is used, but because of the contamination issue, I don't recommend extending the oil change interval for any reason.

Despite the fact that synthetic oil is quite a bit more expensive than mineral based oil, the real pay-off when using synthetic oil comes in longer engine life. In a street engine this means more miles. In a race engine, this means less frequent rebuilds and greatly reduced chance of engine damage due to lubrication failure.

At one time, synthetic oils were very steeply priced and not widely available from many retail auto parts stores. Nowadays, that is not the case. The prices have dropped dramatically and there is now wide spread availability. Most auto parts stores stock synthetic oil, and it can even be found on the shelves of discount department stores such as Wal-Mart. Sure, it still costs four to five times as much as good mineral-based oil, but considering the cost of building a race engine, it is cheap insurance. Actually, it doesn't make sense *not* to use synthetic oil in a race engine!

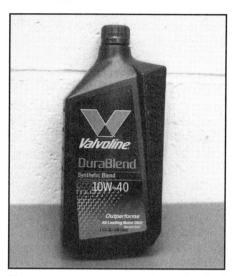

Many companies now offer a blend of synthetic and mineral-based oil. Valvoline DuraBlend is one example.

Although the benefits of synthetic oil can certainly be realized in stock engines used for mundane daily transportation, it may be difficult for many of us to justify the high cost. For this reason, many companies now offer blended oil that contains both mineral-based oil and synthetic oil. Granted, this oil does not contain all of the qualities of 100 percent synthetic oil, but it is certainly better than 100 percent mineral-based oil. If you wish to blend your own oil, you can do so by using one to two quarts of synthetic oil to every two quarts of mineral-based oil.

A word of caution must be mentioned regarding the use of synthetic oil. New engines should not be broken in with synthetic oil. When an engine is new, many of the parts must wear-mate together or "seat themselves in." The piston rings must wear a little bit in order to properly seal against the cylinder walls, and the cam lobes and lifters must also wear together. Because synthetic oil is so slippery and lubricates so well, when it is used during this break-in period, there is often not enough friction to allow the parts to wear-mate. Even if everything was done textbook perfectly during the build-up, if synthetic oil is used during break-in, the rings may not seat readily, if at all. For this reason, only mineral-based oil should be used during break-in.

To play it safe, many engine builders prefer not to make the switch to synthetic oil until the first regularly scheduled oil change after an engine is built. Many engine builders recommend for rebuilds that the oil is changed at frequent intervals during the first thousand miles or so. Doing so is a good practice as long as you use mineral-based oil. After that time, revert back to your normal maintenance schedule. If you normally change the oil in your street engine every 2,000 miles, then wait until your new engine has accumulated 2,000 miles before filling the crankcase with synthetic oil.

Oil Pump, Volume, and Pressure

The volume of oil flow in an engine is determined by the balance between the capacity of the oil pump and the amount of pressure "leakage" in the engine. This leakage is most often thought of in the form of bearing clearance, specifically the crankshaft main and rod bearing clearances, but also includes clearance in the camshaft bearings and valvetrain, such as the lifter-to-bore clearance and rocker arm-to-rocker shaft clearance.

The oiling systems of all contemporary automobile engines are designed so that the capacity of the oil pump exceeds the flow capabilities of all of the oil clearances in the engine. Because the pump continually tries to push more oil than the engine can use, there is pressure at the outlet side of the oil pump, and it is this pressure that we read on the oil pressure gauge. By displaying this pressure, the oil pressure gauge simply allows us to monitor the relationship between the flow capacity of the oil pump and the oil flow requirements of the engine. To put this concept into simple terms, the oil pump initiates the oil flow, while the clearances in the engine restrict the oil flow. The gauge simply tells us how hard the pump is working, for oil pressure is really nothing more than a measure of the oil's resistance to flow.

Several variables come into play in determining the relationship between the oil pump output volume and the ability of the oil to flow through the engine. The effects of those variables can be seen on an engine's oil pressure gauge. Increasing the flow capacity of the pump by installing a larger pump, or simply raising the engine speed, will cause an increase in oil pressure. Reducing the oil flow capability of the engine with minimal bearing clearances will also be reflected in higher oil pressure. Conversely, increasing the oil flow capability of the engine through excessive bearing clearances or the use of full groove main bearings, which feed oil to the rod bearings at all times, will be seen as a decrease in oil pressure, since there is more pressure "leakage" within the engine.

Motor oil also plays a major part in determining the relationship between oil pump volume and the oil flow capability of the engine. A thin oil, such as an SAE 5W-30, can cause the oil-pressure gauge to read lower because a thin oil flows more easily through the engine than a thick oil, so the oil pump doesn't have to work as hard. A thick oil, such as an SAE 40 weight, doesn't flow through the engine as easily as a thinner oil does, so the oil pump has to work harder and the gauge will read higher. Oil temperature also has a drastic effect on oil flow, for the hotter the oil gets, the thinner it becomes and the more easily it flows through the engine.

The oil pump pressure relief valve governs the maximum oil pressure. It opens at a predetermined pressure to bleed off excess oil volume and keep the oil pressure from reaching stratospheric levels. The pressure relief valve operates against spring tension, and the pressure at which the valve opens is determined by the tension of that spring. The greater the spring tension, the greater the pressure that will be required to push the valve open, and the higher the system operating pressure.

When shopping for an oil pump, you could have up to four choices, and the differences between them may not be clear. They are as follows: stock replacement, high-volume, high-pressure, and high-volume/high-pressure.

A **stock replacement pump** needs no explanation, for it should be comparable to the pump that was originally installed in the engine in terms of oil pressure and volume delivery. Yet, it serves as a benchmark against which the other pumps are measured.

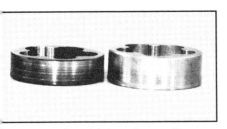

The rotors in a high-volume oil pump are typically taller than those of a stock pump.

A true **high-volume oil pump** has a greater flow capacity than a stock oil pump, but the pressure relief valve is calibrated to open at or about the same pressure as that of the stock pump. The additional flow capacity is typically realized through the use of pump rotors that are taller than those used in stock pumps.

A true **high-pressure oil pump** has roughly the same flow capacity as a stock oil pump, but the relief valve is calibrated to open at a higher pressure than the relief valve of a stock pump.

A **high-volume/high-pressure oil pump** has the features of both the high-volume and the high-pressure oil pumps. Most oil pumps sold as high-volume pumps actually fall into this category, for the relief valves in those pumps are usually calibrated to open at a significantly greater pressure.

Because high-volume and high-pressure oil pumps require more torque to operate than a stock pump, if anything other than a stock oil pump is to be used in a Chrysler V-8 engine, the stock oil pump driveshaft should be upgraded with a stronger part. Even if a stock pump is used, an improved driveshaft will provide cheap insurance against breakage. When the oil pump driveshaft fails, it does so without warning. The oil flow within the engine ceases immediately, which often leads to sudden engine failure.

Before you decide on which oil pump to buy, you must analyze the needs of the engine. If the oil pump initiates the flow, and the oil pressure is a measure of the oil's resistance to flow, then how much oil pressure is required to push an adequate volume of oil through the engine in order to protect its internals? Fortunately, all families of Chrysler engines have well-designed oiling systems.

Therefore, *assuming that all clearances inside the engine are within factory specification,* the rule of thumb – 10 psi oil pressure per 1,000 rpm engine speed – applies to all engines. If an engine will not see anything beyond 6,000 rpm, for example, then 60 pounds of hot oil pressure would be sufficient to push a great enough volume of oil through the engine to its critical points for protection. More than 60 pounds would be overkill.

Oil pressure is one of those areas where novice engine builders often apply "More's Law": If some oil pressure is good, and more's better, then too much ought to be just about right! Many of these same people are also of the belief that oil pressure generated by the oil pump reaches the bearings and tends to "float" the journals of the crankshaft away from the bearing surfaces. They further contend that the greater the bearing clearance, the more room the journal will have to float within the bearing, and the less likely it will be to touch the bearing surface. Some even believe that excessive bearing clearance reduces friction and allows the engine to make more power. Unfortunately, they are wrong on all counts.

Oil pressure in an engine pushes the oil to the bearings, but once inside a bearing, the spinning crankshaft journal causes the oil to form a hydraulic wedge between the journal and the bearing surface. The ability of the oil to do this is a function of its film strength, not the oil pressure in the engine. The oil pressure generated by the oil pump simply assures that the oil gets to the bearings in sufficient quantity.

Because the oil pump is driven by the engine, the harder it has to work, the more power it robs from the engine. When oil pressure approaches 100 psi, it can easily take an additional 10 or more horsepower to operate the oil pump. Although liquid is said to be non-compressible, when pressurized the molecules of a liquid have increased kinetic activity which drives up the temperature of the liquid. If the temperature of the oil is already borderline hot, this additional heat can further weaken the film strength of the oil and compromise its ability to protect the bearings and crankshaft. The high oil pressure

will then push an excessive volume of oil past the bearings.

Oil slung from the rod bearings normally lubricate the cylinder walls, pistons, and rings, but too much oil floods the rings. When this happens, the rings can hydroplane and skim over some of the oil on the cylinder walls, allowing it to enter the combustion chamber. Aside from the obvious oil consumption problem, when oil enters the combustion process, it does so as a low-octane fuel. Low-octane fuels promote detonation – or exploding – of the fuel/air mixture, as opposed to a controlled burn of the mixture. Detonation reduces horsepower, and if severe enough, wreaks havoc with the engine. Furthermore, all of this oil flying around the crankcase creates windage, a heavy oil mist that the crankshaft must continually cut through as it turns. Windage further reduces power and leads to oil foaming.

Excessive bearing clearances further aggravate the above condition, for when the clearances are loose, even more oil will be flying around inside the crankcase. In extreme cases, the oil cannot sufficiently cushion the pounding between the crankshaft journals and bearings, and the bearings will fail prematurely. It is true that an engine that is being built for extremely hard use needs more clearance than the minimum allowable in a stock rebuild, but this is to allow for expansion of the crankshaft journals under extreme conditions. In nearly all street and moderate race applications, if the crankshaft is machined so that the bearing clearances are set at the wide end of the factory specification, there will be sufficient space within the bearings for the crankshaft journals to expand while maintaining oil control.

Controlling Windage

Crankcase windage (the thick mist of oil inside the crankcase) originates from the oil that is thrown from the crankshaft as it spins. You might think that centrifugal force would fling all of the oil from the crankshaft, and indeed much of the oil is thrown from the crankshaft. Some of the oil stays trapped in the center of the crankcase where the crankshaft continues to whip it like an egg beater. To make matters worse, if no windage control device is used, oil flung downward into the pan splashes into the oil that has already been collected and agitates it so that it can again become trapped by the spinning counterweights of the crankshaft. In cars capable of generating high lateral force numbers (such as those used in road racing, often capable of exceeding 1.0 G on the skid pad), the oil climbs the walls of the pan during hard cornering, allowing the crankshaft to whip it further.

Windage must be controlled, for it leads to oil foaming and a lower oil level in the sump. Windage also robs horsepower from the engine by tending to slow the crankshaft as its throws and counterweights rotate through the oil mist.

A stock oil pan serves as nothing more than a catch basin for oil returning to the sump. The most effective solution to lessen crankcase windage would be to build an oil pan that is deep enough to keep the oil at least eight inches below the bottom of the crankshaft counterweights and that runs the entire length of the engine. While this may be practical in a drag race engine, depending on the chassis configuration, it is certainly not practical in a street engine due to limitations imposed by the shape of the chassis and the need for ground clearance. In a road race vehicle this is impossible, for the engine must be kept as low as possible in the chassis in order to achieve a low center of gravity and acceptable handling.

Because of these limitations we are forced to use other means to control crankcase windage. In many cases, two or more of these devices are employed in order to keep the negative effects of windage to a minimum. The most common device used is a windage tray. This is a sheet-steel tray mounted beneath the crankshaft which catches the oil that is thrown downward from the crankshaft, preventing it from agitating the oil in the pan. Slits in the tray allow the oil collected by the tray to run into the pan.

In some cases the slits in the

windage tray are not large enough to allow the oil to return to the pan as quickly as it is collected in the tray. This is especially true at high RPMs in engines with high oil pressure and excessive bearing clearance. When this happens, oil floods the top side of the windage tray, and the crankshaft begins to whip it once again. At this point the problem of crankshaft windage is nearly as bad, if not worse, than if no tray were used at all. If you use a windage tray, especially a stock piece as used in many 340 and 360 cubic-inch engines, be sure that the slits are of generous size. If not, pry them open so that they do not obstruct the flow of oil returning to the pan.

The second type of crankcase windage control device is called a crankshaft scraper. This is nothing more than a flat piece of steel that runs the length of the crankcase and is placed in close proximity of the crankshaft counterweights. Although it does not actually touch the crankshaft (at least it had better not!), its function is to catch and remove some of the oil mist being churned by the counterweights. Oil collected by the scraper then returns to the oil pan.

The third type of crankcase windage control device is a windage screen. This is a special type of screen that is punched from flat sheet steel. As the holes are pierced, the metal is twisted and stretched in such a way that the holes allow oil hitting the screen from one direction to pass through virtually unobstructed, but oil hitting from a different direction cannot easily pass through. Because the screen is directional, when it is properly installed oil thrown from the crankshaft can pass through the screen easily, but oil splashed upward from the pan is blocked from entering the path of the crankshaft throws and counterweights.

When installed, windage trays are usually attached to the crankshaft main bearing cap bolts or studs, or to the oil pan rails of the block. Crankshaft scrapers are usually attached to the oil pan rails or welded to the inside of the oil pan, and a windage screen is usually anchored to either the main bearing cap bolts or studs, or to the inside of the oil pan.

This 360 has been fitted with windage screen.

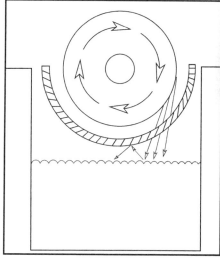

This screen is directional. Oil thrown from the spinning crankshaft can pass through the screen easily, but oil splashed from the sump is blocked from entering the path of the crankshaft.

Oil Pan Baffles

Another type of oil pan modification that is frequently employed is the addition of baffles. Baffles are sometimes used to direct the flow of oil from a windage control device to the sump, but their most common use is to ensure that there is always a sufficient volume of oil around the pick-up to keep it submerged so that it does not suck air.

A baffle has been added to this stock oil pan. Though crude in appearance, it is intended to keep the oil from climbing the walls of the sump on acceleration, braking, and cornering.

The oil pan must be configured so that it will fit with the components of the vehicle chassis. This pan has a hollow tube through which the steering linkage will pass.

On the floor of this pan is a hinged baffle which allows oil to slosh toward the pick-up on acceleration, but blocks its movement away from the pick-up on deceleration.

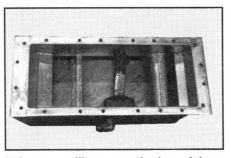

This pan utilizes a swinging pick-up tube. As inertia causes the oil to slosh from one end of the sump to the other, it also causes the pick-up to swing in the same direction, effectively moving with the oil.

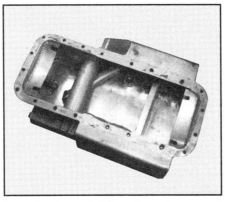

In order to maintain adequate ground clearance while providing a large oil capacity, this oil pan has a large pocket on each side. It, too, uses a swinging pick-up.

In any system, gravity causes the oil to return to the sump, but inertia due to a hard launch in a drag race engine, or hard braking or cornering in a road race engine, can cause the oil to slosh away from the pick-up, leaving it uncovered. Properly baffling an oil pan helps to keep the oil around the pick-up, keeping it covered at all times. Some oil pans have hinged baffles which allow the oil to slosh toward the pick-up while blocking the movement of oil sloshing away from the pick-up. In some cases, swinging pick-ups are used so that the pick-up can follow the movement of the oil. The possibilities for baffling are practically endless, depending on your intended application and resourcefulness.

Accumulators

A device can be added externally of the engine that will add an extra margin of safety should the pick-up become momentarily uncovered for any reason. This device is called an oil accumulator, and it can be mounted just about anywhere in the engine compartment as space permits.

An oil accumulator is a large metal cylinder, and is typically about the size of a five-pound fire extinguisher.

This large aluminum canister is an oil accumulator. The pressurized oil within the accumulator provides an extra margin of safety should the pick-up become uncovered momentarily.

Chrysler Performance Engines **89**

Inside, a large piston divides the accumulator into two chambers. One side of the accumulator is pressurized with air to about half the normal operating oil pressure of the engine. For example, if the engine normally operates with 60 pounds of oil pressure, the accumulator would be charged with 30 psi of air. Because the piston is free to move within the cylinder, this static air charge pushes the piston to the opposite end of the cylinder. The other end of the cylinder is plumbed to a large oil passage in the block near the oil pump with a single piece of steel braided tubing, the larger the better.

Upon start-up, once the oil pressure in the engine surpasses the static air pressure in the accumulator, oil flows into the accumulator and pushes the piston, moving it against the air charge. When the engine achieves normal operating oil pressure (which usually takes only a second or two), there are a couple of extra quarts of pressurized oil on reserve.

Should the pick-up become uncovered for any reason, the oil pressure will drop. When this happens, the pressurized air in the accumulator pushes the piston, forcing pressurized oil into the engine in order to protect the bearings. When the pick-up is again submerged in oil, the oil pump begins to feed the engine once

The pump assembly contains the scavenging pumps, which draw the oil from the pan, and the oil supply pump, which feeds pressurized oil to the engine.

again and refill the accumulator. Oil accumulators are not designed to be a substitute for a well-designed oil pan, but offer a little extra protection.

Dry-Sump Oiling

Many all-out race engines used in various forms of road racing and stock car racing rely on dry-sump oiling systems. In a dry-sump system, windage problems are virtually eliminated because the oil is not stored in a sump at the base of the crankcase. The oil pan acts to collect the oil only. A scavenging pump (or pumps) draws oil from various places around the special purpose-built pan and transfers it to a remote reservoir. From this reservoir, another pump pushes the oil into the engine oil galleries. In most cases the scavenging pump(s) and the oil supply pump are stacked together in one large pump assembly and driven by a common belt from the crankshaft.

The advantages of a well-designed dry-sump oiling system include better windage control, no oil starvation due to the pick-up becoming uncovered, easy oil cooler hook-up because the oil lines are external, and the capability to use an extremely shallow oil pan, since the pan does not serve as a storage sump.

The disadvantages of a dry-sump oiling system are its high cost, space limitations for the external pump assembly, and difficulty in fabricating the pulleys and hardware to drive the pump in conjunction with the existing accessories.

In this dry-sump oiling system, oil is drawn from the pan at various points.

CHRYSLER PERFORMANCE ENGINES

Stroker Engines

If we look at an internal combustion engine simply as an air pump, nearly all the changes and modifications we make in the quest for more horsepower hinge on increasing the air flow, or volumetric efficiency. (Volumetric efficiency is discussed more thoroughly in Chapter 12, "Cylinder Heads and Breathing.") Taking steps to increase the volumetric efficiency of an engine nearly always involves some type of trade-off. Single-plane intake manifolds, hogged-out cylinder heads, long-duration "rumpity-rump" camshafts, and large-tube headers may make tons of horsepower, but the power curve of the engine will move toward the upper RPM range. Low-speed and midrange torque will certainly suffer, and the car won't be much fun to drive on the street, especially with power brakes. What's more, an engine with modifications such as this will require other complementary pieces, such as a high stall-speed torque converter and steep rear-axle gears.

While it is generally true that the more air we can move through a given engine the more power it has the potential to make, what if we simply started with a bigger air pump? When talking horsepower, there is an adage that states, "There's no replacement for good 'ole displacement." Because an engine's displacement is a function of bore, stroke, and number of cylinders, there are three ways to go about increasing an engine's displacement: first, add more cylinders (it doesn't take a genius to figure out that a V-8 has the potential to make more horsepower than a Slant Six simply by virtue of two extra cylinders and a greater displacement); second, choose a large bore size; third, choose a long stroke.

Block and Bore Size Considerations

Selecting an engine with a large bore size will provide you with a good starting point for a large dis-placement engine. Overboring it will further increase its displacement while correcting any taper or out-of-round in the cylinders. However, excessive overboring is not without its drawbacks. The cylinder walls are only so thick in the first place. The thinner they become, the more likely it is that hot spots will develop. In addition, thinner cylinder walls tend to flex more when heavily loaded, which will compromise cylinder ring sealing. Generally speaking, not much additional displacement can be gained from overboring production blocks before problems develop. If you are planning to bore more than 0.040 inches oversize, it is a good idea to have the block sonic checked to be sure that the cylinder walls will still be sufficiently thick after the cylinders have been bored.

Cylinder wall thickness varies from block to block and from year to year. For example, blocks cast in the late 1970s have thinner walls than those cast in the 1960s and early 1970s. It is for this reason that many engine builders prefer to use early blocks when building high-performance engines. Cylinder wall thickness can also vary between two seemingly identical engines, and even from cylinder to cylinder in the same engine, due to the method used for casting iron blocks.

Because coolant must flow through the block and around each of the cylinders in order to remove heat, an engine block must be hollow. Blocks are cast using molds made of packed sand on all external surfaces. The internal water jackets are defined by cores made of packed sand positioned within these molds. Once these molds and cores have been brought together and everything has been positioned properly, molten iron is poured into the sand mold.

Upon cooling, the sand is broken away from the external surfaces. The block is then shaken to break up the sand trapped inside the coolant passages, and that sand escapes through holes in the sides, front, and/or rear of the block, depending on the engine. These holes are later blocked with the familiar cupped core plugs. (While many people refer to these plugs as "freeze" plugs because they are sometimes forced out of the block when engine coolant freezes, often saving the block from being cracked, that is not their intended purpose. Their real purpose is for sand shake-out after the casting process.) Considering the fact that sand casting is not a deadly accurate means of casting, it is easy to see that casting thicknesses can vary somewhat. Furthermore, if the sand cores inside the engine are not placed perfectly, or if they move when the molten iron is poured in, the cylinders will not be of uniform thickness. This is called core shift.

Core shift is not necessarily a terrible thing, depending on which direction the core moved, and how much it moved. During the power stroke, the piston is thrust against one side of the bore due to the angularity of the connecting rod. If the engine is viewed from the front, the crankshaft spins clockwise. Because

of the angle of the connecting rod, the piston is thrust to the left side of the cylinder during the power stroke. On the driver's side bank of a V-8 engine, this means the side of the cylinder closest to the intake manifold. On the passenger's side bank, this means the lower side of the cylinder. The greater the angle of the rod, the greater this thrust becomes (more on that later). When the core has shifted during the casting process, one side of the cylinder will be somewhat thicker than the other. If the thick side happens to be the side against which the piston is thrust during the power stroke, the cylinder wall will be more rigid.

Long-Stroke Engines

Perhaps the easiest and most feasible way of increasing an engine's displacement is to increase its stroke. Unlike boring the engine, increasing its stroke can significantly alter its operating characteristics, often for the better. Engines with long strokes generally produce more torque and more useable horsepower, especially at low speeds, than short stroke engines, and their torque and horsepower curves are often broader and flatter than short-stroke engines. These attributes are very desirable for engines used on the street. With the horsepower curve lower in the RPM range, ultra-high stall-speed torque converters and numerically high axle ratios are not necessary. This reduces component fatigue throughout the drive-train and makes a car more pleasant to drive. In addition, deep breathing long-stroke engines often suffer to a lesser degree the poor low-speed driveability side effects of big carburetors, single-plane intake manifolds, big port, large valve heads, long duration camshafts, large tube headers, etc.

When considering the build-up of a long-stroke engine, one major consideration is the rod length-to-stroke ratio. This number is simply the length of the connecting rods from center to center divided by the length of the stroke. To find the rod length-to-stroke ratio of a 340, divide the

length of the rods (6.123 inches) by the stroke (3.31 inches). The product is 1.850. Therefore, the rod length-to-stroke ratio for the 340 would be expressed as 1.850:1. In fact, this number is also the rod length-to-stroke ratio of the 273 and 318 cubic-inch engines, since they share the same rod length and stroke as the 340.

Opinions vary on the ideal rod length-to-stroke ratio, but it is generally accepted that the closer this number gets to 2:1, the better. We have already noted that when a cylinder is in its power stroke, the piston is thrust against the bore wall due to the angularity of the connecting rod. The greater the angle, the greater this thrust. This increases the stress on the piston and cylinder bore, increases the friction between them, and robs power from the engine.

If an engine was designed using short rods with a given stroke, this thrust would be greater than if it had been designed to use longer rods with the same stroke. Chrysler engineers were certainly aware of this when they designed our favorite engines. Today you may hear members of the Chevy crowd boasting about their 5.7-inch or "trick" six-inch rods. The fact of the matter is that all Chrysler LA engines were built with 6.123-inch rods!

Aside from reducing the loading of the piston against the cylinder wall during the power stroke, a greater rod length-to-stroke ratio offers the benefit of increased piston dwell time. The dwell time of the piston can be thought of as the number of degrees of crankshaft rotation during which the piston remains at or near top dead center. This is more of a concept than an actual number. In any piston engine, when a piston is at mid-stroke, it is moving much faster than when it is near top dead center or bottom dead center. Once it passes top or bottom dead center, it accelerates until mid-stroke, then decelerates through the rest of that stroke. In an engine with short rods, at a given RPM each piston is moving faster as it nears the top or bottom of the bore, spends less time there, and accelerates in the other direction sooner than

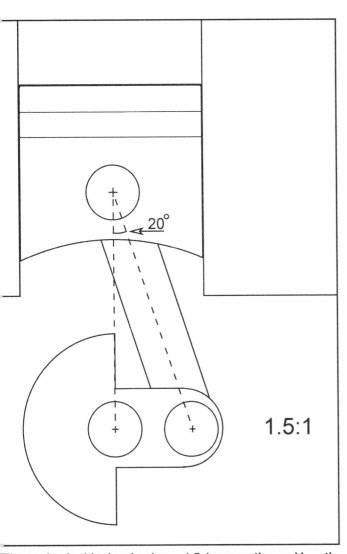

The engine in this drawing has a 1.5:1 connecting rod length-to-stroke ratio. Note the angle of the connecting rod.

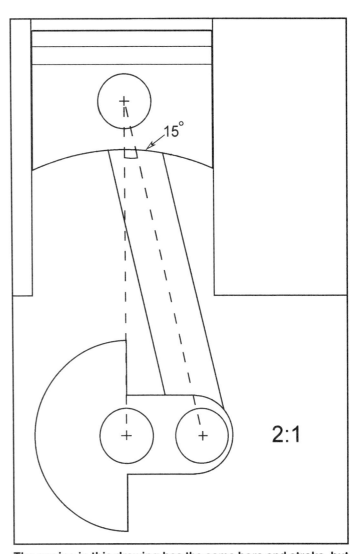

The engine in this drawing has the same bore and stroke, but a longer rod which yields a 2.0:1 rod length-to-stroke ratio. Note that the rod is more vertical at mid-stroke and that a shorter, lighter piston can be used.

an engine with comparatively longer rods. In an engine with long rods, each piston approaches the extremes of its travel sooner in terms of degrees of crankshaft rotation, and doesn't begin rapid acceleration in the opposite direction for several more degrees of crankshaft rotation.

This additional piston dwell time can go a long way toward taming the undesirable characteristics of a long-duration/long-overlap camshaft. As the piston descends on its intake stroke, the intake valve is open. It may remain open for several degrees after bottom dead center, but in a long-rod engine, with a longer piston dwell time, the piston remains near bottom dead center longer than in a short-rod engine. Therefore, the loss in low-speed

cylinder pressure associated with long-duration camshafts will not be as great in a long-rod engine.

As the piston travels upward on its compression stroke, it nears top dead center sooner in a long-rod engine, and stays near top dead center longer. After the spark plug fires, it begins to accelerate downward on its power stroke a little later, so not as much timing advance is needed, and the engine won't be as sensitive to timing errors as an engine with a smaller rod length-to-stroke ratio. As the piston nears bottom dead center, the exhaust valve begins to open.

In a long-rod engine the piston will be lower in its bore sooner than in a short-rod engine, so not as much cylinder pressure is lost at the end of

the power stroke. After the exhaust valve opens and the piston passes bottom dead center, it begins its ascent through the exhaust stroke. Near the top of its exhaust stroke the intake valve opens, and for the next several degrees of crankshaft rotation both valves will be open. The reason for this is to promote exhaust scavenging at high speeds. The exhaust leaving the cylinder flows past the exhaust valve, through the exhaust port, and into the primary header tube.

As the cylinder is emptied, the inertia of the exhaust gases causes a low-pressure area in the cylinder. By opening the intake valve sooner and leaving the exhaust valve open longer, this low pressure will help to initiate the flow of the incoming fuel/air mixture. At low engine speeds, however, the velocity of the exhaust gases leaving the cylinder is too low to create the inertia needed for good exhaust scavenging. Because the intake valve is opened so soon and the exhaust valve is closed so late, the incoming fuel/air mixture becomes diluted with inert exhaust gases.

In a short-rod engine, the piston reaches top dead center later than in a long-rod engine. Therefore, it is likely that more of the exhaust gases will be pushed past the open intake valve at low speeds in a short-rod engine. Because the piston leaves top dead center on its intake stroke sooner in a short-rod engine, it will likely draw more exhaust gases past the open exhaust valve, further diluting the incoming fuel/air charge. Because the pistons in a long-rod engine spend more time at or near top dead center during valve overlap, the negative side effects of low-speed driveability will be less severe than on an otherwise identical engine with short rods.

The greatest limiting factor of connecting rod length is the deck height of the block. Within the distance between the crankshaft centerline and the block deck surface there is the center-to-center length of the crank throw, which is equal to one-half of the stroke, the length of the connecting rod, and the height of the upper portion of the piston from the center of the wrist pin to the top of the piston. The relationship between the height of the top of the piston and the block deck is of utmost importance in determining the compression ratio.

Since we are discussing stroker engines, we are planning to increase the length of the crankshaft throw. To keep the connecting rod length-to-stroke ratio in check, we certainly don't want to use shorter rods. If anything, we would prefer to use longer rods. This increase in the length of the crankshaft throw will push the position of the wrist pin higher in the bore, and it will move higher still if longer rods are incorporated. Because our engine now has a longer stroke and, therefore,

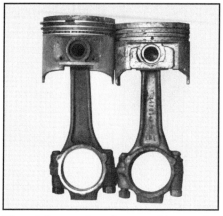

The piston and rod assembly on the left is from a 318, while the assembly on the right is from a 360. Even with the difference in stroke, both engines use identical 6.123-inch rods, but the 360 piston is shorter.

greater displacement, the piston top must actually be lower in the bore at top dead center to maintain a livable compression ratio.

What all of this means is that special pistons with the wrist pins positioned much higher will be needed. Incidentally, this is exactly what Chrysler did when it designed the 360. The 360 uses the same block deck height and rod length as all other LA engines, but the 273/318/340 stroke of 3.31 inches was stretched to 3.58 inches. This necessitated the use of pistons with the wrist pins positioned higher. Obviously, with all other things being equal, a tall-deck block, such as a 440 RB engine, will afford a greater rod length than a short-deck 383 or 400 cubic-inch B engine, but vehicle packaging often plays a part in the decision, too. The B engine is much easier to fit into many cars, especially A-bodies, than the RB engine. Furthermore, the 400 offers a larger bore than the 440.

Another topic should be discussed here. Although it is not directly related to stroker engines or rod length-to-stroke ratio, it is related to connecting rod angularity. Production pistons and most replacement pistons are manufactured with the wrist pin bore slightly offset to one side. This is done in the interest of reducing noise.

Again, when the engine is viewed from the front, the crankshaft turns

The wrist pin bore in this piston is offset slightly to the left.

clockwise. When the piston is being moved upward on the compression stroke, the angle of the connecting rod is such that the minor thrust face of the piston is being pushed against one side of the cylinder bore. As the crankshaft throw swings past top dead center, the rod angularity changes and the piston is thrust against the opposite side of the cylinder bore. If there was no wrist pin offset, this would take place precisely at the moment the piston reaches top dead center. By that time the ignition system has already fired the spark plug and the fuel/air mixture is burning, causing the pressure within the cylinder to rise rapidly. With a great deal of pressure in the cylinder, when the piston shifts to the opposite side of the bore, its major thrust face will meet the cylinder wall forcefully, causing a noise that could be audible to the occupants of the vehicle. This is known as piston slap.

By moving the wrist pin bore toward the major thrust face of the piston, the piston will shift to the opposite side of the cylinder bore a little bit sooner, a few degrees of crankshaft rotation before top dead center. Because the fuel/air mixture hasn't had as much time to burn, the pressure within the cylinder at this point is much lower. This greatly reduces the force with which the major thrust face of the piston meets the cylinder wall, thereby reducing piston slap. Unfortunately, this wrist pin offset increases the connecting rod angularity during the power stroke.

In most cases it is possible to install the pistons backward in their bores, as long as care is taken to pay attention to piston dome shape, valve reliefs, and the orientation of the oil spit holes in the connecting rods. Doing so will reduce connecting rod angularity. In V-8 engines, this often means that the pistons intended for the left bank will be used in the right bank, and vice-versa. Pistons are seldom perfect in size, and often the diameters of the pistons will vary by as much as a couple thousandths of an inch within a set. Therefore, when an engine is being built, the pistons should be measured, then indexed to their respective bores. Each cylinder is then bored to the proper size for ideal piston-to-cylinder wall clearance. With this in mind, the decision to reverse the pistons in their bores should be made early in the engine build-up.

Be advised, though, that while this will improve connecting rod angularity during the power stroke, reversing the pistons in their bores will cause each piston to shift to the opposite side of its bore well after top dead center, when cylinder pressures are much higher than at top dead center. This will intensify piston slap, especially if loose fitting forged pistons are used, and can lead to piston skirt failure. For this reason, most engine builders choose to install the pistons oriented as they were intended.

Interchanging Production Connecting Rods

In our quest to improve the rod length-to-stroke ratio, we may have some options with regards to swapping production rods from other engines within the same basic engine family. Unfortunately, this does not apply to the LA engine family. Since all LA engine connecting rods measure 6.123 inches from center to center, there is no way to improve the rod length-to-stroke ratio by swapping production rods. The same is true of RB engines, all of which use rods that measure 6.768 inches from center to center. That is not to say that all LA engine connecting rods are the same,

or that all RB engine connecting rods are the same. They are not. In this discussion we are simply talking about rod length.

Increasing the rod length-to-stroke ratio in a B engine could be accomplished by using rods from an RB engine, for the 6.768-inch RB engine rods measure an additional 0.410 inches over the B engine rods, which measure 6.358 inches center to center. Given the 3.38-inch stroke of the B engine, switching to the longer RB engine rods would improve the rod length-to-stroke ratio from 1.88:1 to 2.00:1. Of course, doing so would require special pistons.

Slant Six fans can improve the rod length-to-stroke ratio of the 225 by swapping in a set of rods from a 198 cubic-inch engine. With its long 4.12-inch stroke, switching from the 225 connecting rods, which measure 6.699 inches from center to center, to the 198 rods, which measure 7.006 inches from center to center, will increase the rod length-to-stroke ratio from 1.63:1 to 1.70:1. All 198 cubic-inch engines have forged-steel crankshafts, which have wider connecting rod journals than do the 1977 and later 225 cubic-inch cast crank engines. Therefore, a 1976 or earlier 225 cubic-inch engine must be used.

With regards to pistons, Slant Six guru Doug Dutra from Sunnyvale, California recommends using the dished pistons for a 2.2-liter turbocharged Chrysler engine. They are lighter than the Slant Six pistons, the wrist pin is located higher in the piston, and when used in conjunction

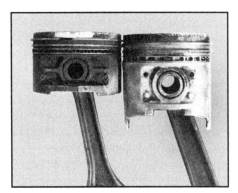

Shorter 2.2-liter pistons like the one on the left, and longer rods from a 198 engine, could be used to replace the 225 piston and rod assembly on the right.

with the 198 rods, the compression ratio of a 225 will be around 9.5:1. Using these pistons requires that the cylinders be bored approximately 0.045 inches oversize, which the 1976 and earlier cast-iron Slant Six blocks can easily accept.

Changing the Stroke

Changing the stroke of an engine can be done by any one (or a combination) of the following: offset-grinding the rod journals undersized; welding up the rod journals and then grinding them offset; or swapping in a production or aftermarket crankshaft with a longer stroke.

Offset-grinding the rod journals of the crankshaft provides the easiest and least expensive way to alter the stroke of your engine, and it can be done to the crankshaft from any engine except for the Hemi. Production crankshafts for Hemi engines have bearing journal surfaces that are nitride hardened, and Chrysler advises against turning them. Unfortunately, offset grinding offers very little in terms of increased stroke if production Chrysler rods are to be used.

Starting with a crankshaft that is not badly worn, if you turned the rod journals undersized, but removed nearly all of the metal from the side of each rod journal closest to the crankshaft centerline, you would increase the length of the throw of the crankshaft, thereby increasing the stroke of the engine.

For example, if you ground the rod journals 0.020 inches undersize, but removed 0.018 inches from the side of each journal closest to the crankshaft centerline and only 0.002 inches from the side furthest away, you would effectively move the center of the rod journal 0.008 inches away from the centerline of the crankshaft. This would increase the stroke of the engine 0.016 inches.

Although the gains in stroke that are possible by offset grinding the connecting rod journals while keeping the original rods are minimal, this method can be used to dial in the engine displacement to a specific number. This may be necessary in certain classes in different types of racing where there are limits on engine displacement. Offset-grinding can also be done to slightly alter the compression ratio, although this is normally achieved via other means, such as piston and head gasket selection, milling the heads and/or block deck surface, etc.

Offset-grinding can offer much larger gains in stroke if rods with a smaller big end (non-Chrysler) are used. A good example of this is the use of big-block Chevy rods in a Chrysler B or RB engine. If the 2.375-inch diameter rod journals are offset-ground to the big-block Chevy sized 2.200 inches, it is possible to offset-grind the rod journals such that the main journal center to rod journal center dimension will be increased from 1.875 inches to 1.9575 inches, thereby increasing the stroke from 3.75 inches to 3.915 inches. If this crankshaft was installed in a standard bore 440, the displacement would jump to 459 cubic inches!

Big-block Chevy rods are much narrower than Chrysler rods, allowing roughly 0.060 inches of side clearance. Although this might not be a detriment in itself, it would certainly allow more oil to be flung around inside the crankcase and onto the cylinder walls, quite likely contributing to oil consumption in a street engine. Some of the aftermarket companies now offer connecting rods with Chevy sized big ends, but in the correct width for Chrysler engines.

The next choice, and perhaps the most feasible for the street enthusiast or weekend racer working within the confines of a budget, involves swapping production crankshafts between engines within the same family.

Starting with the Slant Six family, the 170, 198, and 225 cubic-inch engines all have the same 3.400-inch bore size, but the strokes vary by half-inch increments. The 170 uses a short-deck block, while the 198 and 225 share the same tall-deck block. There is nothing to be gained by trying to use a 198 or 225 crankshaft in a 170 block. Since they have the same bore size, after all the trouble and expense of custom pistons and balancing, you

will still only have 198 or 225 cubic inches. Vehicle packaging is not an issue here, since a 198 or 225 will easily fit into any engine bay formerly occupied by a 170. Therefore, it would make more sense to start with a 198 or 225 engine. Since the 198 and 225 cubic-inch engines share the same block, if you currently have a 198, a 225 crankshaft and a set of 225 connecting rods are a direct drop-in. Of course, you could go with the previously mentioned Doug Dutra combination using your existing 198 rods and 2.2-liter Turbo pistons.

Within the LA engine family, all 273, 318, and 340 engines have a 3.31-inch stroke, while the 360 engine uses a crankshaft with a 3.58-inch stroke. All LA engines have 6.123-inch connecting rods. Since the 340 cubic-inch engine has the largest standard bore of the LA engine family, measuring 4.040 inches, it only seems natural to start with a 340 block and add a 360 crankshaft. This combination would net 367 cubic inches with a standard bore, and 372 cubic inches with a 0.030-inch overbore.

The problem is that all 273, 318, and 340 engines have a main journal diameter of 2.50 inches, while the 3.58-inch stroke 360 crankshaft has main journals that measure 2.81 inches in diameter. It would be necessary to grind 0.31 inches from the main journals of the 360 crankshaft in order for it to fit the main bearing saddles of a 340 block. The 360 cast crankshaft is a stout piece in stock form, and has proven its strength in a number of supercharged and nitrous oxide-injected engines, but grinding this much material, nearly 5/16 of an inch, from its main journal diameter would seriously compromise its strength. A 360 crankshaft with main journals ground this far might work fine in a moderately tame street engine, but could be prone to failure in high horsepower applications.

Perhaps a better approach, depending on what parts you have at your disposal, would be to start with an early 1970s 360 engine. In today's world, decent 340 blocks are scarce, and complete, running 340 engines command a hefty price when compared to

the typical junkyard 360. The early 360 blocks typically have thick cylinder walls and can usually support a large overbore. In fact, in the 1970s, Chrysler engineer Tom Hoover built a 372 cubic-inch 360 using an early 360 block, the standard 360 stroke of 3.58 inches, and modified 0.030-inch over-size 340 pistons. Because the 4.040-inch bore of a standard 340 is 0.040 inches larger than the 4.000-inch bore of the 360, the 360 block had to be bored 0.070 inches oversize to accommodate the pistons. Replacement pistons for the low-compression 1973 340 were selected because they are 0.100 inches shorter than the earlier high compression versions. Even so, the tops still had to be machined for proper piston-to-head clearance, and the bottoms of the wrist pin towers had to be shortened for crankshaft counterweight clearance.

When everything was said and done, the compression ratio came in about 12:1, which gave it a voracious appetite for race fuel. Today it would be possible to order a set of custom pistons for this application that would net a lower compression ratio and perhaps help you avoid having to do the machine work to the pistons. The point is that this combination still netted 372 cubic inches without sacrificing any strength in the crankshaft.

RB Crankshaft Into a 400 Engine

Chrysler's family of big-block engines is actually made up of two smaller families, with one close cousin. The members of the B engine family, which include the 361, 383, and 400 cubic-inch engines, all use short-deck blocks, and all have the same 3.38-inch stroke. The members of the RB engine family include the 413, 426 wedge, and 440 cubic-inch engines. All use tall-deck blocks, and they share the same 3.75-inch stroke. The 426 Hemi also uses a crankshaft with 3.75 inches of stroke, but it is a special crankshaft with an eight-bolt crank flange.

Of all the engines in the B/RB engine family, the 400 boasts the largest standard bore size. In staying with our long-stroke-crank-into-big-ore-block theme, it only seems logical to drop an RB engine crankshaft into a 400 cubic-inch engine. Unfortunately, it isn't that simple. Although the connecting rod journals for all B/RB engines measure the same at 2.375 inches, the B engines have a main journal diameter of 2.625 inches, while main journal diameter of the RB engines measures 2.750 inches. Therefore, an RB engine crankshaft will not fit a B engine block in stock form. There are a couple of ways around this, although opinions vary on which way is better.

First, since the main bearing saddles and webbing of the B engines are nearly identical to those in the standard duty RB engines, the B engine block could be line-bored to accept the larger main bearings from the RB engine. This would ensure that no crankshaft strength or rigidity would be lost, for the RB engine crankshaft would retain its standard dimensions. This will work fine in nearly all street and moderate race applications, but in extremely high horsepower engines the main webbing in the production RB engines becomes prone to cracking. Because the webbing inside the B engines is nearly identical to the webbing inside the RB engines, the smaller main bearing bore diameter adds to the strength of the block. Enlarging the main bearing bores to accept the RB engine crankshaft would negate this advantage.

The other method of fitting the RB engine crankshaft into the B engine block is to simply grind the main journals from 2.750 inches to the standard B engine main journal size of 2.625-inches diameter. Although it is recommended that the cast 440 crankshaft not be used for this type of build-up, it has been proven time and time again in B family stroker engines that the production forged-steel RB engine crankshaft remains an extremely durable piece even after 1/8 inch has been ground from its main journals. This is the generally preferred method for installing the RB engine crankshaft into the B engine. It won't sacrifice any strength in the block webbing, and is certainly less expensive than line boring the block.

With the difference in main journal diameter solved, there are still minor clearance problems in the block. The counterweights of the crankshaft and/or the block can be machined to gain the necessary clearance. Many engine builders prefer to reduce the counterweight diameter by 1/4 inch using a lathe. Some recommend grinding the block in the area of the oil pick-up tube and bottoms of the cylinders, while others insist on machining a 45-degree bevel on the two counterweights that encroach on the block in these areas. How you obtain the necessary clearance is not important. What is important is that you and your machinist are aware of the clearance problems and that together you take whatever steps are necessary to ensure adequate clearance in all the tight spots. Furthermore, be sure to check for adequate clearance between the crankshaft and windage tray or screen and the oil pick-up tube.

All B engines have connecting rods that measure 6.358 inches from center to center, while all RB engine rods measure 6.768 inches from center to center. Because custom pistons will be needed regardless which rods are used, the longer RB engine rods would be preferred. Using the B engine rods with the longer 3.75-inch RB engine stroke will net a rod length-to-stroke ratio of 1.695:1, while the longer RB engine rods will maintain the RB engine rod length-to-stroke ratio of 1.80:1.

Although the 400 has the largest bore of all the B/RB engines, it narrowly beats the 440. At 4.34 inches, the bore of the 400 is a mere 0.020 inches larger than the 4.32-inch bore of the 440. If we do the math, a standard bore 400 with an RB engine stroke will net us 444 cubic inches. Given this modest difference in bore size, but considering the trouble and expense involved in making the long-stroke crankshaft work in a 400, it seems that the benefits are practically nil. Yet, this is one of the most popular stroker engine builds today. Why bother?

Actually, there are several good reasons for this build-up. First, vehicle packaging is often a consideration, especially among street and show car enthusiasts. The B engines have a crankshaft centerline-to-deck surface dimension of 9.980 inches. This is 0.745 inches, nearly 3/4 of an inch shorter than the RB engines, which have a dimension of 10.725 inches.

In trial-fitting a 440 crankshaft in a 400 block, the larger counterweights touch the bottoms of the cylinder bores and come dangerously close to the oil pick-up tube hole.

This forged-steel 440 crankshaft has a damaged rod journal, making it a perfect candidate to be welded and reground as a stroker crank.

If your budget permits, you can order a custom crankshaft in virtually any stroke you desire.

Because of this, they are smaller externally than RB engines, both in height and width. They fit into cramped engine bays with a little more room for headers. This is especially true in A-bodies.

Although a big-block Dart or Duster used strictly for bracket racing will likely have large holes hacked through the inner fender wells through which the headers pass, few show car owners are willing to cut up their cars. CPPA, in Mansfield, Pennsylvania, offer chassis exit headers for big-block A-bodies, but they are an extremely tight fit, especially with an RB engine. Building a stroker 400 makes for an easier fit while offering a larger displacement.

A second reason for this build-up is that the B engine block is somewhat lighter than the RB engine block due to its lower deck height. The third reason is the cylinders of the B engine are shorter than those of the RB engine, resulting in less flex. Remember, the block is hollow. The cylinders are really nothing more than cast-iron tubes inside the block. Since these tubes are surrounded by coolant, they are only supported at the tops and bottoms. The longer they are, the more prone they are to flexing. Making them shorter affords better ring sealing and less chance of the cylinder collapsing in extremely high horsepower applications. The fourth, and perhaps best, reason to select a B engine is that shorter, lighter pistons can be used. Lighter pistons mean less stress, better longevity, and increased performance from your engine.

Welded and Reground Crankshafts

The subject of welding and regrinding crankshafts has long been a source of controversy. This practice originated as a means of repairing crankshafts that had suffered a bearing failure and were so badly damaged that they would have had to be discarded otherwise. Over the years many of the welded crankshafts that were returned to service held up just fine, while others did not, leading to catastrophic engine failures. It seemed that the quality of the repaired crankshaft depended on the quality of the welding, and since it was not possible to determine the quality of the welding by visual inspection, there was no way to differentiate between two seemingly identical welded and reground crankshafts. Using a welded crankshaft was usually somewhat of a crap shoot.

As time marched on and welding techniques improved, it became generally accepted that as long as the welding was done properly, there was really nothing wrong with a welded crankshaft. It was also realized that welding crankshafts could offer some flexibility in reestablishing the dimensions of the crankshaft. Just as a badly damaged rod journal could be restored to its former size, if enough material was added to that journal, the journal could be reground such that

its center was moved, thereby changing the length of the throw and th stroke of the engine.

Since that time it has become increasingly more common to fin stock crankshafts that have bee welded and reground into stroke crankshafts. That is not to say that a welded crankshafts on the marke today are of good quality. No doubt there are some vendors who still offe a sub-standard product, but what a of this means is that just because crankshaft has been welded does no mean that you should be afraid to us it. Welded stroker crankshafts ca offer great performance potential at price well within the reach of th weekend racer, and excellent durabi ity in moderate horsepower applica tions. Of course, there is no way t guarantee that the crankshaft yo purchase will be flawless, but if yo choose a vendor with a good reputa tion for producing stroker crankshafts the odds will be greatly in your favor.

If you choose a custom cran grinder, you can order your crank shaft in virtually any stroke yo would like. For example, suppos the rod journals of an RB engin crankshaft were welded an reground to their standard size, bu the stroke was increased from 3.7 inches to 4.125 inches. This is 0.375-inch increase in stroke, or a additional 3/8 inch. If this cranksha was used in a standard bore 440 the resulting displacement would b 484 cubic inches. If the main jour nals were ground to fit the B engin block and this crankshaft was the used in a standard bore 400, the dis placement would come in at 48 cubic inches, a full 88 cubic inche over the stock configuration of th 400! If the block sonic checked suc that it could withstand a 0.060-inc overbore, an additional 14 cubi inches could be realized, and th displacement would jump to 50 cubic inches. If 6.768-inch RI engine rods were used with thi crankshaft, the rod length-to-strok ratio would be 1.64:1. If shorte 6.358 inch B engine rods were used the rod length-to-stroke ratio woul be 1.54:1. Using the longer rod would be the wiser choice.

CHRYSLER PERFORMANCE ENGINES
Crankshafts and Balancing

When selecting a crankshaft, you must carefully consider several factors. What will be the intended use of the engine? How much horsepower will it make? Will it be a stroker engine or will it have the stock stroke? Will it be internally or externally balanced? (More on balancing later.) How much are you willing to spend? You must answer all of these questions when choosing the crankshaft for your engine build-up.

In recent years a number of crankshaft vendors have begun to offer a wider variety of crankshafts in various strokes for the popular Chrysler V-8 engines. Although many of these crankshafts are cost prohibitive for the average street enthusiast or bracket racer, the selection is nonetheless pretty good. Aftermarket crankshafts are usually ground from either 1053 or 4340 steel forgings. Both materials are well suited for crankshaft construction, but 4340 crankshafts are stronger and more expensive than 1053 crankshafts.

For any engine that will approach the 1000 horsepower mark, 4340 should definitely get the nod. Billet crankshafts are machined from a large solid piece, or "billet," of 4340 steel. Because forged 1053 and 4340 crankshafts start out as forgings, they have some limitations in terms of stroke and counterweight shape, for the rough forgings already have a basic shape before any machining is done. Since a billet crankshaft starts out as a solid piece of steel, you can choose an extra long stroke or any counterweight configuration you desire.

All factory production crankshafts have undercut fillet at the ends of the journals to reduce the chance of cracks forming at these points. Crankshafts used in Race Hemi engines have radiused fillets, which require special bearings. Radius fillet crankshafts are stronger by design than those with undercut fillets, so all aftermarket crankshafts are of this design.

Aftermarket race crankshafts are available for just about any popular V-8 application. This Winberg 5.00-inch stroke crankshaft fits Hemi and RB engines. Note the knife-edged counterweights.

This crankshaft features radiused fillets.

Production crankshafts are either cast iron or forged steel. In the early and mid-1960s, forged steel was the material of choice for crankshafts in Chrysler engines. Forged crankshafts are strong and well suited for use in stock, high performance, and the vast majority of race engines. Because they are more rigid than cast crankshafts, they are less prone to flexing, which can help to extend the life of the bearings, thereby increasing the life of the engine. Because forged-steel crankshafts are harder than cast-iron crankshafts, they are less susceptible to wear on the bearing surfaces. Additionally, if a forged crankshaft suffers damage from a bearing failure, it can usually be repaired by welding and grinding the affected journal, and can even be transformed into a stroker crankshaft by welding and grinding all of the rod journals.

By the late 1960s, 273 and 318 cubic-inch engines had begun receiving cast-iron crankshafts. From the manufacturing viewpoint,

All production crankshafts have undercut fillets. This crankshaft is from a 426 Street Hemi.

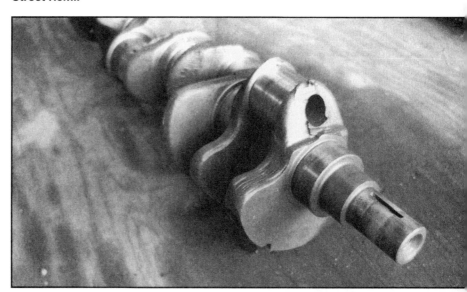

Forged crankshafts typically have rounded edges on the unmachined portions of their counterweights. Often some areas have a grainy appearance.

Another characteristic of a forged crankshaft is the wide parting line.

Cast crankshafts usually have sharper, better defined edges in the unmachined portions.

The parting line of a cast crankshaft is usually very narrow.

If you are working on a B or RB engine with a cast crankshaft, you will likely find the engine displacement cast right into the crankshaft.

Cast crankshafts are attractive because they are less expensive to produce and easier to machine. As they proved their durability, they began to appear in more and more engines, and have been used exclusively in production engines since 1977. All 273 and 318 engines from 1968 on were fitted with cast crankshafts, as were all

Pre-1962 V-8 engines have eight-bolt flanges configured like this.

Although 426 Hemi engines also have eight-bolt flanges, they look nothing like the pre-1962 pieces.

All other V-8 engines have a six-bolt flange that looks like this, although 1964-1967 273 engines have a smaller recess for the torque converter hub.

360 engines. The 340 was the last LA engine to have a forged crankshaft, but lost it in favor of a cast crankshaft in 1973, the final year of the 340. All B and RB engines through 1970 used forged-steel crankshafts, but cast crankshafts found their way into the last of the 383 engines with two-barrel carburetors at the end of 1971. The 400

engines, which used cast crankshafts, replaced the 383 for 1972. It has been rumored that there were a few 400 engines with four-barrel carburetors that received forged crankshafts, but the chances of actually finding one are highly unlikely. By the end of 1973, cast crankshafts were used in all B and RB engines.

In all V-8 engines except the 360, it is possible to substitute a production forged-steel crankshaft from the same engine family in place of the cast crankshaft. All LA engines use the same rod bearing and main bearing widths, and the rod journals all measure 2.125 inches in diameter. All 273, 318, and 340 engines have a 3.31-inch stroke and a main journal diameter of 2.50 inches. Therefore, it is possible to swap crankshafts between any of these engines as long as the balancing issues are addressed. All 273, 318, and forged crankshaft 340 engines are internally balanced, but because piston and connecting rod weights vary between them, the crankshaft would have to be rebalanced if it was used in a different engine. In terms of crankshaft interchangeability, the 360 is the oddball of the LA engine family. With its 3.58-inch stroke and 2.81-inch diameter main journals, there is no other production crankshaft that will simply drop into a 360.

All B engines share the same rod and main bearing widths, a 3.38-inch stroke, 2.38-inch diameter rod journals, and 2.625-inch diameter main journals. Therefore, a forged-steel crankshaft from a 361 or 383 could be used in place of the cast crankshaft in a late 1971 383 or a 400 cubic-inch engine. As in the case of the LA engines, the crankshaft should be rebalanced in consideration of the different rod and piston weights.

Crankshaft interchangeability is no problem in the RB engine family either, since all 413, 426 wedge, and 440 engines share common rod and main bearing widths, a 3.75-inch stroke, 2.38-inch diameter rod journals, and 2.75-inch diameter main journals. Therefore, a forged

If you are building an engine for a car with a manual transmission, check to see if your crankshaft was drilled and properly sized for a pilot bushing. See your respective engine chapter for more information on this subject.

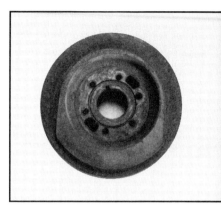

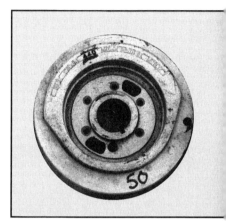

All four of these dampers are for externally balanced engines, and all four have a different intentional imbalance used to cancel the imbalance of their respective engines. As such, they cannot be interchanged.

crankshaft from any of these engines could be used in place of the cast crankshaft in a 440. Again, be sure to address the balancing issues. The 426 Hemi uses the same crankshaft dimensions as the other RB engines, so it is physically possible to use a Hemi crankshaft in an RB engine, but the Hemi uses an eight-bolt crankshaft flange, while all other V-8 engines from 1962 and later use a six-bolt flange. Using a Hemi crankshaft would require the use of a Hemi flywheel or flex plate.

The Slant Six was the last engine to lose its forged-steel crankshaft in favor of a cast crankshaft. The cast crankshaft appeared at the beginning of the 1977 model year and was used from that point forward. Although it shares the same 2.189-inch diameter rod journals and 2.750-inch diameter main journals as the earlier forged crankshafts, and the same 4.12-inch stroke as all previous 225 cubic-inch engines, the main and rod journals of the cast crankshaft are narrower than those of the forged crankshafts, necessitating the use of narrower rods and blocks with narrower main bearing saddles. For that reason, cast and forged crankshafts are not interchangeable in Slant Six engines.

Although forged-steel crankshafts are generally preferred over cast-iron crankshafts for a number of reasons, building an engine with a

cast crankshaft does not necessarily mean that you are building a time bomb. In fact, Chrysler's stock cast crankshafts are sturdy pieces that can endure a great deal of punishment. Sure, there are a number of reasons to toss a cast crankshaft in favor of a replacement forged-steel crankshaft, but the fact of the matter is that for most high-performance street engines and medium-duty race engines, a cast crankshaft will hold up fine. There are more than enough nitrous oxide-injected or supercharged 360s running around to prove this point!

Internal versus External Balancing

Engine balancing is of special concern in an engine with a cast crankshaft, for most are externally balanced. All Slant Six, 273, and 318 cubic-inch engines are internally balanced, regardless of whether they have cast or forged crankshafts. All 340, 360, 400, and 440 engines with cast crankshafts are

externally balanced, meaning that some of the weight necessary to balance the engine is located on the vibration damper and flywheel or torque converter. Stated another way, the vibration damper and flywheel/torque converter are intentionally made out of balance. This imbalance cancels out the imbalance inside the engine. Because of this, crankshaft vibration dampers and flywheels or torque converters cannot be interchanged between internally balanced, or "zero" balanced, and externally balanced, or "Detroit" balanced, engines.

To complicate matters further, all externally balanced engines require that a different amount of weight be added to the damper and flywheel/torque converter, so these components cannot be interchanged between the different externally balanced engines either. For example, a torque converter that has been weighted for a 360 could not be used behind a cast crankshaft 440. The 1970 and 1971 440 Six Pack/Six Barrel

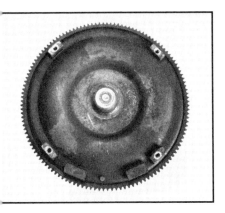

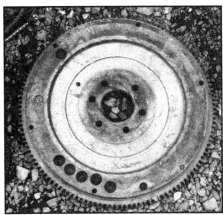

The same is true of torque converters and flywheels for externally balanced engines. It is vitally important that you don't install these components in the wrong applications.

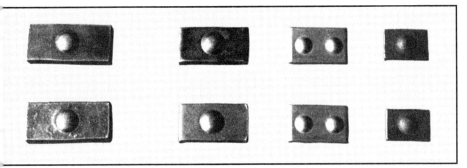

The Mopar Performance torque converter weight package includes weights for all popular externally balanced engines.

An enclosed template instructs which weights to use and where to position them so that they can be welded.

B&M offers SFI-approved flex plates for externally balanced engines.

engines are also externally balanced because of the heavy connecting rods used in those engines. Additionally, these rods were used in some heavy-duty 440 four-barrel applications, necessitating the same external balancing as the Six Pack/Six Barrel engines. These are the only engines with forged-steel crankshafts that require external balancing, but the amount of weight necessary to balance one of these engines is different than that of any of the other externally balanced engines.

It often happens that the need arises to use a zero-balanced torque converter behind an externally balanced engine. Perhaps you need a different stall speed and there isn't a torque converter available that is properly weighted for your engine in the stall speed that you need. There are a couple of possible solutions. First, Mopar Performance offers a weight package complete with various weights and instructions on how to position these weights so that they can be welded to your torque converter.

The other alternative is to use an offset balanced B&M flex plate. This approach is often preferred over the Mopar Performance weight package because the SFI-approved B&M flex plate is a solid disc, which is much stronger than the stock flex plate, and is approved for racing. It is easier to install since no welding is required, and since the weight is not permanently attached to the torque converter, different zero-balanced torque converters can be used behind the engine without the external balance issue having to be addressed again.

Chrysler's extensive use of external balancing – and the fact that each externally balanced engine requires a different amount of weight to be brought into balance – can be a real nuisance. In street and mild race applications, external balancing causes no real trouble, as long as all of the components are properly matched. In an all-out high-RPM race engine, however, external balancing puts undue stress on the crankshaft, for having the weight at the ends of the crankshaft will cause it to flex at high engine speeds. Ideally, a high-RPM race engine should be balanced with all of the weight moved to the inside of the engine. Furthermore, SFI-approved vibration dampers are not always readily available for externally balanced engines.

Nearly all engines with cast crankshafts require external balancing because cast iron is not as dense as forged steel. The crankshaft is balanced in "halves," meaning that the front half of the crankshaft must be balanced irrespective of the rear half, and the rear half must be balanced irrespective of the front half. If both halves were balanced together, and the imbalance from one half was used to cancel out the imbalance from the other half, the overall length of the crankshaft would cause the engine to gyrate at certain speeds, with the engine tearing itself loose from its mountings in the chassis. The counterweights of the crankshaft are designed to offset the weight of the throws, rods, and pistons. Because the density of a cast crankshaft is such that its counterweights often lack some of the necessary weight, the additional weight that is needed is added to the vibration damper and flywheel/flex plate.

Vibration Dampers/Harmonic Balancers

The crankshaft vibration damper, or harmonic balancer as it is also called, performs a vital function in ensuring crankshaft longevity. In a running V-8 engine, a cylinder is fired every 90 degrees of crankshaft rotation, or every quarter turn. When a cylinder is fired, the piston is driven downward and exerts a tremendous force on the crankshaft via the connecting rod. Because the initial load on the crankshaft is perpendicular to its centerline, this is considered a lateral load. The crankshaft is hammered by this lateral load four times per revolution in four different places along its length. At a 600-rpm idle, the

engine is turning 10 revolutions per second, so the pistons and rods are driving it 40 times per second. At 6,000 rpm, the engine is turning at 100 revolutions per second, so it is receiving 400 blows per second from the pistons and rods!

Working together, the connecting rod and crankshaft convert the reciprocating motion of the piston to rotating motion, and the force of the piston being driven downward is converted to torque. Considering the fact that each time a cylinder is fired, the application of torque on the crankshaft lasts for only a fraction of a second, that this happens at four different places along the length of the crankshaft, and that this happens anywhere from 40 to 400 times per second, it is easy to see why the crankshaft experiences torsional vibration.

Harmonics certainly play a crucial role in determining at what engine speeds this vibration will be at its worst, and factors such as crankshaft weight and length play major roles in determining these harmonics. Left unchecked, this vibration would put unbelievable strain on the crankshaft, bearings, and even on the engine block, leading to cracks forming in the crankshaft, and ultimately causing its failure. The job of the crankshaft damper is to "dampen" these vibrations, thus relieving the crankshaft of this undue stresses. It is also called a harmonic balancer because it balances out the harmful harmonics of the crankshaft.

In order for the crankshaft damper to work, it must have enough mass so that it can effectively absorb the vibrations of the crankshaft. One reason lightweight components are desired in race engines is because with less reciprocating and rotating weight, the engine can accelerate more quickly. From the standpoint of performance, it would seem that a lightweight damper would be desired, but if the damper is not heavy enough it will do a less than adequate job of quelling the torsional vibration of the crankshaft. Yes, this is a trade-off of sorts, but it is not a good place to gamble.

A couple of dampers of different weights were used by Chrysler in

This Street Hemi damper has a much wider ring than those commonly used on other engines.

In a production damper, a layer of rubber is sandwiched between the iron hub and outer ring.

the production of internally balanced engines, with the dampers on Street Hemi engines being much heavier than those on other engines. Many dampers can be swapped, although their interchangeability is not always straightforward because of things like timing marks, minor differences in crank pulley attachment, etc.

There are a few different methods of constructing crankshaft dampers. Production dampers are constructed of a cast-iron hub which is keyed to the snout of the crankshaft and a heavy cast-iron outer ring. A narrow band of rubber is sandwiched between them. This method of construction is typical of the dampers used by nearly all auto makers because they are cheap to manufacture and they do an acceptable job of controlling crankshaft vibration. Over time, however, many factors conspire to reduce the effectiveness of production dampers. Oil, heat, ozone, and time all work to cause the deterioration of the rubber between the hub and outer ring of the damper.

Although the gradual process of deterioration is seldom obvious, here are two dead giveaways. First, if the rubber appears swollen or badly cracked, the damper is beginning to fail. Second, if the timing mark has moved, the outer ring has begun to slip on the hub. In extreme cases the ring will become non-concentric with the hub, causing it to orbit or wobble. If this condition is ignored, the ring can eventually walk completely off the hub. If any of these conditions is noted, the damper should be replaced.

Another type of failure occurs when a jaw type puller is used on the outer ring. I mention this because anything is possible when you are working on an older car or engine. Once a car has been in circulation for a couple of decades, it is usually impossible to know whose hands have been into it before yours, and butchers can be very creative in the ways that they destroy things.

In racing applications, higher engine speeds and power levels can overcome the effectiveness of the stock vibration damper, and sometimes even lead to its failure. Under extreme circumstances stock dampers have been known to explode! Due to the obvious safety concerns, the National Hot Rod Association requires SFI-approved dampers on all cars that run 10.99-second or faster elapsed times. Many other race sanctioning bodies have addressed the crankshaft damper safety issue as well.

Viscous crankshaft dampers are available from several companies, including Mopar Performance, BHJ, and (the most widely recognized name) Fluidampr (registered trademark). Inside a viscous damper, a steel ring is suspended in fluid. Although the actual weight of a viscous damper is comparable to that of a stock damper, its rotational inertia is much less, since as the engine accelerates rapidly, the free floating ring inside the damper does not have to accelerate at the same rate. In operation, the speed differential between the damper ring and the crankshaft afforded by the fluid is much like that of a viscous fan drive.

In addition to the performance advantage of a viscous damper over a stock piece, there is the reliability issue. Viscous dampers are more effective in absorbing crankshaft vibration over a much wider RPM range than stock dampers. Because of their superior construction, they are safer and more durable, and there is no outer ring to slip. They are also approved for use by most race sanctioning bodies. In weighing the cost of a viscous damper against all of these benefits, it really doesn't make sense to skimp here.

Another type of damper uses friction discs instead of fluid to dampen crankshaft torsional vibration. It is made by ATI, and has proven to be even more effective than viscous dampers at speeds above 8,000 rpm. The crank pulley attachment bolt pattern is the same as that found on Chevrolet engines. Although a Chrysler crank pulley might not be a direct bolt-up, the Chevy bolt pattern is commonly found on race engines using crank triggers or dry-sump oiling systems.

Solid-hub type dampers are also available, but they do little to dampen out the harmful vibrations of a crankshaft. Using a solid-hub damper will practically guarantee that your crankshaft will eventually fail. For this reason, you should not even consider using this type of damper on anything!

Swapping stock type dampers between engines with cast and forged crankshafts should be avoided, even if both engines are internally balanced. Swapping

SFI-approved dampers are available from a number of sources.

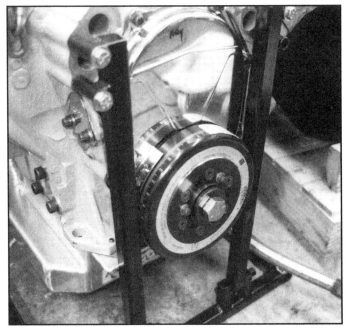

Nearly all have a timing degree scale.

dampers between engines with forged crankshafts usually poses no problems as long as both engines are of the same family, and as long as you pay careful attention to timing marks. The obvious exceptions to this rule are the 1970 and 1971 440 Six Pack/Six Barrel engines, which are externally balanced, and the externally balanced 1970 and 1971 440 HP engines, which use the same heavy rods.

In the case of the Slant Six, any pre-1977 damper can be used on any pre-1977 engine, since they all have forged-steel crankshafts. Because the outer ring of the damper on the Slant Six engine contains the groove for the V-belt that drives the alternator and water pump, you will not likely find a source for a viscous damper. If you need one, a viscous damper for a V-8 engine can be used, but the timing indicator will need to be re-indexed to the pointer. In addition, it will be necessary to drive the water pump and alternator, if used, by other means.

It is possible to interchange dampers between LA engines with forged-steel crankshafts, but the timing mark configuration changed for the 1970 model year. Through 1969, all LA engines used cast-iron water pumps, which placed the lower radiator hose on the driver's side of the car. Thus, the timing marks were located on the passenger's side of the engine. In 1970 the cast-iron water pump was replaced by a cast-aluminum water pump, and the lower radiator hose was moved to the passenger's side. At that time the timing chain cover and damper were reconfigured to move the timing marks to the driver's side.

The timing mark issue on B and RB engines is a bit more murky than on the LA engines. Through 1971, B and RB engines typically had the lower hose on the driver's side, while 1974 and later engines had the hose on the passenger's side. Engines from 1972 and 1973 could have the hose on either side. In most cases the timing marks are on the right side of the engine, but there are certainly exceptions.

Dampers should not be swapped between LA engines and B or RB engines if belt-driven accessories will be used. Although the dampers from either family will physically fit the crankshafts in the other family, the lengths of the snout of the dampers differ slightly. Swapping between families will cause pulley misalignment due to this difference in length.

One final issue must be addressed when swapping crank dampers: variations in crank pulleys. Slant Six engines use the same crank-pulley bolt pattern for all years, but in many cases there is an additional pulley bolted to the back side of the damper which is usually found only on engines used in air-conditioned cars. If your engine uses this pulley, be sure to bolt it in place before installing the damper.

On V-8 engines, however, there were two different bolt patterns used to retain the crank pulleys. Through 1971, all V-8 engines used six bolts to attach the crank pulleys to the damper, but one of the bolts was offset slightly. Beginning in 1972, all six bolts were evenly spaced. Should you encounter a mismatch between crank pulley and damper bolt patterns, a rattail file can be used to widen one hole into an oval shape, then the unused portion of the hole can be welded shut. Afterward, the weld must be ground flat for the pulley to sit flat on the face of the damper.

Engine Balancing Procedure and Considerations

With eight pistons and eight connecting rods, and the related pieces such as rings, wrist pins and locks, rod bearings, and a crankshaft all moving about, the crankcase of an engine is a busy place. All of these parts have inertia, and in the case of a piston, for example, the higher the engine speed, the greater the force it applies to the crankshaft via the connecting rod. In fact, each piston can easily exert well over 1,000 pounds of force on the crankshaft as it decelerates in one direction,

stops, then accelerates in the opposite direction when passing either top dead center or bottom dead center! It is very important that engines are designed so that many of these forces cancel each other. This is why in each bank of a V-8 engine, as one piston reaches top dead center, another reaches bottom dead center.

Even so, engine balancing plays a crucial role in "smoothing things out." Proper engine balancing not only insures that an engine runs smoothly, but it reduces unnecessary stress on the crankshaft and cylinder block and greatly reduces the likelihood of pounded-out bearings.

Furthermore, proper engine balancing frees up horsepower. If we can recall part of a long forgotten lecture from high school physics class, we might remember that one of the Newtonian laws of physics states something to the effect that energy can be neither created nor destroyed, but it can change form. Gasoline is said to have chemical potential energy. When this fuel is burned inside an internal combustion engine, the combustion transforms this chemical potential energy into kinetic energy – or energy of motion – and thermal energy (heat). Consider the fact that excess engine vibration is really nothing more than wasted kinetic energy. If unnecessary vibration is eliminated through balancing, this energy will no longer be wasted, and the engine will be able to do more work.

Unfortunately, most factory balance jobs leave a lot to be desired, and, sad to say, Chrysler's balancing was often among the worst in the industry. If you are rebuilding an engine to stock specs, or even modifying it slightly, the factory balance is probably acceptable as long as you are using pistons of the same weight and you keep the original rods and crankshaft. If you are rebuilding an engine for racing purposes or if you have changed the stroke or the weight of anything inside the engine (such as the pistons or rods), the engine must be alanced. The same is also true when swapping crankshafts, especially between engines of different displacements. A good example would be the use of an early forged 273 or 318 crankshaft in place of the cast crankshaft in a 1973 340.

When an engine is balanced, two different types of weight must be addressed: reciprocating weight and rotating weight. The pistons, rings, wrist pins, and wrist pin locks are all part of the reciprocating weight, for they all move up and down within the cylinders. The crankshaft is part of the rotating weight, as are the rod bearings, for they turn with the crankshaft. The connecting rods do a little of both, for the small end reciprocates with the pistons, while the big end rotates with the crankshaft. When an engine is balanced, the weights of all of these components are taken into consideration, as are the weights of the crankshaft vibration damper and flywheel in the case of externally balanced engines.

The first step is to weigh all of the pistons. Once the weight of the lightest piston has been determined, material is removed from each of the other pistons in order to match their weights to that of the lightest one. The bottoms of the wrist pin towers are the points normally chosen for grinding. Be sure to leave a *minimum* of one-eighth inch thickness between the bottom of the wrist pin bore and the bottom of the wrist pin tower.

The next step is to equalize the weights of the connecting rods. If the beams of the rods are to be polished, that needs to be done before balancing. Furthermore, any machine work to the rods, such as reconditioning or replacing the rod bolts, must be done before balancing. Since the small end of the rod is considered to be reciprocating weight, while the big end is considered rotating weight, this is a two-step process in which each end of the rods will be weighed separately. A fixture is used to support the big end of a rod while the small end rests on a scale. Then the rod is reversed and the fixture supports the small end while the big end is weighed.

When a crankshaft is balanced for a particular engine, a bobweight is clamped to each of the rod journals. The canisters at each end of the bobweight are partially filled with shot.

A drill press attached to the balancer is used to drill material from the counterweights as needed.

When the rod with the lightest small end has been found, material is ground from the small end of each of the other rods until this weight is matched. Normally there is ample material on the pad above the wrist pin bore for this purpose. The same procedure applies to the big ends of the rods, with the material being ground from the balancing pads on the bottoms of the rod caps. When the weights of all the big ends and all the small ends have been matched, the total weight of each rod is checked and compared with the others in the set as a means of verifying the process. The wrist pins, locks, rings, and rod bearings are also weighed, and their weights com-

Sometimes it is necessary to add weight to the counterweights in order to balance an engine. It appears that the balance holes in this crankshaft were filled with shot, then capped with plugs. Although this is certainly not a good practice, at least the plugs were welded in place.

The correct method is to drill through the counterweight and install a Mallory metal slug.

pared, but if there is any variance is usually negligible.

After all of the components have been weight-matched, their weight must be taken into account before the crankshaft can be balanced. Bobweights must be clamped to the rod journals of the crankshaft to simulate the weights of these components, and the required weight of the bobweights is determined by plugging the weights of these components into a formula. When the necessary weight of the bob weights has been calculated, shot is used to fill the bobweight canisters to achieve that weight.

With the properly bobweighted crankshaft placed in the balancer, it is spun and the balancer determines how much weight needs to be added to or removed from the crankshaft and where. A drill press attached to the balancer is used to drill the counterweights as needed. Sometimes it is necessary to add weight to the counterweights to bring a crankshaft into balance. This is especially true if an externally balanced engine is being internally balanced. In this case, a hole is drilled in the counterweight parallel to the crankshaft centerline and a plug of heavy metal, or Mallory metal, is inserted. Mallory metal contains material such as tungsten or depleted uranium and is much more dense than steel or cast iron. It is also expensive. The hole for the Mallory metal plug must be drilled through the side of the counterweight parallel to the crankshaft centerline so that at high engine speeds, centrifugal force does not cause it to be shot from the crankshaft. Should that happen at, say, 6,000 rpm, the slug will destroy anything in its path.

In some cases it is possible to weld material into an existing balance hole in a counterweight in order to add the necessary weight. This is an acceptable practice, provided the welding is of good quality. There have been cases where steel shot was used to fill a balance hole, then the hole was capped with a cupped plug. At speed, centrifugal force then propelled the plug and shot from the crankshaft, destroying the engine. Obviously, this practice is not recommended.

CHRYSLER PERFORMANCE ENGINES
Camshafts and Valve Gear

The selection of a camshaft is perhaps the most important decision you must make when building an engine. The camshaft determines the characteristics, or "personality," of the engine, and in order to get the most from the engine, other pieces of the engine must be selected to work in harmony with the camshaft.

Camshaft Terms

Picking a camshaft is not an easy task, and before making your choice it is important for you to have an understanding of basic camshaft terminology. Following are a few terms you should know:

Lift. There are actually two types of lift discussed in camshaft conversation. "Gross lift" refers to the lift of the cam lobe only. Measured from the base circle of the cam to the tip of its nose, gross lift defines how far the lifter rises in its bore. "Net lift" is often referred to as valve lift, and is

the distance the valve moves from its seat when it achieves its maximum opening. Gross lift multiplied by the rocker arm ratio equals net lift.

Duration. The duration of a camshaft is the number of degrees of crankshaft rotation that the valve is off its seat. There are generally two types of duration discussed: advertised duration and duration at 0.050 inches lift.

Advertised duration can vary greatly from one camshaft manufacturer to another, for the starting and stopping points could be anywhere a manufacturer chooses. Typically, these points are in the range of 0.004 to 0.006 inches of gross lift. The point is that there is no real standard for advertised duration. Advertised duration can be used to compare camshafts from the same manufacturer, but should not be used to compare camshafts from different manufacturers.

Duration at 0.050 inches is a standard commonly used to compare

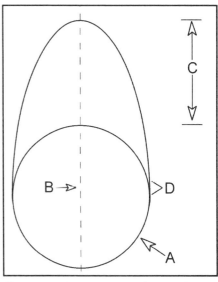

The parts of a cam lobe: A) Base Circle; B) Centerline; C) Gross Lift; D) Lash Ramp, solid lifter camshafts only.

camshafts for race engines. At high engine speeds there is so little air flow past the valves at anything less than 0.050 inches lift that the difference it makes is negligible. Furthermore, because the camshafts used in these engines have a much greater lift, the lobes go from zero lift past 0.050 inches in relatively few crankshaft degrees. In a street engine, however, that is not the case, for at low engine speeds the air flow at less than 0.050 inches lift can have a significant impact on the characteristics of the engine. Because stock passenger car camshaft lobes typically don't have anywhere near the maximum lift of those used in race engines, they accelerate the movement of the valves more slowly, taking a little longer to go from zero to 0.050 inches lift.

Overlap. The overlap of a camshaft refers to the number of degrees of crankshaft rotation during which both valves are off their seats. The starting and stopping points in terms of gross lift used to measure overlap are the same as those used to measure advertised duration. Consequently, as with duration, direct overlap comparisons cannot be made from manufacturer to manufacturer.

Base Circle. The base circle is the round part of the cam lobe. The lifter follows the base circle of the camshaft lobe during the time that the valve remains on its seat. The base circle is important because it is the starting point from which the lifter movement takes place. Some cam grinders offer high-lift camshafts with modified base circles. What this means is that the base circle is smaller in diameter. This is important to know, for modified base-circle camshafts place the lifters lower in their bores and require longer pushrods.

Lobe Centerline. This can be thought of as an imaginary line that extends from the center of the base circle of the camshaft right through the peak of the cam lobe. In nearly all cases, the cam lobes are symmetrical, so by finding the lobe centerline we have one of the reference points needed to synchronize the camshaft to the crankshaft, otherwise known as "degreeing the camshaft."

Lobe Separation. The number of degrees between the exhaust lobe centerline and the intake lobe center-

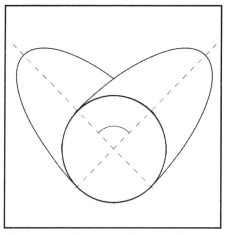

The angle between the intake and exhaust lobes of a cylinder is known as the lobe separation angle.

line represents the lobe separation angle. The smaller this angle, the closer the lobes are together in terms of crankshaft rotational degrees. The greater this angle, the greater the number of crankshaft degrees between the exhaust and intake lobe centerlines. Lobe separation is closely related to overlap. If two camshafts had identical lobe contours but different lobe separation angles, the camshaft with the smaller separation angle would have more overlap, for the lobes would be closer together, resulting in a greater number of degrees during which both valves are off their seats.

Inertia. This refers to the force required to accelerate a component that is at rest or the force necessary to decelerate and stop a component that is in motion. The more mass (weight) that an object has, the greater its inertia. The more quickly the parts of a valvetrain are accelerated and decelerated (high-lift camshafts, high engine speeds), the greater the likelihood that problems associated with inertia will develop.

Valve Float or Bounce. The term valve bounce accurately describes what happens as the valve springs are overcome by high engine speed. When the valves meet their seats, instead of closing fully and remaining closed, the first time they contact the seats they bounce open again. Once this has happened the valves are said to have floated, for when they bounce they "float" from their seats. Valve

float or bounce limits the maximum speed an engine can attain. It can be detrimental to the parts of the valve train, and can even cause the valve head to break from the stem.

Harmonics. The term harmonic refers to the vibrational characteristic and interactions that occur within and between the valvetrain components.

Types of Camshafts

The lobes of a camshaft must be ground to accommodate the type of lifter to be used with that camshaft. For this reason, solid lifters cannot be used on a hydraulic camshaft and vice-versa. Furthermore, flat lifters and roller lifters cannot be interchanged without using the appropriate style camshaft, either.

The lobes of a roller-lifter camshaft are ground so that the nose of each lobe is parallel to the centerline of the camshaft. This must be the case in order for the rollers to maintain full contact with the lobes as the camshaft rotates. All roller-lifter camshafts must use some means of retaining the camshaft in the block, either in the form of a thrust button or a thrust plate. Production roller lifters are extremely heavy compared to either hydraulic or solid lifters of the flat variety.

The lobes of a flat lifter camshaft are another story. When new, flat lifters are not actually flat. Their faces are ground with a slight radius, and the lobes are ground

These are the three lifter types that have been used in production engines. From left to right they are solid flat lifter, hydraulic flat lifter, and hydraulic roller lifter.

Production hydraulic roller lifters were used in late LA engines and all Magnum engines. Flats machined into the tops of the lifter bodies fit through the yokes and keep the lifters from turning.

The bar permits independent movement of the lifters while preventing them from spinning.

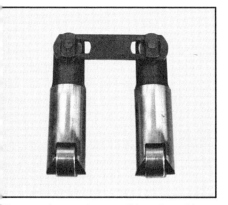

These aftermarket solid roller lifters are linked together by a small flat bar.

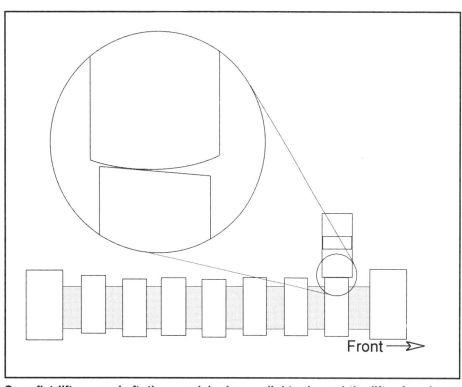

On a flat lifter camshaft, the cam lobe has a slight rake and the lifter face has a slight radius.

with a slight rake. This is done in order to promote rotation of the lifters as the engine runs. If the lifters did not rotate, the camshaft lobes and lifter faces would wear quickly and gall themselves together. The rake of the camshaft lobes provides an additional benefit in some engines in that it causes the camshaft to walk toward the rear of the block, seating the back side of the cam sprocket against the face of the block and eliminating the need for a camshaft thrust plate.

Hydraulic lifters maintain proper adjustment automatically through the use of a spring under the lifter plunger to eliminate any clearance in the valvetrain. Oil is fed into the cavity inside the lifter under the plunger, and this oil ensures that the plunger main-

tains its position inside the lifter while the valve is being opened and closed. Because there is no clearance – or lash – in the valvetrain, as soon as the opening ramp at the base of the cam lobe contacts the lifter, valve actuation begins. Hydraulic lifter valvetrains generally require little or no maintenance, but hydraulic lifters are usually heavier than solid lifters.

Solid-lifter camshafts, on the other hand, do require clearance (lash) in the valvetrain. This is done to allow for the different rates of expansion and contraction of the valvetrain components as well as the block and heads. The lash of a solid-lifter valvetrain does change with engine temperature, and under heavy acceleration the temperature of the exhaust valves increases dramatically, causing them to grow in length. The absence of lash in the valvetrain would prevent the valves from seating fully. This example also explains why valve lash specifications usually call for the exhaust valves to have more lash than the intake valves.

Camshafts designed for use with solid lifters must have lash ramps designed into the bases of the lobes in order to remove the lash before valve actuation can begin and to allow the lash to return after the valve has seated. Without these lash ramps, the valvetrain would be extremely noisy. Solid-lifter valvetrains require occasional (sometimes frequent) maintenance. Solid lifters are usually lighter than hydraulic lifters.

There are five types of lifters commonly used. The first four are hydraulic flat lifters, solid flat lifters, hydraulic roller lifters, and solid roller lifters. Two of the four characteristics listed above apply to each of these lifters – hydraulic roller lifters have the characteristics of a hydraulic lifter and a roller lifter, and so on.

The fifth type of lifter is a mushroom lifter. In some cases with extremely high-lift camshafts, the lobes are so tall that the contact point between the lobe and lifter would run right off the face of the lifter, causing the edge of the lifter to ride against the camshaft lobe. This would obviously spell quick destruction of the camshaft and lifters, so special stepped lifters with large diameter faces must be used. This type of lifter usually requires that the undersides of the lifter bores be machined, and the lifters must be installed into their bores from the bottom before the camshaft is installed. Mushroom lifters are available in solid form only.

Selecting a Camshaft

When contemplating an engine build-up, the first decision you must make is what the engine will be expected to do. Will the engine need to make lots of upper-RPM horsepower, or will it need low-end torque? Will it be used for racing only, street use only, or a combination of the two? How about economy and emis-

sions considerations? What is your budget? List all of your objectives in order of priority.

Ideally, the camshaft should be the first part you select in any engine build-up, and your choice should be made based on the prioritized list of objectives for the engine, while also taking into consideration the bore and stroke of the engine. (See Chapter 9, "Stroker Engines.") The rest of the parts should then be chosen with the idea that they must work with and complement the camshaft. You certainly wouldn't want to build a 318 using a two-barrel intake manifold, stock small-port heads, and restrictive exhaust manifolds with single exhaust if the camshaft you selected had a recommended power band of 3,000 to 6,500 rpm! When selecting a camshaft, follow the "Three Cs": Camshaft, Carburetion, and Compression.

Once you have selected the camshaft, your next consideration, carburetion, addresses the size of the carburetor you will choose. Actually, this concept must be expanded to include *everything* in the upper portion of the engine. The size of the carburetor, the design of the intake manifold, the port and valve sizes of the cylinder heads, and the headers must all be selected to work within the parameters dictated by the camshaft. (See Chapter 12, "Cylinder Heads and Breathing.")

Understanding the static compression ratio requirements of the camshaft is a bit more complex. Long-duration camshafts with lots of overlap typically enable an engine to produce more high-speed horsepower while sacrificing low-speed torque. When an engine with a camshaft such as this is operated at low speeds, however, there is far less cylinder pressure than in an otherwise identical engine with less duration.

At high speeds, when the piston reaches bottom dead center on the intake stroke, the intake valve remains open so that the inertia of the incoming fuel/air mixture can fill the cylinder more completely. This additional cylinder filling continues to take place even as the piston begins its ascent on the compres-

sion stroke, so the intake valve remains open well after the piston begins moving upward.

At low speeds, however, the incoming fuel/air charge is moving much more slowly and, therefore, doesn't have nearly as much inertia to pack the cylinder. When the piston begins to move upward on the compression stroke, some of the mixture is pushed backward past the open intake valve leaving less mixture in the cylinder to be compressed and burned. Because the cylinders are not adequately filled at low speeds, engines with long-duration camshafts can withstand a higher static compression ratio without experiencing detonation and, in fact, require a higher compression ratio to make satisfactory power at the lower extremes of their power bands.

Overlap is another factor involving the duration of a camshaft and the engine's tolerance for a higher compression ratio. At high speeds when the piston travels upward on the exhaust stroke and expels the spent gases from the cylinder, the inertia of the exiting gases creates a low-pressure area within the cylinder. This helps to initiate the movement of the fuel/air mixture into the cylinder, promoting a more complete scavenging of the exhaust gases. This can take place if the valve timing is such that both valves are open for a period of time, called valve overlap.

At low speeds, however, the exhaust gases leave the cylinder at a lower velocity, so there is simply not enough inertia to promote scavenging. Instead, with both valves open together, the incoming fuel/air charge is diluted with exhaust gases. It is this dilution of the fuel/air mixture that causes the low speed misfires, or "lope" that is characteristic of long duration/long-overlap camshafts. The presence of a fairly large percentage of exhaust gases in the cylinder during combustion also has the effect of quelling detonation. (This is one of the benefits of an exhaust gas recirculation valve on stock passenger car engines.) For this reason, too, engines with radical camshafts tend to be more tolerant of higher static compression ratios.

With the myriad of camshafts on the market today, making the right choice is not an easy task. Fortunately, most of the larger cam manufacturers have tech lines that can help you to decide. When choosing a camshaft for a street engine, if the choice comes down to two camshafts, always be conservative and select the smaller of the two. A camshaft that is too big is much more difficult to live with on the street than one that is a tad too small.

Valve Springs

In considering a valvetrain, if the camshaft lobe is responsible for opening a valve, then the spring is responsible for closing it. If we look at it this way, then the valve spring performs a function that is just as important as the camshaft. Granted, it is the contour of the cam lobe that determines the closing rate of the valve as well as its opening rate, but it is the job of the spring to ensure that the lifter remains in contact with the lobe. If the springs cannot properly control the valvetrain, then the lifters can actually ski jump off the noses of the cam lobes at high speeds, leading to coil bind that can result in damaged lobes and lifters, bent pushrods, broken rocker arms, or rocker arms impaled by pushrods. In addition, once the valve meets its seat, it is the tension of the valve spring that keeps the valve from bouncing off its seat.

Due to the inertia of the wire of the valve spring, when a valve is opened and its retainer begins to compress

Even with a damper, fatigue eventually claimed this spring.

the spring, not all of the coils are compressed together. The uppermost coil begins to compress, pressing on the next coil down, and so on. A wave of energy begins at the top of the valve spring and traverses downward through the coils to the cylinder head, at which point it bounces off the head and begins traveling upward through the coils.

The oscillation of this wave of energy up and down through the coils of the valve springs dramatically weakens the springs and is often responsible for mysterious valvetrain component breakage. Many valve springs use dampers made of flat steel wound inside the springs to control these oscillations, while the individual springs of a double or triple valve spring are designed to work together so that the overall oscillation will be minimized. The conical valve

springs used in Magnum small-block engines also resist these oscillations. The lesson here is that camshafts and valve springs are designed to work in harmony. Always use springs suited to the camshaft you choose.

Rocker Arms

The shaft mounted rocker system used in all Slant Six and Chrysler V-8 engines (except the Magnum) is a strong, rigid system. The rocker arms used in the vast majority of V-8 engines are constructed of stamped steel, which is satisfactory for stock and mild-performance usage and cheap to manufacture. These rockers are certainly not without their limitations, however. First, they are often criticized for their ratio not being a consistent 1.5:1, but varying slightly from this number. Second, as valve lifts and spring pressures are increased, their limit of strength is soon realized.

Strong, lightweight rocker arms with and without roller fulcrums and tips are available in different types of construction and from nearly all of the major camshaft vendors. Lighter weight reduces valvetrain inertia, and roller fulcrums reduce friction. Roller tips reduce the friction between the valve tip and rocker arm, but offer the added benefit of reduced valve guide wear, since the valve is no longer loaded against the guide as the rocker arm tip sweeps across the valve

This valve spring has a damper wound from flat spring steel.

This is a multiple valve spring.

These 1964-1967 adjustable 273 rocker arms are of a 1.5:1 ratio.

Magnum small-block engines have rocker arms of a 1.6:1 ratio.

Any serious performance engine build up should include upgraded rocker arms, such as these roller tipped rockers.

tip while the valve is being opened and closed. Stock rocker arms are usually fine for any stock or mild-performance engine, but any engine that will see speeds above 6,000 rpm, or have valve lifts much over 0.500 inches, should receive upgraded rocker arms.

All Slant Six and non-Magnum V-8 engines have a stock rocker arm ratio of 1.5:1. Magnum engines have rocker arms with a ratio of 1.6:1. The obvious difference between these two rocker arm ratios is that a camshaft with 0.300 inches gross lift will produce 0.450 inches lift when a 1.5:1 rocker arm ratio is used, but if a 1.6:1 rocker arm ratio is used, the lift jumps to 0.480 inches.

On the surface it might appear that the duration will be unchanged if 1.6:1 rocker arms are installed in place of 1.5:1 rockers, but bear in mind that the movement of gases into or out of a cylinder doesn't really get underway until the valve has moved far enough away from its seat to create a gap large enough for the gases to move in substantial volume. Increasing the rocker arm ratio causes the valves to be opened and closed at a faster rate, so the gap between a valve and its seat widens more quickly, promoting the movement of gases into and out of the cylinder sooner. Therefore, although the actual duration of the camshaft has not been changed, the effective

duration has been increased. Switching from a 1.5:1 to a 1.6:1 rocker arm ratio has roughly the same effect as mildly increasing both the lift and duration of the camshaft.

Camshaft Degreeing

The lobes of the camshaft carry the programming for the activity of the valves in an engine. Degreeing the camshaft is nothing more than coordinating this valve programming with the movement of the pistons. Because all of the popular Chrysler rear-wheel-drive engines are of the overhead valve design with a single camshaft located in the block, the intake and exhaust lobes are ground on a common shaft. This makes it impossible to change the intake valve timing events without changing the exhaust valve timing events equally.

The movement of the piston up or down in the cylinder causes the flow of gases into and out of the cylinder. As such, this flow of gases lags behind the movement of the piston. The higher the engine speed, the greater the lag. Therefore, retarding the camshaft timing in relation to the crankshaft and pistons increases high-speed horsepower at the expense of low-speed torque, while advancing the camshaft timing reduces high-speed horsepower while increasing low-speed torque.

Degreeing a camshaft is a three-part process. First, we need a point of reference on the crankshaft, then a point of reference on the camshaft, and then these two points must be coordinated. On the crankshaft, number one cylinder top dead center is used. This point is more commonly known as Absolute TDC. Do not rely on the crank damper timing mark for this, for these ignition timing marks are often inaccurate. On the camshaft, we need to establish the position of the number one cylinder intake lobe centerline. Once these points are identified, their relationship can be changed as needed. Before starting, number one piston must be brought up to top dead center, a degree wheel must be affixed to the front of the crankshaft, and a moveable pointer must be fashioned to point at the "0" mark.

If the heads are on the engine, remove number one spark plug and install a positive piston stop tool which is available from any speed shop. SLOWLY rotate the engine, BY HAND, using a long breaker bar until you can feel the piston just touch the stop tool. Read the degree wheel. Next, rotate the engine in the other direction until, once again, the piston just touches the stop tool. Again, read the wheel. Absolute top dead center is exactly in the middle

This piston stop tool is used in finding absolute top dead center if the heads are on the engine.

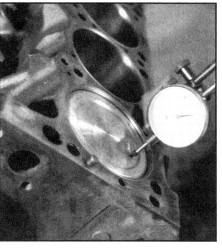

If the heads are removed, a dial indicator can be set up on number one piston. Be sure that the piston is at the top of its bore.

Install a degree wheel and fabricate a pointer.

between these two points on the degree wheel. Remove the stop tool, then rotate the engine until the pointer indicates this middle mark. Number one cylinder is now at absolute top dead center. Adjust your pointer to read "0."

Next, install a new lifter in the bore for number one cylinder intake valve. The lifter must move freely. A few drops of very light oil can be used to lubricate it if desired, but no cam lubricant should be used yet. Mount a dial indicator at the top of the cylinder with a long extension to reach the center of the lifter. If you don't have a dial indicator extension, a pushrod for an adjustable valvetrain works well for this as long as the

Rotate the engine clockwise until the dial indicator drops 0.020 inch. Read the degree wheel.

Continue rotating the engine until the piston approaches top dead center. Stop when the dial indicator shows that the piston is 0.020 inch from the top. Read the degree wheel again. Absolute top dead center is at the midpoint between your degree wheel readings. Rotate the crankshaft to this point, then adjust your pointer to read top dead center.

engine is on a stand and can be positioned so that the pushrod is kept vertical. From here on, the crankshaft must be rotated clockwise only, for backing it up will cause erroneous readings due to the slack in the timing chain and the seating of the chain links on the teeth of the sprockets.

Next, rotate the crankshaft to the point of maximum valve lift indicated on the dial indicator. Zero the dial at

Install a lifter on number one intake lobe and set the dial indicator to read lifter movement. Now rotate the engine and read the degree wheel and dial indicator as explained in the text.

This double roller timing chain set has multiple keyways in the crankshaft sprocket. The camshaft sprocket is retained by three bolts and indexed by a dowel.

this point. Rotate the engine again until the indicator reads 0.010 inches before maximum lift. Read the degree wheel. Rotate the engine until the indicator passes maximum lift and

Camshaft timing adjustments are made at the camshaft sprocket.

again reads 0.010 inches below maximum lift. Read the degree wheel again. The intake lobe centerline is in the middle between these two points. If your first reading was 100 degrees and your second reading was 112 degrees, then your intake lobe centerline is at 106 degrees.

Compare your calculation to the recommended installed centerline listed on your cam card. If they match or are within a degree either way, you are done. Changing camshaft timing by one degree will have a negligible impact on the operation of the engine. If you are off by two or more degrees, you will have to adjust your camshaft timing.

There are a variety of ways to adjust camshaft timing, depending on the engine you are building. Timing chain and sprocket sets with multiple keyway crankshaft sprockets are readily available for all Chrysler V-8 engines, and are easy to use. Small-block engines have the camshaft and camshaft sprocket indexed by a small woodruff key, and offset keys are available to adjust camshaft timing.

There are two types of camshaft sprocket to camshaft attaching methods used in big-block and Hemi engines. From the factory, Hemi and 440 Six Barrel/Six Pack engines used three bolts to retain the sprock-

et to the camshaft, while all other engines used one larger, centrally located bolt. All have the camshaft and sprocket indexed by a pin located in the camshaft that protrudes through the camshaft sprocket. Mopar Performance offers offset bushings for this arrangement, in which the hole in the cam sprocket is enlarged, then the appropriate offset bushing is pressed in.

Whichever method of adjustment you choose, be sure to double-check your cam timing after you have made your adjustment.

Camshaft Break-in

In engines that use flat-lifter camshafts, the faces of the lifters and cam lobes wear-mate together. The first several minutes of operation of an engine with a new camshaft and lifters are the most critical in the life of the cam and lifters. During assembly a thin film of camshaft assembly lubricant should be applied to each of the cam lobes only, but not to the journals. A dab of assembly lube should also be applied to the face of each of the lifters. Upon start-up, because the majority of the oil that lubricates the camshaft is slung from the rod journals of the crankshaft, the engine speed should be maintained at 2,000 to 2,500 rpm for the first 20 to 30 minutes of engine operation. This will ensure that the camshaft receives sufficient lubrication during this critical period, and will also promote rotation of the lifters.

This Milodon gear drive uses a single idler gear.

CHRYSLER PERFORMANCE ENGINES
Cylinder Heads and Breathing

When building an engine, the modifications we make typically fall into one of two categories: with each improvement we are looking to increase either horsepower or durability. Items such as carburetors, intake manifolds, heads, valves, camshaft profile, headers, and exhaust do nothing to strengthen the engine. However, each of these pieces comes into play in determining the power output of the engine.

Conversely, items such as cylinder head and crankshaft main bearing cap studs, forged-aluminum pistons (disregarding changes to dome shape or compression ratio), heavy-duty rods, forged-steel crankshafts, crankshaft dampers, and heavy-duty valvetrain pieces do little to raise the horsepower numbers. Improvements made in these areas help to ensure that the engine stays together for a long time.

Although it is true that selecting lightweight reciprocating and rotating components will allow the engine to accelerate faster, we generally think of making changes in the bottom end of the engine (short block) to improve durability, and changes in the top end (cylinder heads and related components) to increase horsepower.

All gasoline-powered internal combustion engines burn a mixture of gasoline and air in order to produce power. It stands to reason that the more fuel/air mixture we can feed into an engine, the more horsepower it will produce. This means filling the cylinders as fully as possible during each intake stroke. Of course, in order for this to occur, the cylinders must be emptied as completely as possible on each exhaust stroke, since if there is a large amount of exhaust gas left in a cylinder after the end of the exhaust stroke, it will displace some of the fuel/air mixture that would otherwise enter the cylinder when the intake stroke begins. Maximizing horsepower hinges directly on maximizing the flow through the engine.

Volumetric Efficiency

The term "volumetric efficiency" refers to how completely (or efficiently) the cylinders in an engine are filled during the intake stroke. The more fuel/air mixture we can get into the cylinders, the higher the volumetric efficiency. Volumetric efficiency is expressed as a percentage, and the greater the number, the more fully the cylinders are filled during their intake strokes. If a V-8 engine displaces 400 cubic inches, then each cylinder in the engine has a displacement of 50 cubic inches. During their intake strokes, if 50 cubic inches of fuel/air mixture are inhaled by each of the cylinders, then the engine is said to be operating at 100 percent volumetric efficiency. Anything less than complete cylinder filling is expressed as a number less than 100 percent.

Stock high-performance street engines typically have volumetric efficiencies of around 80 to 85 percent, while modified street engines can typically have volumetric efficiencies as high as 90 percent. Many race engines approach the 100 percent mark, and some naturally aspirated race engines are capable of surpassing 100 percent volumetric efficiency if the correct components are selected to take advantage of the pulses in the intake and exhaust tracts (more on this later). The key to building a high horsepower engine is to select components that will work together in order to achieve a high volumetric efficiency percentage.

Forced induction systems, such as superchargers and turbochargers, push volumetric efficiency numbers even higher. By force-feeding the fuel/air mixture to the engine, it is possible to obtain volumetric efficiency numbers of 150 percent or more! Of course, it takes horsepower to drive a supercharger or turbocharger, but the additional horsepower the engine can produce when it is forced to ingest additional fuel/air mixture more than offsets this horsepower loss.

Designing engines with good volumetric efficiency is an exacting science. The intricacies of the theories applied here can become quite complex, and many have made careers of researching, experimenting with, and applying these principles. It would be possible to fill a library with all of the scientific data and results of experiments and testing that have been done on this subject.

In order to understand how airflow through an engine can be improved, it is first necessary to understand what causes air to flow in the first place. Many people think of a cylinder as "sucking" air in during the intake stroke, then "blowing" it out during the exhaust stroke. To a point this is true, but to get a better idea of what happens inside an engine we must think of this process in a different way.

The movement of air is caused by a pressure difference. Air moves from areas of high pressure to areas of low pressure. As the piston in a cylinder moves downward during the intake stroke, the volume within the cylinder increases, causing low pressure within the cylinder. The air outside the engine is at atmospheric pressure, which is typically as much as 14.7 psi, depending on elevation and atmospheric conditions.

Because of the difference in pressure between the inside of the cylinder and the air outside the engine, atmospheric pressure pushes air through the carburetor into the intake manifold plenum, down the intake runners, through the cylinder head intake port, past the open valve, and finally into the cylinder. Near the end of the power stroke, the pressure inside the cylinder is much higher than atmospheric pressure, so when the exhaust valve opens, this pressure difference initiates the flow of exhaust from the cylinder past the exhaust valve, through the exhaust port, into the exhaust manifold or header, through the remainder of the exhaust system, and finally into the atmosphere.

The combustion of the fuel/air mixture causes it to expand in the cylinder, driving the piston downward during the power stroke. Because of the combustion process, there is a far greater volume of exhaust leaving the engine than there is air and fuel entering the engine. Even so, the intake valve is always significantly larger than the exhaust valve. This is because at the end of the power stroke, there can be as much as a couple hundred pounds per square inch of pressure in the cylinder to initiate the flow of exhaust from the cylinder. As the piston moves upward, the volume in the cylinder decreases, which serves to maintain pressure in the cylinder and expel the exhaust gases. During the intake stroke, however, there is only atmospheric pressure available to initiate airflow into the engine. Since there is only so much real estate available in the combustion chamber for the valves, the intake valve gets the preference.

This talk on volumetric efficiency brings up another point. In computing the static compression ratio of an engine, the volume of the combustion chamber with the piston at top dead center is divided into the swept volume of the piston as it travels from top dead center to bottom dead center. The swept volume can be thought of as the difference between cylinder volume with the piston at top dead center and at bottom dead center. The static compression ratio assumes 100 percent volumetric efficiency. Supposing an engine has a static compression ratio of 10:1, we can get an approximate idea of the pressure within the cylinder at the end of the compression stroke by computing as follows:

14.7 (atmospheric pressure) X 10.0 (comp. ratio) X 1.00 (vol. efficiency) = 147 psi

Suppose an engine with a static compression ratio of 10:1 had a low volumetric efficiency and could achieve only an 80 percent cylinder fill:

14.7 (atmospheric pressure) X 10.0 (comp. ratio) X 0.80 (vol. efficiency) = 117.6 psi

Now suppose a supercharger was added to that same engine, and the volumetric efficiency jumped to where it could achieve a 130 percent fill:

14.7 (atmospheric pressure) X 10.0 (comp. ratio) X 1.30 (vol. efficiency) = 191.1 psi

Of course, other factors such as valve timing and temperature are not taken into consideration with this formula. As we can see, static compression ratio tells only part of the story of cylinder pressure at the top of the compression stroke. The volumetric efficiency of the engine also plays a key role.

Inertia and Velocity

It is logical to assume that any restriction in the flow of the incoming fuel/air mixture or the outgoing exhaust gases will result in a lower volumetric efficiency percentage. Furthermore, it might seem that if we use the largest carburetor we can find, mount it atop the largest runner intake manifold available, bolt it to a pair of large-port heads with the iggest valves that will fit, and use eaders with primary tubes the size f stovepipes, we will have the least mount of restriction possible, and e will make gobs of horsepower. Unfortunately, it's not that simple, nd the reason can be summed up in vo words: inertia and velocity.

During the intake stroke, airflow gs behind piston movement. When piston begins its descent on the ntake stroke, the pressure imbal-nce between the atmospheric pres-ure outside and the low pressure reated in the cylinder causes the uel/air mixture to flow into the cylin-er. The piston accelerates down-ard from top dead center until it eaches mid-stroke, at which point it as attained its maximum speed.

At this point, if the intake tract is unctioning as designed, the fuel/air ixture passing through the port is aveling at a high rate of speed. The iston decelerates from mid-stroke ntil it reaches bottom dead center. ecause the mixture in the intake anifold runner and intake port is aveling at a high velocity, its inertia auses it to keep moving past the pen intake valve into the cylinder. It ontinues to pack the cylinder even fter the piston reaches bottom ead center.

Next comes the compression troke, then the power stroke. The xhaust valve opens before the pis-n actually reaches bottom dead enter on the power stroke. Pressure vithin the cylinder initiates the flow of xhaust gases past the open exhaust alve, through the exhaust port, into ne exhaust manifold or primary eader tube, and through the rest of ne exhaust system. The piston accel-rates from bottom dead center until it eaches mid-stroke. By this point the xiting exhaust gas is flowing through ne exhaust port at a high rate of peed. The piston decelerates from id-stroke until it reaches top dead enter, but the inertia of the exiting xhaust gases in the exhaust port nd header tube or manifold causes a ow-pressure area just outside the ylinder, which causes the gases nside the cylinder to keep flowing. his continues even after the piston eaches top dead center.

Beginning at a point near the end of the exhaust stroke, and continuing through the beginning of the intake stroke, is a valve timing event called overlap. During this time, both the intake valve and the exhaust valve are open. The reason for this is that as the exhaust gases leave the cylinder, if there is sufficient inertia, the pressure in the cylinder will be less than that in the intake port above the intake valve. By allowing the intake valve to open early, the pressure within the intake port will cause the fuel/air mixture to begin flowing into the cylinder before the piston begins its descent. This helps to purge, or scavenge, the exhaust gases from the cylinder, resulting in a more complete fill of the cylinder. This goes on for several degrees of crankshaft rotation as the piston passes top dead center. Of course, it takes inertia for this to happen, which is why camshafts with a lot of overlap don't become effective until high RPMs.

Ram Effect and Header Tuning

In the late 1950s Chrysler engi-neers began to realize that another key element to engine breathing could be utilized to further increase volumetric efficiency. These pio-neers of intake manifold research developed the technology to take advantage of this so-called "ram effect." By the early 1960s this tech-nology had taken shape as the long-ram and short-ram intake manifolds on the big-block engines, and as the long runner Hyper Pak intake mani-fold for the Slant Six engines. Today this same technology is employed most notably on the long runner intake manifolds of the Magnum truck engines, but is actually used by every large auto maker and intake manifold manufacturer in the world.

When the piston reaches the end of the intake stroke and the cylinder has been filled, the intake valve clos-es. The inertia of the fuel/air mixture in the intake manifold runner and intake port causes it to stack up and create a point of high pressure at the back side of the intake valve. This pressure bounces off the back of the

intake valve and travels in the form of a pressure wave up the intake manifold runner to the plenum. Upon reaching the plenum, this wave again bounces off the fuel/air mix-ture in the plenum and travels once again down the intake runner to the intake valve. If the cylinder has com-pleted its compression, power, and exhaust strokes by the time this pressure wave returns to the back side of the intake valve, then the pressure wave will be greeted by an open intake valve. This wave of pressure will then enter the cylinder, helping to pack it full.

Engine speed and the combined length of the intake runner and intake port of the cylinder head are the two main factors in determining how well the timing of the pressure wave returning to the intake valve coincides with the opening of the valve. At low engine speeds, say 2,000 rpm, there is considerably more time required to complete the four-stroke cycle than at high speeds, such as 6,000 rpm.

Because this pressure wave moves through the intake manifold at about the speed of sound regardless of engine speed, the length of time between the origination of this wave at the back side of the intake valve and its return to the intake valve is determined by the total length of the intake port and intake manifold run-ner. Long runners are best suited for lower engine speeds, while short run-ners are most effective at high engine speeds. This is why long cross-ram intake manifolds were used on pas-senger car engines, which need to make low- and mid-range power, while Max Wedge and Race Hemi engines received short cross-ram intake manifolds.

Furthermore, it is common knowl-edge that single-plane intake mani-folds are typically recommended for high-RPM horsepower, while dual-plane manifolds are usually recom-mended for good low- to mid-range power. In a single-plane manifold, the area directly below the carburetor is a large, open plenum. From this plenum, short runners carry the fuel/air mixture to the intake ports of the cylinder heads. We already know that short runners are better for high-RPM breathing than long runners.

In a dual-plane intake manifold, the plenum is divided in half, creating two plenums. Each plenum is fed by one side of the carburetor. From the driver's side plenum, runners feed the outer two cylinders on that bank (numbers one and seven), and the inner two cylinders on the passenger's side bank, (numbers four and six). From the passenger's side plenum, runners feed the outer two cylinders on that bank (numbers two and eight), and the inner two cylinders on the driver's side bank (numbers three and five). Dividing the manifold in this way allows for longer runners, which are best suited for lower engine speeds.

A similar principle can be applied to the exhaust side of the engine. While it is common knowledge that the average pair of steel-tube headers will easily outflow just about any pair of cast-iron exhaust manifolds, headers can offer additional benefits as well. When the exhaust valve opens near the end of the power stroke, the pressure within the cylinder sends a large pressure wave past the exhaust valve, through the exhaust port, and down the header tube. The exhaust gases following this pressure wave flow through the port and into the header tube together, in a long column of sorts. At the end of the exhaust stroke, because the entire contents of the cylinder are flowing through a single steel tube, the inertia of all of the exhaust gases from that cylinder create low-pressure areas within the exhaust port and cylinder. This aids in scavenging the cylinder of exhaust gases. Furthermore, the lower the pressure in the cylinder when the intake valve opens, the greater the pressure differential between the cylinder and the intake port, and the more quickly the cylinder will begin to fill.

The relationship between the length of the header primary tube and the speed of the engine determine how well this principle works in a given application. Generally, longer header primary tubes are more effective at lower engine speeds, while shorter primary tubes work better at higher

engine speeds. Keeping all of the primary tubes the same length assures that the cylinders are working together and receiving this benefit uniformly. Headers with uniform length primary tubes are known as equal-length headers or tuned headers. Once the exhaust gases reach the collector, the principle of venturi effect causes their flow through the collector to create low-pressure areas in each of the other primary tubes. This helps to initiate exhaust flow in the cylinder that will be exhaling next. The critical factors here are the diameter of the collector and its length.

On a related note, we've all seen race cars that have their headers wrapped with heat insulating material. This is not solely a safety precaution, but is actually done to help the heat remain in the header tubes. When the temperature of a gas drops, it contracts and its volume decreases. Many racers feel that by keeping the headers hot the steel tubing will not conduct heat away from the exhaust gases. Keeping the exhaust gases as hot as possible ensures that the volume of the gases does not diminish as it travels through the header tubes. If the volume of the exhaust decreases, so does its velocity, and the positive effects of inertia are compromised.

Size Does Matter

By now we should have a basic understanding of some of the principles that must come into play, and obstacles that must be overcome, for an engine to make good horsepower. An engine has to be able to breathe freely, with minimal restriction to intake and exhaust flow, in order to achieve good volumetric efficiency. The flow of air into the engine and exhaust out of the engine is caused by differences in pressure. Inertia is always a factor, and it can be used to benefit the process. The velocity (speed) of the flow of gases has a direct effect on inertia.

What about the size of the intake manifold runners, intake ports, exhaust ports, and header tubes? It stands to reason that the greater the size, or the greater the cross sec-

tional area, the greater the flo[w] potential. This is true for static (o[r] constant) flow, such as that genera[t]ed by a vacuum cleaner. The cyli[n]ders in an engine don't breathe th[is] way. They breathe in pulses, taking [a] short gulp of air during the intak[e] stroke and exhaling it sharply durin[g] the exhaust stroke. It is becaus[e] they breathe in this manner that ine[r]tia is so important, and inertia hinge[s] directly on the velocity of the gases[.]

If we picture a small stream, som[e] portions of the stream are wider tha[n] others. The width and depth of th[e] stream determine the speed a[t] which the water moves. Wate[r] moves slowly through sections tha[t] are wide or deep, but passes mor[e] quickly through sections that ar[e] shallow or narrow.

The same is true of internal com[-]bustion engines. An engine of a give[n] displacement, operating at a give[n] load and speed, will require a certai[n] rate of flow of fuel/air mixture into th[e] engine. At the same time, exhaust w[ill] be flowing from the engine at a certai[n] rate. The speed at which the fuel/a[ir] mixture moves as it flows into th[e] cylinders is determined by the size o[f] the intake manifold runners an[d] intake ports, just as the speed a[t] which the exhaust gases move a[s] they flow from the cylinders is dete[r]mined by the size of the exhaust por[t] and header tube diameter. This [is] important in order to harness th[e] properties of inertia.

Engine speed and displacemen[t] are the two major factors in dete[r]mining the size requirements of th[e] intake manifold runners, intak[e] ports, exhaust ports, and exhau[st] header primary tube diameters[.] Engines of small displacements, o[r] those that are used primarily at lo[w] speeds, don't move as much volum[e] into or out of their cylinders as larg[e] displacement engines, or engine[s] that operate at high speeds.

For these engines, intake an[d] exhaust tracts with small cross sec[-]tional areas are generally chosen i[n] order to keep the gases moving a[t] an acceptable speed to take advan[-]tage of the effects of inertia. If sma[ll] runner intake manifolds, small po[rt] heads, and small tube headers we[re] sed on large displacement engines r engines designed to operate at igh speeds, the velocity of the ncoming fuel/air mixture and outgo-ng exhaust gases would be more nan adequate to take advantage of nertia. However, the small sizes of nese components would restrict the novement of the air and exhaust, egating any positive effects of iner-a. This would be akin to you or me rying to breathe through a drinking traw. Sure, the air would be moving nrough the straw at a high speed, ut could we take in enough air this vay? Certainly not, for the small pening in the end of the straw vould restrict our breathing.

Cylinder Head Selection

The engineers who designed our ngines were well aware of the ffects of large and small ports and unners, and the trade-off that must e made between large passages nat breathe well at high speeds but on't allow enough velocity to take dvantage of inertia at low speeds, nd small passages that work well at ow speeds but don't flow enough olume at high speeds. They real-ced that the 318 two-barrel engine n Aunt Beatrice's four-door Coronet vould likely spend more of its time at lle and low speeds than it would creaming wide open at 6,000 rpm, o the sizes of the passages in the ntake manifold and heads were cho-en accordingly. The 340, however, vas intended to be a performance

engine, even while retaining its street qualities.

With performance a major consid-eration, and the fact that the 340 displaces 22 cubic inches more than the 318, larger passages were needed for this engine. Although most 360 engines were not intend-ed to be performance engines, these same size passages were needed in the 360s because they displaced an additional 20 cubic inches over the 340.

Engines with 273 cubic-inch dis-placement were available both in mundane two-barrel form, and in high-performance four-barrel form, yet all 273 engines were equipped with the same small ports that were used on the 318 due to the rela-tively small displacement of these engines. The engineers who designed these engines were con-cerned with choosing passages that were appropriately sized to provide sufficient flow into and out of the engines, while maintaining good velocity throughout their operating ranges. As we can see, they chose intake manifold runner and port sizes based on the dis-placement and likely uses of each of these engines.

In some cases it seems that these engineers were a bit conservative, since a good performance upgrade for a 318 would include installing the cylinder heads and intake manifold from a 360 or late 340. In reality, though, the 318 was never intended to be a performance engine.

Porting Cylinder Heads

So it seems that for the best potential port flow, we need large, free breathing passages. In order to maintain velocity at low speeds, however, it seems that we need small passages. With flow and velocity working against each other in determining the size requirements of the ports in the engines, is there a way to have your cake and eat it too, so to speak? Considering the cast-ing and manufacturing processes typically employed in the production of the cylinder heads, the answer is yes – to a point. For an engine that will see a broad range of operating conditions, the goal is to improve port flow without significantly increasing the size of the ports.

Sure, we've all seen pictures of beautifully finished cylinder heads with huge ports polished to a mirror-like finish. Cylinder heads such as these may look like works of art, and in many ways they are. If done properly, these gorgeous heads breathe extremely well in their intended application.

To do a job such as this, however, the person porting the heads must take several things into considera-tion, not the least of which is the intended application. He must know when it is and isn't necessary to sig-nificantly change the port size while working within the confines of a par-ticular cylinder head casting.

When cylinder heads are designed, the port layout often must

orting cylinder heads correctly requires time, patience, and experience. This Hemi ead is being ported at Ray Barton Racing Engines in Wernersville, PA.

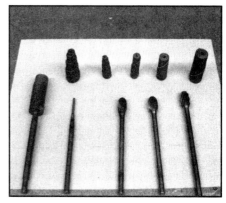

In addition to an air compressor, die grinder, and eye protection, various carbide cutters, sandpaper rolls, and mandrels are among the tools used to port and polish cylinder heads.

be compromised to accommodate such things as head bolts, pushrods, and water passages. The cylinder head porter must be aware of all of these things, and must have the familiarity with the heads being ported to know where the thin spots are. He must also have an excellent understanding of the characteristics of airflow and how to improve it without sacrificing velocity more than necessary. This all boils down to one thing: experience. Additionally, he must have the necessary tools, including a flow bench in order to take comparative measurements of the flow capability of each port as he reworks it and to equalize the flow potential between the ports.

At the other end of the spectrum is the guy who picks up a die grinder and starts blindly hogging out the ports in a pair of otherwise perfectly good cylinder heads. The only thing he understands about porting is that the bigger a port is, the more air it should flow. When he has finished, assuming that he hasn't broken into a water passage, his ports will certainly generate less velocity and perhaps even less air flow than they did in stock form!

In addition, if the intake ports of his heads were designed with "swirl" technology (as is the case on late LA engine cylinder heads and Magnum engine heads), they probably won't swirl anymore. Furthermore, even if he didn't actually break through to a water passage, there may be places, especially in the exhaust ports, where the iron is so thin that it will eventually burn through and cause an internal coolant leak at a later time, perhaps a couple of hundred or

even a few thousand miles down the road. Even if they don't burn through, these ultra-thin places in the casting can lead to hot spots in the water passages and mysterious overheating problems.

With all of this in mind, is it possible for the average enthusiast to lug a pair of cylinder heads down the steps to the basement, toss them onto the work bench, pick up his die grinder, let the shrapnel fly, and obtain the same results as the pros? No way! Is it possible for that same average enthusiast – using patience, careful attention to detail, and a conservative approach – to greatly enhance the flow characteristics of a pair of stock cylinder heads, without sacrificing velocity or creating any of the aforementioned headaches? Certainly!

Because cylinder blocks and cylinder heads are cast in sand molds, they don't have perfectly smooth surfaces and there are often slight variances in thickness and in the locations of internal passages with respect to the exterior surfaces between castings. On a cylinder head, critical areas – such as the deck surface, valve guides and seats, valve spring seats, and manifold mating surfaces – must be machined after the casting process. Because of the variances from casting to casting, there is often extra material in the critical areas in order to make sure that all castings have sufficient thickness, despite the variances that occur from casting to casting.

For example, if the engineers who designed an engine said that the deck surface of a cylinder head had

to be at least 0.500 inches thic before machining, the foundry cou not use this specification as its goa If the foundry used 0.500 inches fo its goal, due to the variance between castings, some casting would be thicker than 0.500 inche while some would be thinner. Th castings that measured thinne would then have to be scrapped. T avoid this scrappage, the foundr would be a little more conservativ and allow for additional material i this area. Some castings might hav a little extra material, while other might have a lot of extra material, bu as long as they all had at least th minimum material, they would b suited for machining and would no have to be scrapped.

The same is true of the valv seats, and the area just below th valve seats as seen when the hea is inverted on a work bench. Extr material cast into these area assures that there will be sufficier material to support the machining c the valve seats. During productior once the valve seats have bee machined, the remaining materia just below the valve seats is simpl left there, for the process of remov ing this material would be an extr expense deemed unnecessary b the auto makers. They figure that little extra material in this area won hurt anything in a stock passenge car engine. Unfortunately, it doesn help it breathe, either.

Removing this excess material wi improve airflow through the ports. I fact, there is more performance t be gained by opening up this are of the ports than anywhere else i the cylinder head! This area is typ

Sometimes it is necessary to braze portions of a port, adding material to achieve the desired contour.

When completed, a professionally ported race head is a wor of art.

cally referred to as the bowl area, and although enlarging this area will decrease the velocity of the gases traveling through this section of the port, the velocity of flow through the rest of the port and intake manifold runner or exhaust header tube will not be greatly

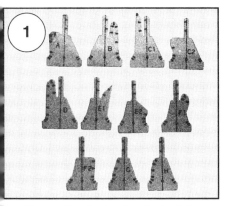

For the enthusiast who is building a street engine on a budget, Mopar Performance offers porting templates for popular V-8 cylinder heads.

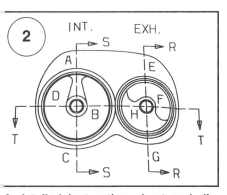

A detailed instruction sheet and diagram are included with each kit, and letters on the diagram correspond with letters on each template.

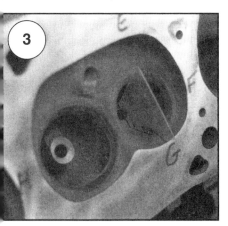

The templates are indexed from the valve guide and seat. Remove just enough material so that the template touches the walls of the port, but doesn't bind.

affected, so low-speed performance will not suffer greatly with a clean-up of the bowl areas.

Reworking the bowl areas by enlarging and smoothing the surfaces is sometimes called pocket porting. Ideally, we would enlarge the area just below the valve seats to the same diameter as the valve seats, but in most cases this cannot be done around the entire circumference of the seats, for doing so could create thin spots in the cylinder head casting.

While a little smoothing of the area can certainly be done in all cases, for maximum reworking of the bowl areas Mopar Performance offers cylinder head porting templates, which, when used correctly, guide the novice cylinder head porter on just how much material to remove from which places around a bowl. The porting template works like a go/no-go gauge. The stem of the

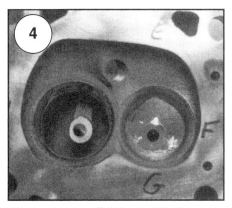

When you are finished with the templates, the port will look like a beaver has been gnawing at it.

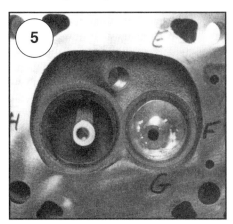

It is then necessary to blend all of the areas of the port together without removing additional material from the portions shaped to fit the templates.

template fits into the valve guide, and therefore uses the valve guide as a point of reference. The template shows how far to open the bowl at various points around the seat. From there, you must play a game of connect-the-dots to gently blend these points together. Working slowly and patiently, you can use these templates to significantly improve air flow through the ports, at the same time staying conservative enough to avoid creating hot spots or breaking through the wall of the casting into a water passage.

Another type of porting is called gasket-matching. Because the intake manifold and cylinder heads are cast in molds of sand, the interior walls of the ports are not precise. Once the fuel/air mixture reaches the ends of the intake runners, it flows into the cylinder head ports. It usually happens that there is a slight mismatch between the walls of the intake manifold runners and the ports, and this mismatch causes turbulence in the airflow.

To minimize the effects of this mismatch, the port entrances in the cylinder head and the runner exits in the manifold are cleaned up and squared. This is most often done by scribing the mating surfaces of these castings using an intake manifold gasket as a guide, hence the term gasket-matching. The port and runner openings are then enlarged to the dimensions indicated by the scribed marks. Gasket-matching can also be done on the exhaust side of the head, but a slight mismatch on the exhaust side isn't nearly as critical as on the intake side. Furthermore, in any serious high-performance build-up, headers will certainly be used, and the opening into a header tube should be at least as large as the exhaust port anyway.

Overall, unlike pocket porting, the benefits of gasket-matching are minimal. Unless there was an abnormally large mismatch between the ports and manifold runners, there will be no improvement in the "seat-of-the-pants" feel in the way the engine runs as a result of gasket-matching only. The same can be said of polishing the insides of the ports to a mirror-like finish. Once again, the benefits are small. In an all-out race engine where every little bit counts, the small gains realized in polishing the ports make it worthwhile, but in a street engine those gains will never be felt. In fact, some argue that a small degree of roughness on the walls of the intake runners and ports helps to resist fuel puddling and drop-out at low-engine speeds by creating a small amount of turbulence along the walls.

This slight turbulence helps to keep the fuel particles suspended, which actually helps low-speed driveability. A smooth finish inside the exhaust port might aid in exhaust flow, but once the engine has accumulated a little time operating at low speeds a thin layer of carbon will coat the exhaust port walls, negating most of the small improvement gained by polishing.

Even so, if you wish to polish the ports, time, patience, a hand held grinder, and grinding stones and/or sandpaper rolls are the tools most commonly employed. Still, it is quite difficult to reach deep into a port or runner, and it is nearly impossible to effectively reach around curves in these passages. A few years back a company called Extrude Hone began to offer a service through which it is possible to reach these areas. The Extrude Hone process begins with a paste that contains abrasive materials. The consistency of this paste is adjusted depending on the job at hand. This paste is injected under high pressure into the passage that is to be "honed," and as it is pumped through, the roughness and high spots within the passage are

scrubbed level and smooth. The Extrude Hone process can be applied to cylinder head ports, intake manifolds, and exhaust manifolds.

Valve Selection and Preparation

The first decision you must make with regards to the valves in an engine is what size to use. In many cases this will be governed to some degree by the choice of cylinder heads. When an engine is being built, the decision is often made to increase the size of the intake and/or exhaust valves in order to improve the breathing ability of the engine. There are obvious limitations here, for there is only so much room in the roof of the combustion chamber for valves, and there is only so much material in the cylinder head casting. Even if there is enough material in the seat areas of the casting to support larger diameter seats, in order for an engine to fully reap the benefits of larger valves the area of the port below the valve seat must be enlarged also, and there may not be enough material in the casting to allow this to be done properly (more on this later).

Given the vast interchangeability of cylinder heads on B and RB engines, and the fact that the ports in all of these heads are similar (with the obvious exception of the Max Wedge heads), it only makes sense to start with a pair of 1968 or later cylinder heads. These heads were all endowed with the most generous valve sizes of any of the B/RB engine cylinder heads, with 2.08-inch diameter intake valves

and 1.74-inch diameter exhaust valves. A common modification is to install larger 2.14-inch diameter intake valves in place of the standard 2.08-inch valves, and all 1968 and later castings can support these larger valves.

In the world of LA engines, there are basically two common port/valve size combinations. The small-port heads of the 273 and 318 cubic-inch engines have 1.78- and 1.50-inch diameter intake and exhaust valves respectively, while 1972 and 1973 340 cubic-inch engines and all 360 engines have 1.88- and 1.60-inch intake and exhaust valves respectively. If you are building a 273 or 318 cubic-inch engine, the larger valve heads will certainly breathe better, but due to their larger ports, low-speed power and throttle response may suffer a little. The larger 1.88-inch intake and 1.60-inch exhaust valves cannot be safely installed into the small-port/valve heads in most cases, for there is simply not enough material in the castings to do the job properly. Besides, the small ports of these heads really can't flow a volume great enough to justify the larger valves.

Chrysler's 1968 through 1971 340 engines were equipped with 2.02-inch diameter intake valves and 1.60-inch exhaust valves. If you have a pair of cylinder heads with the 1.88/1.60-inch valve combination from a later 340 or a 360, the 2.02-inch intake valves can be safely installed into your castings.

Slant Six and 426 Hemi owners are in much the same boat, for there

When gasket matching, use a gasket as a template.

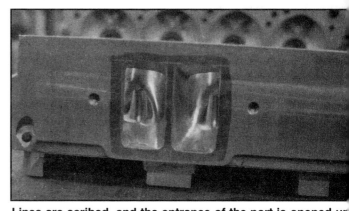

Lines are scribed, and the entrance of the port is opened up to these lines.

This Hemi block has small bore notches.

wasn't much of a variety of valve sizes used over the years of production in these engines. Mopar Performance offers oversized Hemi intake valves in 2.28-inch and 2.35-inch diameters to replace the standard 2.25-inch diameter valves. Similarly, 1.70-inch diameter intake and 1.44-inch diameter exhaust valves were at one time offered by Mopar Performance to replace the minuscule 1.62-inch diameter intake and 1.35-inch diameter exhaust valves originally installed in these engines.

I have successfully installed the 1.78-inch intake and 1.50-inch exhaust valves from a 273 or 318 cubic-inch engine into a Slant Six cylinder head, but due to the small 3.4-inch bore, the valve-to-bore clearance was closer than I would have liked. The real problem, however, was that I could not sufficiently enlarge the areas of the ports just behind the valves in order to take full advantage of the larger valve sizes. In retrospect, the Mopar

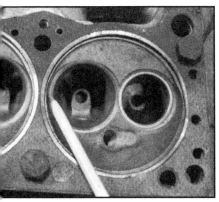

Using a head gasket as a guide, remove material from this area to help deshroud the intake valve.

Performance 1.70-inch intake and 1.44-inch exhaust valves probably would have worked better.

Valve Shrouding

The term "valve shrouding" refers to an obstruction of flow past the valve located on the combustion chamber side of the valve. Many closed-chambered cylinder heads have material in the combustion chamber in close proximity to the valves, and this material often hampers the breathing of the cylinder. Shrouding also often occurs at the outer edges of the cylinders, caused by the valves being located closely to the edges of the combustion chamber and cylinder wall. This is an area of special concern when oversized valves are being installed. A head gasket can be used to mark the edge around each of the chambers. Grinding away material between the valves and the edge of the chambers will help to deshroud the valves and promote air flow past the valves. In some cases, similar notches at the tops of the bores are also used for valve clearance and for deshrouding purposes. Bore notches were used in production on Max Wedge engines.

Seat Preparation

We've all heard guys bragging about the ultra trick techniques they used during the build-ups of their engines, and one of the tricks almost always mentioned is a three-angle valve job. Little do they know that every properly done valve job has a *minimum* of three angles used to properly true the valve seats. This goes for everything from Hemis and 440-Six Barrel/Six Pack engines right down to the Slant Six in Mom's old grocery-gettin' Valiant. The reason for this is simple: three angles are necessary to control the width of the valve seat.

Most valve face and valve seat angles are typically 45 degrees. Ideally, the valve seat should contact the middle of the valve face. There is a specification given for the width of the seat, and this specification must be adhered to in order to promote good valve sealing over a long period of time. If the

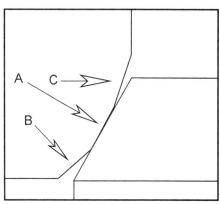

When reconditioning a valve seat, in order to achieve the desired seat width and placement against the valve face, you must cut a minimum of three angles.

seats are too narrow, the valves will seal well, but the seats will wear quickly as the valves pound against such a small area. Furthermore, exhaust valves must dissipate a large portion of their heat to the valve seats, and if there is not enough contact area the exhaust valves will burn. If the seats are too wide, the valves may not seal well and carbon deposits could accumulate on the surfaces of the valve faces and seats.

When a valve seat is reconditioned, it is ground with a 45-degree stone first to obtain a smooth surface that is concentric with the valve guide. Once this has been completed, top cuts are typically made with a 30-degree stone and bottom cuts are made with a 60-degree stone. These cuts are made alternately until the 45-degree seat is trimmed to the proper width and it meets the center of the valve face. If these top and bottom cuts were not made, the seat would be far too wide to seal properly against the valve face.

Sometimes more than three angles will be employed during a valve job in order to provide a more gradual approach to the seat. Grinding these additional angles serves to blend the areas on each side of the valve seat into the surrounding areas. Doing so will enhance the flow of air past the seat.

Back-Cut Valves

Another trick to improve airflow past the valves is to use back-cut

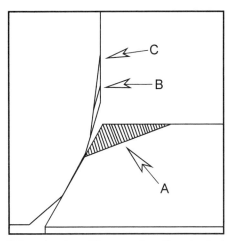

When back-cutting a valve, the shaded portion (A) is ground away. Making additional throat cuts (B and C) will also improve flow through the port.

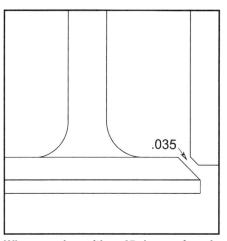

When a valve with a 45-degree face is raised 0.050 inch from its seat, a 0.035-inch gap exists between the valve face and seat.

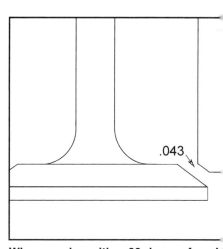

When a valve with a 30-degree face is raised 0.050 inch from its seat, a 0.043-inch gap exists between the valve face and seat.

valves or to back-cut the existing valves. The valve seat is much narrower than the face of the valve, and ordinarily the seat should contact the middle portion of the valve face. By grinding away the portion of the valve face below the seat contact area, this unused portion of the valve will not obstruct the flow of air between the seat and valve face once the valve begins to move away from its seat. This is especially helpful in promoting air flow at low valve lifts. Furthermore, adding a radius to the margin of the valves will smooth the air flow past the valves. Although these tricks lead to small gains in air flow, they are not difficult to perform, and the positive effects of all these small details do add up.

Changing Valve Face and Seat Angles

At low valve lifts, the only real cylinder head related impediments to air flow are the contours of the valves (back-cut) and seats (radiused approach to the seat), the diameters of the valves, and the distance between the valve face and seat at a given valve lift. Perhaps we don't often think about the valve opening in this manner, but just because the valve has moved a certain distance from its seat – say 0.050 inches – doesn't mean that there is a corresponding 0.050-inch gap between the face of the valve and its seat. In fact, due

to the 45-degree angle of the face and seat, there is only about a 0.035-inch gap between them at 0.050 lift! Decreasing the angle of the valve seats will increase the width of the gap between the valve seat and face at any given valve lift, but it is important to consider why the seats and faces are angled in the first place.

Machining the valve faces and seats in the shape of a cone causes them to fit together tightly, promoting a good seal. The valve springs pull the heads of the valves against the seats, and pressure within the cylinder wedges them even more tightly into their seats. If the valve face and seat angle was increased to, say, 60 degrees, the valves would wedge themselves into their seats even more tightly, promoting a good seal, but it is conceivable that they could wedge themselves so tightly against their seats that they would bind when the rocker arm began to push them open. Rapid valve seat and face wear would be a problem, and airflow past the valve would certainly suffer.

If the valve face and seat angle was decreased to, say, 15 degrees, the airflow past the valves could be improved, and rapid seat and face wear would most likely not take place, but the valves would not wedge themselves into their seats. Obtaining a good seal between the valve seat and face could be a

problem from the start, and if any deposits formed on the seat or the face, it is likely that without sufficient pressure between the seat and face the valve seal would be quickly lost. With all of these factors taken into consideration, a 45 degree valve seat and face angle was the compromise chosen for production engines.

Many engine builders believe that on a performance engine, a 30 degree valve face and seat angle on the intake valves is a better compromise. Because most performance engines use valve springs that exert much higher pressures than those of stock springs, even with the decreased face and seat angle there is sufficient force between the seat and face to promote a good seal and pulverize any deposits on the faces or seats. Furthermore, at 0.050-inches valve lift, the gap between the intake valve faces and seats is roughly 0.043 inches.

Switching the intake valve seat angle from 45 degrees to 30 degrees is most easily done when installing larger intake valves. Simply cut the new seats at 30 degrees instead of the standard 45 degrees. If you are not increasing the intake valve diameter, cutting the existing 45-degree seats to 30 degrees will cause the valves to sink too far into the head. Instead, the existing seats will have to be cut out and 30-degree seat inserts will have to be installed. It is unlikely that you will find replacement Chrysler valves with 30-degree faces, so the faces of the valves will have to be ground at a 30-degree angle.

Unfortunately, the stock valves will not work for this, because they are of a tulip shape. Grinding the face of a stock valve to 30 degrees will leave the head of the valve too thin, allowing it to warp. Replacement valves with flat heads, sometimes referred to as nail head valves, will have to be used, and they are available from a number of valve suppliers. The faces of these valves can be ground at 30 degrees with no trouble.

Aftermarket Cylinder Heads

Over the last several decades a number of aftermarket cylinder heads have appeared for use on Chrysler V-8 engines. There are Hemi heads and Hemi conversion heads. There are W-2 small-block heads in both race and econo-versions, as well as W-5, W-7, W-8, and W-9 heads, all from Mopar Performance.

There are also heads offered by Edelbrock. For the big-block wedge engines, there are Stage V heads, which could refer to either the high-performance wedge head offered by Mopar Performance, or the Hemi conversion heads for B/RB engines offered by Stage V Engineering. There are also Stage VI heads, B-1 heads, Indy heads, and Covalt heads. All of these heads are mentioned frequently during bench racing sessions, but understanding who offers which heads and for which applications can be confusing. This section will familiarize you with most

of the popular offerings on the market today designed for use on production blocks.

LA Engine Cylinder Heads

Chrysler has offered many different cylinder heads over the years that were based on production cylinder heads. There have been heads based on both the late swirl port 318 and 360 LA engine heads as well as Magnum heads. Because all of these heads began as production castings, they can all be duplicated by simply starting with the appropriate production casting. This section deals with heads of non-production origin; as such, none of the production based heads will be covered.

W-2 Cylinder Heads

The famed Mopar Performance W-2 cylinder head was introduced in the fall of 1976 (Mopar Performance was known as Direct Connection in those days), and by 1977 there were three versions available: the standard W-2, the ported W-2, and the W-2 Econo heads. The W-2 heads feature large oval-shaped intake ports and special D-shaped exhaust ports that easily outflow any of the ports in production cylinder heads. The combustion chamber is essentially the same as the 340, although today there are versions with 55, 65, and 70cc combustion chambers. Standard 2.02-inch intake and 1.60-inch exhaust valves were carried over from the early 340. The standard exhaust manifolds or headers can be used with W-2 heads, but some grinding may be necessary to port-match them to the wide D-shaped ports.

Due to the large oval-shaped intake ports and different intake manifold bolt spacing of the W-2 heads, a standard 340 intake manifold will not work without a lot of welding, grinding, and redrilling of bolt holes. Special W-2 intake manifolds have been available for as long as these heads have been around. W-2 heads have no exhaust heat crossover passages.

The intake pushrods are angled differently with W-2 cylinder heads so that they don't encroach on the intake ports the way they do in production engines. This design is similar to that of the 1970 340 T/A engines. Because of this, different rocker arms, pushrods, and rocker shafts are used with W-2 cylinder heads. The W-2 Econo heads have the rocker shaft pedestals cast into the cylinder heads, while the standard W-2 Race heads do not. Therefore, the race heads require rocker shaft pedestals to be purchased, too. In fact, this is the main difference between the W-2 Econo and Race heads.

While nearly all W-2 cylinder heads are cast iron, at one time aluminum W-2 cylinder heads were available. These heads used the same rocker gear as the cast-iron W-2 heads, but had rectangular intake ports much like the production heads. Two different combustion chamber styles were available.

W-5 Cylinder Heads

The W-5 heads are the next step in the "W" series of cylinder heads. These heads are aluminum, as opposed to the cast-iron construction of current W-2 cylinder heads. The intake ports in these heads are rectangular and raised somewhat from

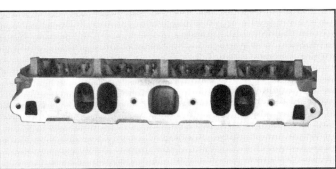

The oval-shaped intake ports of a W-2 cylinder head are unlike those of any production head.

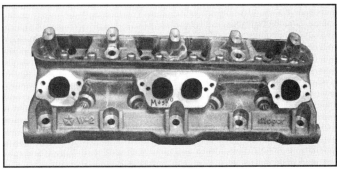

Raised D-shaped exhaust ports help the cylinders exhale.

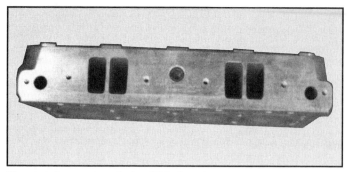

The intake ports of the W-5 head more closely resemble those of a production head.

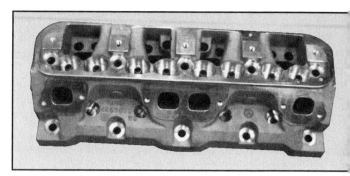

D-shaped exhaust ports are used in the W-5 head, too.

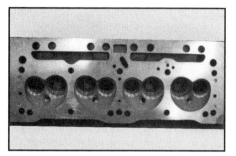

The W-5 head has closed, heart-shaped combustion chambers.

the stock location in order to smooth the curve leading up to the intake valve. The D-shaped exhaust ports have been raised as well, and these heads require W-2 style rocker gear. The standard 2.02-inch intake and 1.60-exhaust valves have also been retained. These heads feature the same swirl port technology that was first used in late 1980s LA engine heads, and they have heart-shaped combustion chambers. Two versions are available: one with 51cc combustion chambers, and one with 59cc combustion chambers.

W-7 Cylinder Heads

The W-7 cylinder heads are the next step up for the serious racer. All production LA engine cylinder heads have a common head-bolt pattern that places only four head bolts around each cylinder. With the high cylinder pressures that are encountered in high horsepower applications and in supercharged and nitrous oxide-injected engines, head-gasket failures become common. The W-7 cylinder heads, when used with the Mopar Performance R-3 cylinder block, have the capability to accept two additional bolts around each of the cylinders. These additional bolts provide the extra clamping force necessary to keep the head gasket tightly sandwiched between the block and heads. The W-7 heads are aluminum, and are available with 62, 65, or 73cc combustion chambers, intake valves ranging from 2.08 inches to 2.20 inches in diameter, and exhaust valves of 1.60 or 1.625 inches in diameter.

W-8 Cylinder Heads

The W-8 cylinder heads were designed for use in the NASCAR Craftsman Truck and NHRA Pro

The four humps along the lower edge of the W-7 head provide the material necessary for an additional row of head bolts.

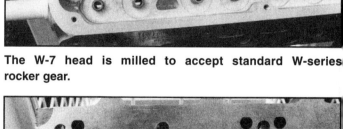

The W-7 head is milled to accept standard W-series rocker gear.

Raised rectangular intake ports are another feature of the W-7.

W-7 heads have closed combustion chambers.

V-8 heads have provisions for an additional upper row and lower row of head bolts right out of the box. Of course, a Mopar Performance R-3 block would be needed.

The exhaust port and header bolt-up configuration is unlike any discussed up to this point.

Stock Truck competitions. These heads are aluminum and have 63cc combustion chambers. All cylinder heads mentioned up to this point are designed to accept the standard LA engine style five-bolt rocker covers, but the W-8 heads do not. They use rocker gear and rocker covers that are specific to the W-8 heads only. The ports have generous wall thicknesses to permit extensive porting, and there is enough material in the valve guide and seat areas to permit the valve angles to be moved from the standard 15 degrees to 12 degrees, if desired.

The basic head is sold as a partially machined piece, while a machined and ported version is also available for use in the NASCAR Craftsman Truck series. This head features seats machined for 2.18-inch intake valves and 1.625-inch diameter exhaust valves, with combustion chambers of 65cc, and six-bolt per cylinder head bolt pattern capability.

W-9 Cylinder Heads

The W-9 cylinder heads are based largely on the W-7 heads, but with raised intake and exhaust ports. These heads are aluminum, and they accept the same rocker gear and rocker covers as all of the W-series heads up to this point, with the exception of the W-8. They feature swirl-type intake ports, closed 62-65cc combustion chambers, and six-bolt per cylinder head bolt patterns. Two different combustion chambers are available, one for gasoline, and one for alcohol. In addition, two different spark plug locations are available. The nominal valve sizes are 2.18-inch intake and 1.625-inch exhaust.

Edelbrock Heads

Edelbrock Corporation now offers aluminum cylinder heads for the Chrysler LA engines that are designed as direct replacements for the 273, 318, 340, or 360 cylinder heads with additional breathing capacity. These heads feature the larger 340/360 size ports, closed 65cc combustion chambers, 2.02-inch intake valves, and 1.60-inch exhaust valves.

Like the production heads, the rocker shaft pedestals are cast into the heads, and they are designed to use the stock rocker gear and rocker covers. The intake and exhaust port openings are shaped the same as the production heads with bolt holes in the stock locations so that production or aftermarket manifolds and headers will attach with no hassles. The valve seats are ductile iron, and the one-piece stainless steel valves are fitted with valve springs capable of 0.575 inches lift. These heads offer an excellent value for a street engine and quite likely the easiest installation of the bunch.

Brodix Heads

The Brodix B1-BA cylinder heads are aluminum and feature 65cc combustion chambers, 2.08-inch

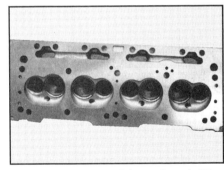

The Edelbrock head has closed 65cc combustion chambers.

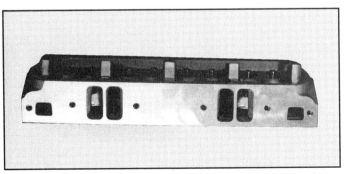

The intake port configuration of the Edelbrock head is identical to that of a production 340/360 head. Note the absence of an exhaust crossover passage.

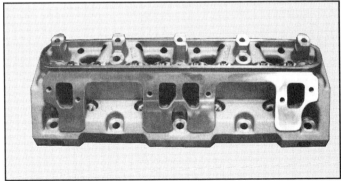

The exhaust port configuration is also like that of a production head.

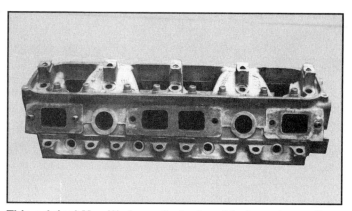

This original Max Wedge cylinder head features larger-than-stock exhaust ports.

Ditto for the intake ports. Note the absence of an exhaust crossover passage.

intake valves, and 1.60-inch exhaust valves. These heads are designed to accept standard headers and intake manifolds. Production rocker covers and adjustable rocker arms may be used, although special rocker shaft pedestals will be needed. Relocated spark plugs and improved port and combustion chamber shapes are among the attributes of these heads. There are no accessory mounting holes.

B/RB Engine Cylinder Heads

There has been much confusion over the B and RB cylinder heads with designations of different "stages." To make matters worse, there are two distinctly different heads both known as Stage V. Here is a quick summary of the evolution of the different stages of Chrysler cylinder heads, from Stage I through Stage VI.

The 1962 413 Max Wedge was the first in the series of the Max Wedge engines. Actually, the Plymouth version was called the Max Wedge, while the Dodge version of the same engine was called the Ramcharger. The 1963 426 cubic-inch version was called the Stage II. Although the 1962 version was never officially called a Stage I, it became known as such, since, if the 1963 incarnation was called the Stage II, then logic dictates that its predecessor *must* have been the Stage I. The 1964 version was called the Stage III. This engine was superseded by the Hemi, which for the sake of classification became known as the Stage IV.

All of this seems pretty simple, and this is how things remained for over

20 years. During this time, as Hemi engines became more and more scarce, there became a growing need among enthusiasts and racers for more Hemis. The obvious solution was to develop cylinder heads that were of a Hemi design that would bolt atop the B and RB engine cylinder blocks in place of the wedge cylinder heads. A company rose to the occasion, and in 1987 the Hemi conversion head was born. The name of this company, appropriately enough, is Stage V Engineering, and its heads are known as the Stage V Hemi conversion heads. The Stage V designation represents the next logical step in the evolution of the big-block/Hemi engines. Stage V Engineering is located in Walnut, California.

Stage V Hemi Conversion Heads

Constructed of aluminum, Stage V Hemi conversion heads use all of the stock Hemi external hardware such as rocker covers and manifolds, but the rockers are specific to these heads. Hemi-style pistons are required, as is a Hemi camshaft. The valve layout on a Hemi head is I-E-I-E-I-E, while the valve layout on a wedge head is E-I-I-E-E-I-I-E. Consequently, the positioning of the lobes on the camshaft is different between Hemi and wedge engines. These heads also require external oil returns to the block, but they are barely visible when the exhaust manifolds or headers are in place. When an RB engine has been fitted with a pair of these heads and is fully dressed in Hemi garb, it looks just

like a stock Hemi. Everything needed for the conversion is available in kit form, and Stage V Engineering also offers replacement cylinder heads for actual 426 Hemi engines.

Mopar Performance Stage V Wedge Cylinder Heads

Now for the confusion. Several years after the introduction of the Stage V Hemi conversion heads, Mopar Performance recognized that there was a market for a new high performance cast-iron wedge engine cylinder head, so it introduced one. Refusing to acknowledge the existence of a cylinder head from another manufacturer in the "Stage" series of heads, Mopar Performance elected to call its new cylinder head a Stage V, also.

The Mopar Performance Stage V cylinder heads are designed to be used as direct replacements for stock B and RB engine cylinder heads. They feature 2.18-inch diameter intake and 1.81-inch diameter exhaust valves, hardened

The Mopar Performance Stage V wedge head features open combustion chambers like those in 1968 and later production heads.

Although original Street Hemi rocker covers will fit Stage V Hemi Conversion heads, Stage V Engineering offers its own dress-up parts.

exhaust valve seats, and exhaust heat crossover passages. The intake and exhaust ports are in the stock locations and of the stock sizes. They use stock valvetrain pieces and accept stock six-bolt rocker covers. The Stage V heads are used on the 440-based 500 cubic-inch, 505-horsepower crate engine and are available as complete assemblies or bare castings.

It should also be noted that replacement Stage II and Stage III cylinder heads have been introduced, and these heads are actually derivatives of the current Stage V.

Mopar Performance Stage VI Cylinder Heads

The Stage VI cylinder heads are constructed of aluminum. On the intake side, the ports are raised from their stock locations for better breathing, while the port openings and manifold bolt spacing is the same as the production B/RB engines. If these heads are installed on an RB engine, spacers are needed between the cylinder heads and intake manifold. If they are installed on a B engine, the same spacers can be used with a B engine intake manifold, or a manifold for an RB engine can be used.

On the exhaust side, the standard port openings and manifold/header attaching bolt spacing have been retained, but the ports have been

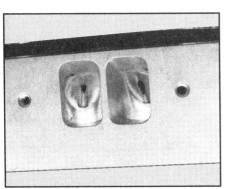

The Mopar Performance Stage VI head features raised intake ...

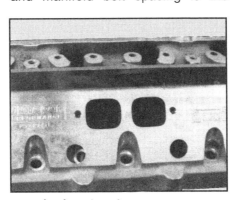

... and exhaust ports.

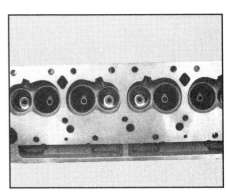

The Stage VI also has closed combustion chambers.

raised, again for better breathing. These heads use stock rocker gear and rocker covers, and accept 2.14-inch intake and 1.81-inch exhaust valves. They have closed 78cc combustion chambers, so piston-to-head clearance may be an issue in some cases. The Mopar Performance Stage VI cylinder heads are used on the 440-based 500 cubic-inch, 545-horsepower crate engine, and, like the Stage V heads, they are available as complete assemblies or bare castings.

Brodix Heads

There are two heads available from Brodix for the B and RB engines – the original B-1 cylinder head, and the B-1 BS head. Both are aluminum.

The B-1 head was designed for the serious racer, and can actually be considered part of an engine package. Special pistons, valvetrain components, rocker covers, and intake manifold are all needed in order to use these heads. Standard headers can be used. These heads have 68cc combustion chambers and accept 2.30-inch intake valves and 1.78-inch exhaust valves. The manufacturer recommends that these

The original B-1 head in no way resembles a production head.

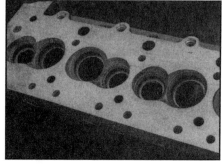

It features small, closed combustion chambers.

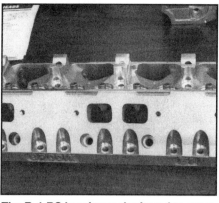

The B-1 BS head was designed to more closely resemble a production head, although it is doubtful that it would be mistaken for a stock piece.

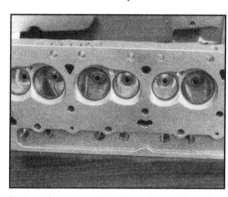

It too has small, closed combustion chambers.

heads be used on engines displacing 440 to 540 cubic inches, that turn 7,000 rpm, and have a compression ratio of at least 13:1.

The B-1 BS cylinder heads were designed for much more conservative applications, for they are intended to replace the stock iron heads. These heads have 65cc combustion chambers, 2.20-inch intake valves, and 1.81-inch exhaust valves. In switching from production heads to these heads, the only additional hardware needed is a head stud kit, longer pushrods, and a set of rocker arms. The standard headers, intake manifold, pistons, and rocker covers can all be retained.

Indy Cylinder Heads

Indy Cylinder Head, in Indianapolis, Indiana, now has four wedge chamber cylinder heads for the big Chrysler engines, three of which were designed to work on production blocks.

The 440-1 cylinder heads were the first, introduced in 1992. Indy

At first glance the intake ports of the Indy 440-1 head look like those of a production head, but they are larger.

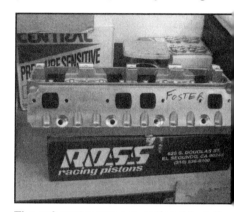

The exhaust ports are noticeably taller than those of a production head, although Indy states that standard headers fit.

recommends that these heads be purchased in kit form, which includes everything from the block on up. These heads are aluminum and have 75cc combustion chambers, accept standard headers, and any Indy intake manifold. The standard intake valves measure 2.19 inches in diameter, with 2.25-inch valves being optional. The exhaust valves measure 1.81 inches in diameter. Special offset intake rocker arms are required. Indy recommends that these heads be used on 451 to 500 cubic-inch bracket race engines. The 440-C cylinder heads are the cast-iron versions of the 440-1 heads.

The 572-13 cylinder heads are also aluminum, and have even larger ports than the 440-1. They have 79cc combustion chambers and are designed to be used on engines with at least a 4.5-inch bore. The standard intake valve measures 2.30 inches in diameter, with 2.35-

The Indy 572-13 head features even larger intake …

.. and exhaust ports than the 440-1.

inch valves optional. The exhaust valves measure 1.81 inches in diameter. Like the 440-1 heads, these accept standard headers, but require an Indy intake manifold and special rocker gear. Furthermore, the lubrication of the rocker arms must be accomplished through the use of spray bar rocker covers.

The 440-SR heads are aimed at the budget minded street enthusiast/bracket racer. They are aluminum, and were designed to replace the production iron heads with a minimum of extra hardware changes. These heads are compatible with standard intake manifolds, headers, pistons (domed or flattop), rocker shafts, rocker arms, and rocker covers. There is enough material around the intake port openings to port-match them to Max Wedge size. These heads use 2.19-inch diameter intake valves and 1.81-inch diameter exhaust valves, and have 75cc combustion chambers. There are also bosses and bolt holes in the stock locations for accessory mounting.

Covalt 32-valve Hemi conversion heads require special rocker covers, intake manifold, and distributor.

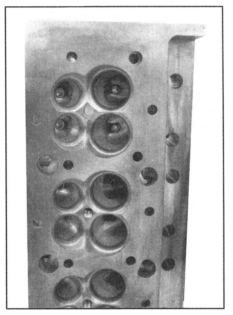

Four valves per cylinder. Wow!

Single intake port entrances for each cylinder branch into separate passages leading to the intake valves.

Covalt Cylinder Heads

The brain child of Marty Covalt, Covalt cylinder heads are manufactured by Newman Racing Components in Duncan, Oklahoma. These Hemi conversion heads are the most exotic cylinder heads available for any of the popular Chrysler V-8 engines, for they feature four valves per cylinder. Valve actuation begins with a conventional camshaft of Hemi lobe sequencing in its stock location in the block. However, through the use of special "trick" rocker

gear it is possible to actuate two intake valves or two exhaust valves from a single cam lobe and lifter. Combustion chamber volume can be specified from 40cc to 65cc. The intake valve diameters can be specified from 1.70 inches to 1.90 inches, and the exhaust valve diameters range from 1.30 inches to 1.45 inches, with cylinder bore size and flow requirements being the determining factors.

Although these valve sizes may seem small, bear in mind that there are two of each in each cylinder, so

Separate exhaust passages from each exhaust valve are funneled into a common Hemi-style exhaust port.

Because Covalt heads are so large, a special offset distributor is needed.

the breathing capability of these heads is outstanding. Furthermore, the valve springs can effectively control a smaller, lighter valve with moderate pressure, so spring pressures can be kept to a sane level.

Because of the comparatively small combustion chambers of the Covalt heads, when switching from production style heads the compression ratio will skyrocket unless dished pistons are used. Even so, the installation of these heads is truly a bolt-on operation with no block modifications necessary. Because the upper portion of these heads is larger than stock Hemi heads, special rocker covers are needed. Due to the girth of the heads, a stock distributor will not fit, so Newman offers a

special offset distributor. With four valves per cylinder, it is logical to assume that the port entrances might not be of a conventional shape, and that is true on the intake side. Special intake manifolds are available in single and dual four-barrel form. Standard Hemi-style headers can be used. Newman Racing offers Covalt heads in kit form, including pistons and everything between the block and the carburetor.

Hemi Cylinder Heads

For many years there was no source for new Hemi cylinder head castings. Because the Hemi remained popular for racing, the availability of used Hemi heads (all Hemi parts, for that matter) began to dry up, pushing prices higher and higher over time. When the restoration craze hit in the late 1980s, the prices for these already scarce pieces were driven higher still. Thankfully, companies like Indy Cylinder Head and Stage V Engineering answered the call of racers, while Mopar Performance catered to racers and restorers alike.

Mopar Performance Heads

There are two basic Hemi cylinder heads currently available from Mopar Performance, a cast-iron head and an aluminum head. The cast-iron head was designed to be a direct replacement for the Street Hemi head, featuring the same 2.25-inch intake and 1.94-inch exhaust valves and 170cc combustion chamber sizes as the original. In fact, the outward appearance of this head is the same as the Street Hemi head, with the exception of the shape of the alternator mounting boss. The deck surface is thicker than the original, and there is extra material to allow for porting. There is even a version of this head available with hardened exhaust valve seats for street use with unleaded fuel.

The aluminum Hemi head is basically the same as the cast-iron head. The aluminum head has the same 170cc combustion chamber and uses the same 2.25-inch intake and 1.94-inch exhaust valves as the iron head.

Current Mopar Performance Hem cylinder heads are nearly identical to production pieces.

Stage V Engineering Heads

The originators of the Hemi conversion heads for B and RB engines, Stage V Engineering also offers replacement aluminum heads for rea 426 Hemi engines. Like its conversion heads, Stage V's replacement heads accept stock Hemi externa pieces, and to an untrained eye, look like original issue Hemi heads.

Indy "Legend" Cylinder Heads

The Indy Hemi cylinder heads called the Legend, are cast-aluminum heads that, as assemblies are almost totally interchangeable with production heads. These heads will accept stock rocker arms and rocker shafts, intake manifolds, headers, and rocker covers, and they fit stock Hemi blocks. They can be ordered with the intake and exhaust ports in their stock locations or raised for improved flow, and due to their raised port capability, the rocker cover rails have been raised .5 inch. Although stock type rocker covers fit, longer spark plug tubes are needed. In addition, a lifter valley plate is needed. These heads will accommodate intake valves measuring 2.25 inches to 2.40 inches and exhaust valves measuring from 1.90 inches to 2.00 inches.

CHRYSLER PERFORMANCE ENGINES
Keeping It Together and Making It Work

This chapter contains a variety of tips and tricks to help you build an engine that shows its strength in both performance and reliability. We all know people who have built engines that ran incredibly, but which broke down frequently or perhaps were short-lived due to some catastrophic failure. Perhaps you've been there yourself. If so, then you know that owning a car in which you spend more time under the hood than in the driver's seat isn't much fun.

By carefully applying good machine shop and engine building practices, your chances of building an engine right the first time are stacked well in your favor. Talk to serious racers and engine builders who are familiar with your type of engine. Their level of success speaks for itself. Although opinions usually vary greatly concerning the details of how a particular engine should be built, if you talk to enough knowledgeable people there will, no doubt, be some common threads in

what they tell you. There is no substitute for experience. By following the advice of those in the know and applying some of the tips discussed here, you should wind up with an engine that performs well for a long time. Following are some suggestions that can help your engine live longer and run stronger.

Swapping Caps

The cap of a connecting rod and the main caps of a cylinder block are properly mated to and machined with the rod or block to which they are bolted. As such, they should never be swapped with other caps unless the rod is to be reconditioned or the cylinder block is to be align-bored. Doing so can result in bearing misalignment, too much or too little bearing crush. If any of the caps are swapped, in many cases the crankshaft will not turn. Even if it does, the chances of premature bearing failure are high.

Don't Overbore Excessively Without Sonic Checking

Most production blocks can handle as much as a 0.060-inch overbore without it causing trouble in mild street use. The exceptions are noted in their respective engine sections. Even so, the thinner the cylinders, the weaker they become, which leads to cylinder flexing, compromised ring seal, and the possibility of cracking. Furthermore, cylinder hot spots can develop near the tops of the bores, leading to cooling problems. In order to be safe, no matter what block you plan to use, if you intend to overbore more than 0.040 inch, have the cylinders sonic checked.

Block Fillers

Many racers use block filler to add strength and rigidity to the cylinders. When you think of how the block is constructed, you see that the cylinders are really noth-

Chrysler Performance Engines **135**

Hard Blok is one of the brands of block filler on the market.

ing more than cast-iron tubes inside the block. These tubes are supported at their tops and bottoms only. With the pressure on top of the piston and the piston-to-cylinder wall loading that is caused by the angularity of the connecting rod, it is no wonder that cylinder wall flexing is an issue.

Filling the water passages of the block part way effectively shortens the free-standing portion of the cylinders, which supports them and makes them less prone to flex. It might seem that doing this could lead to cooling troubles, but the majority of the heat in the cylinder is at the very top, in and near the combustion chamber. The lower portion of the cylinder stays relatively cool, so filling this portion of the water

passages rarely causes problems. It can also be argued that block filler adds weight to the block, but remember that this filler is displacing water from the cooling system, which weighs eight pounds per gallon. The additional weight of block filler is negligible.

Cylinder Blocks

Generally speaking, most production blocks used throughout the 1960s and early 1970s are strong castings that will endure a great deal of punishment. Even the thin-walled castings of the late 1970s and beyond are well suited for high-performance street/mild race applications, provided the cylinders are not bored excessively. As a very loose guideline, however, once the anticipated horsepower exceeds 600 or so, it is time to start thinking about an aftermarket block. Stronger aftermarket blocks can be had in either cast-iron or aluminum for some engines, and are available from a variety of sources including Keith Black, Indy Cylinder Head, and Mopar Performance.

Restricting Oil Flow to the Top End

Many engine builders like to restrict the oil supply to the upper end of the engine. Their reasoning

This is an aluminum Keith Black Hemi block. Note the struts across the lifter valley that tie the cylinder banks together for additional rigidity.

is that the high-volume, high-pressure oil pumps that are frequently used as part of a high-performance build-up tend to flood the cylinder heads with more oil than is needed to lubricate the pushrods, rocker arms, and valve stems. An over-abundance of oil laying on top of the cylinder heads means that there is less oil in the sump, and this excess oil can enter the combustion chambers via the valve guides. The engineers at Mopar Performance, however, do not recommend restricting oil flow to the top end of the engine. They feel that flooding the cylinder heads with oil is not as much of a problem with Chrysler engines as it is with engines of other manufacturers, and they warn that reducing the oil supply to the top end can lead to damaged valve-train pieces.

Torque Plates

When the cylinder heads are installed on an engine block and the bolts are tightened, the stress that is applied to the threads in the bolt holes and surrounding areas of the block cause it to distort slightly. Because the head bolts surround the cylinders, they also distort and lose their perfectly round, true shape.

An engine builder at Ray Barton Racing Engines in Wernersville, PA has leveled the right cylinder bank of a 340 block and prepares to fill the water jacket.

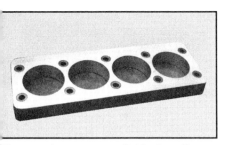

Torque plates are available for all popular Chrysler V-8 engines.

This distortion in the cylinders compromises ring seal, causing a small amount of blow-by and lost power.

Torque plates, or honing plates as they are sometimes called, should be used in order to simulate the stress placed on the block and the distortion that is normally present in the cylinders during the honing process. This guarantees that the cylinders will be true when the cylinder heads are bolted in place. Torque plates are available in both aluminum and steel, with the steel units being superior to the aluminum. It may be difficult to find a machine shop that has torque plates for Chrysler engines, but for the best ring seal possible, they should be used. In addition, whenever any machine work is being done to the block, the main bearing caps should be installed and torqued to the proper specification, again due to the distortion that is induced in the block.

Lightweight Components

It is true that lightweight components – such as aluminum blocks, cylinder heads, and intake manifolds – all shave weight from the engine and, thus, the vehicle. However, the lightweight components referred to in this discussion are those inside the engine. Reducing the weights of pistons, rods, and valvetrain pieces can have a dramatic effect on the performance of an engine while greatly increasing its durability, especially at high RPMs.

When the weight of a component is reduced, so is its inertia. In the case of valvetrain parts, this means that less spring tension may be necessary to control the movements of the valvetrain at a given engine speed, or

that the same springs may be able to control the valvetrain at a higher engine speed than would be possible with heavier components. Lighter valves, retainers, and pushrods all reduce the inertial loads on the valvetrain, reduce the chance of valve float, and help enable the valve springs to do their job.

Lighter pistons exert less pressure on the rods and crankshaft, and lighter rods further reduce the pressure on the crankshaft. This serves to improve the durability of the engine, especially at high speeds. Reducing the weights of the pistons and rods will seldom make a horsepower difference that can be seen on a dyno, for most dynos load the engine statically to measure horsepower and torque as the engine accelerates or decelerates slowly through the RPM range.

If an engine is running at a steady 4,000 rpm, for example, lightweight pistons and rods have little, if any, impact on the power output of the engine. They do, however, allow the engine to accelerate more quickly. Because it takes power to accelerate an engine, by reducing its inertial loads, the power necessary to accelerate the engine is reduced, meaning that there is more horsepower available to accelerate the vehicle. Of course, any time the weights of any of the components in the bottom end of an engine are changed the engine should be balanced.

A right-angle oil filter adapter bolts to the block in place of the oil filter mounting plate.

Right-Angle Oil Filter Adapter

Because the oil filter on Magnum and LA engines is located on the right side near the back of the engine, it sometimes interferes with the exhaust or torsion bar. This is normally an A-body concern, but can happen in any chassis depending on what headers are used. Many (not all) A-body cars came from the factory with a right-angle adapter for the oil filter. Should you need one, Mopar Performance offers them.

Cylinder Head and Main Cap Studs

Most engine builders agree that the use of studs instead of bolts to attach the cylinder heads and main bearing caps provides a number of benefits. First, when you are considering a top-grade stud manufacturer such as ARP, the material used in the construction of their studs is far superior to that of the original equipment bolts they replace, and their tensile strength (force required to stretch a fastener until it breaks) is much higher. This helps to keep the cylinder heads clamped tightly to the block, reducing the possibility of head-gasket failure, and also helps to keep the main bearing caps from bouncing on the block.

A second benefit is that the studs are threaded deep into the holes in the block, which makes it possible to engage more threads in each

ARP is the most widely recognized name in engine fasteners.

This 360 has been fitted with cylinder head studs.

This 440 has been fitted with main cap studs.

hole than can safely be done with bolts. If bolts were threaded all the way to the bottom of the holes, they would likely bottom in the holes while being torqued. This would result in insufficient clamping force on either the cylinder head or main cap, and may even result in a cracked block.

A third benefit is found when you are torquing cylinder head bolts or main cap bolts. Friction takes place between the threads of the bolt and block. Each time this happens the threads in the block accumulate a little more wear and fatigue, which compromises their strength. When the nut is being torqued on a stud, however, the friction takes place between the threads of the stud and nut. This helps to preserve the threaded holes in the block.

When you are installing studs, the threaded holes should first be cleaned with a bottoming tap. Resist the temptation to clamp a pair of Vise-Grips on the studs and screw them tightly into their holes. Bottoming the studs tightly can lead to cracks forming in the block. Instead, they should be installed by hand until they are snug. As an added precaution to keep the studs from turning while the nuts are being torqued, when the studs are being installed use thread locking compound on the threads. Once they are screwed into their bolt holes, use a stack of washers or a deep socket that fits over the stud

and install the nut finger tight so that the stud is pre-loaded slightly. This helps to ensure that the threads of the stud and block are properly seated while the thread locking compound cures.

Aftermarket Main Bearing Caps

Stronger-than-stock main bearing caps are available from a number of sources. There are two schools of thought regarding these caps. RB engine blocks that have endured the rigors of racing sometimes develop cracks in the main bearing webbing. In order to keep this from happening, aluminum main bearing caps are sometimes used. Aluminum is softer than steel, and it absorbs some of the shock load of the pistons hammer-

The center three main caps on this Mopar Performance LA engine block have splay bolted four- bolt main caps.

ing downward on the crankshaft via the connecting rods.

More often, however, billet steel main bearing caps are chosen due to their superior strength. Pro-Gram Engineering has emerged as the industry leader in offering main bearing caps for all popular engines in both two- and four-bolt varieties. Four-bolt caps for small-block engines are splay bolted, meaning that the outer two bolts are angled toward the oil pan rails for additional strength. Due to the deep-skirt design of the big-block B and RB engines, four-bolt main bearing caps for these engines are cross-bolted through the skirts like those of the Hemi engines. In any case, when the main bearing caps are being replaced, the block must be align-bored.

Connecting Rods

Several different rods were used in the various Chrysler V-8 engines, and they are all good. Unlike some of its competition, Chrysler insisted on using forged steel for the construction of rods, so in most street and mild race applications, strength is not an issue. Connecting rod interchangeability is not always straightforward even between engines of the same family. Some engines, such as the early 273 and 340, used floating wrist pins, while other engines of the same family used pressed pins.

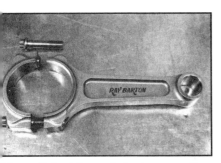

This polished forged-steel connecting rod is stronger and lighter than a stock piece.

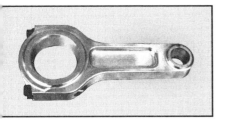

Aluminum rods are lighter than steel rods, but require replacement at regular intervals.

Furthermore, the 340 rods are heavier than those of the 273 or 318. The same is true of the heavy 440-Six Barrel/Six Pack rods versus those used in the standard 440s. This difference in weight had to be taken into consideration when the crankshafts were balanced. Swapping rods of different weights will necessitate that the engine be rebalanced.

There are a variety of aftermarket connecting rods available today. Many of these are stronger and lighter than the original equipment rods. One area that can be improved in the stock rods is the rod bolts. Replacing the stock bolts with high-grade bolts (such as those available from ARP) will reduce the possibility of a rod-bolt failure. Because the bolts are an interference fit in the rod, installing them causes some distortion to the rod. Therefore, the big ends of the rods must be reconditioned after the rod-bolts are replaced to ensure that they are round and true.

Piston Selection

For decades, pistons were commonly available in either of two types of construction: cast aluminum or forged aluminum. Cast-aluminum pis-

tons are generally less expensive than forged-aluminum pistons, making them attractive to the auto makers which are constantly looking for ways to save money.

Cast pistons have another property that makes them better suited for stock passenger car use than forged pistons. At operating temperatures, forged pistons expand much more than cast pistons. In order to have sufficient piston-to-cylinder wall clearance at operating temperature, forged pistons need a few more thousandths of an inch clearance when cold. This additional clearance can make an engine with forged pistons noisy when cold, and can lead to increased oil consumption – two characteristics the average consumer would find unacceptable. Forged pistons, however, are far stronger and much less brittle than cast pistons. Although most cast pistons will work just fine in any mild-performance application, for extremely high-horsepower, supercharged, or nitrous-oxide applications, forged pistons should be used as an extra precaution.

A few years ago hypereutectic pistons entered the market. The aluminum used in a hypereutectic piston is impregnated with silicone, which acts as a lubricant and greatly reduces the chances of the piston skirts scuffing against the cylinder walls. Hypereutectic pistons generally expand at a lesser rate than either cast- or forged-aluminum pistons, which means that even tighter piston-to-cylinder wall clearances can be used when building an engine. Another plus is that they don't transfer heat as readily as cast or forged-aluminum pistons. This means that more thermal energy stays in the cylinders, which allows the engine to make more power. Unfortunately, they are very brittle and will shatter if pushed beyond their limits. Many top engine builders refuse to use them because of this tendency.

Compression Ratio

In the days when 100-octane pump gas was readily available,

compression ratios well in excess of 10:1 were the norm for high-performance street engines. The more tightly the fuel/air mixture is compressed before it is ignited, the greater the expansion rate will be as the mixture burns. The octane rating of gasoline is nothing more than a measure of its resistance to detonation, and as long as gasoline is available which has a high enough octane to suppress detonation or "ping," higher compression ratios generate more horsepower.

In today's world of reformulated, low-octane, unleaded, oxygenated fuels, compression ratios for street engines should be kept to around 9:1. Many factors – such as the quality of gasoline available in your area, camshaft profile, combustion chamber design, and cylinder head material (aluminum or cast iron) – work together to determine the tolerable compression limit of the engine you are building. All things considered, 9:1 is generally a safe number.

Bushing Lifter Bores

One often overlooked area of an engine is its lifter bores. The lifter bores should be inspected for cracks and checked for wear any time the engine is apart. Worn lifter bores cause the valvetrain geometry to be inconsistent and oil-pressure leakage to occur between the lifter bores and lifter bodies. If they are worn, they will have to be bored and have bushings installed. Many engine builders do this as standard practice when building race engines. This helps to ensure that the lifter-to-camshaft geometry

The lifter bores in this block are being drilled for lifter bushings.

This is how lifter bushings appear after installation and machining.

Nearly all are hex shaped in this area ...

... indicating that they are adjustabl with an Allen wrench.

as well as the remainder of the valvetrain geometry is held constant, which is crucial to maintaining proper valve timing throughout all eight cylinders.

Some engine builders claim that 20 or more hidden horsepower can be found by simply correcting the lifter-bore angles, something that the factory apparently wasn't overly concerned with. Another plus to bushing the lifter bores is that if hydraulic lifters are used, the oil feed hole in the bushing is typically much smaller than the hole in the lifter bore of the block. If solid lifters are used, there may not be an oil feed hole at all. Should there be a valvetrain failure that causes a lifter to be tossed from its bore, the oil pressure won't suddenly fall to zero and starve the rest of the engine.

Vacuum Advance

The vacuum advance is one of the most misunderstood components on an engine, yet all street engines

need one. When a distributor is properly calibrated to an engine, the centrifugal advance is curved to give maximum power at wide-open throttle throughout the operating range of the engine. Setting the base timing shifts this whole curve up or down. At wide-open throttle the carburetor is delivering a rich air/fuel mixture, often around 12:1. At part throttle or steady cruise, the engine wants a leaner mixture, and the carburetor responds with a mixture that is typically around 15:1 or even 16:1.

Most racers know that lean mixtures burn hotter than rich mixtures, but lean mixtures also burn more slowly than rich mixtures. Because the lean mixture entering the cylinders while cruising at part throttle burns more slowly than the rich mixture that is fed to the cylinders at wide-open throttle, if peak cylinder pressure is to be achieved shortly after top dead center under both sets of circumstances, the spark plugs must be fired earlier

during part throttle operation. Th vacuum advance accomplishe this by using vacuum to sens engine load. At wide-open throttl there is no manifold vacuum t speak of, so the vacuum advanc canister does nothing. At part throt tle there is usually 10 or more inch es of vacuum, and the vacuur advance pulls the breaker plate i the distributor in order to advanc the ignition timing.

The total number of degrees c advance afforded by the vacuur advance canister is stamped on it arm. Switching to a canister with higher or lower number will chang the number of degrees of advanc accordingly. In addition, canister with a hex-shaped area on the con near the nipple are adjustable. B inserting an appropriately sized Alle wrench and turning the screw clock wise, the vacuum advance will begi at a lower vacuum. By turnin it counter clockwise, the vacuur advance will be held off until the vac uum climbs higher.

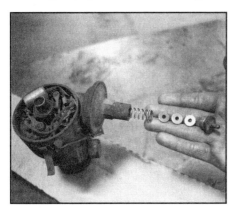
Prestolite distributors use shims that can be added or removed from the vacuum advance canister.

Chrysler distributors have a sealed vacuum advance canister. The arm is stamped to indicate the number of degrees of advance afforded by that canister.

The centrifugal advance is controlle by weights and springs.

Only one slot of this advance plate has been welded and ground for the purpose of comparison. Before it is used the other slot will be welded and ground, too.

Limiting Centrifugal Advance

It is common knowledge that changing the springs for the centrifugal advance weights will change the rate of advance, but in many cases it is desirable to limit the total number of degrees of advance achievable by the centrifugal advance. Most stock distributors permit around 30 degrees of advance. Most lightly modified engines run best with 12 to 15 degrees of initial advance (base timing) and around 35 to 38 degrees total advance (base timing + centrifugal advance). In order to limit the centrifugal advance, the slots in the advance plate need to be welded partially closed, then ground smooth. In this manner the slots can be shortened, limiting the movement of the centrifugal advance. The distributor must then be reassembled and either reinstalled in the engine or placed in a distributor machine and the centrifugal advance checked. This is a trial-and-error modification.

Things to Check After Hot Tanking Block

The caustic solution used to clean large engine pieces and castings also destroys bearing material. Furthermore, to allow the solution to enter all of the passages as the block is being cooked, all oil gallery plugs and core hole plugs (freeze plugs) should be removed first. The cam bearings will have to be replaced in all cases, and all V-8 engines will

All A, LA, and Magnum small-block engines have an oil gallery plug at this location. After hot tanking and cleaning, be sure that this plug is installed!

need a new distributor/oil pump drive shaft bushing installed. On small-block engines, be sure to install a new oil-filter mounting plate gasket and don't forget the oil gallery plug at the rear of the driver's side oil galley. This plug is located inside the engine where it is easily overlooked. Leave this plug out, and there will be a massive internal oil pressure leak.

O-Ringing the Cylinders

O-ringing the cylinders is a procedure that is often done to prevent head-gasket failure on race engines. When an engine is fitted with O-rings, typically a thin groove is machined around each of the cylinders in the deck surface. Special wire is then formed into shape and installed into these grooves. Wider receiver grooves are machined into the heads around each of the combustion chambers, and the engine is assembled with copper head gaskets.

When assembled, the O-ring wire pushes the copper head gasket into the receiver groove, providing a means to lock the head gasket in place and prevent it from blowing out. Because the sheet copper from which the head gaskets are stamped is not nearly as malleable as a composition type head gasket, it is often quite difficult to get copper head gaskets to seal around the cooling passages of the block and heads. For this reason, it is impera-

Before you O-ring the cylinders, the head and block deck surfaces should be milled flat.

Many engine builders put the O-rings in the block.

Ray Barton prefers to put the O-ring grooves in the heads.

He then cuts receiver grooves in the block.

tive that the surfaces of the block and heads be absolutely flat. Milling these surfaces greatly reduces the likelihood of sealing problems when copper head gaskets are used.

Slant Six engines, LA engines, and Magnum engines have cylinder head bolt patterns arranged so that there are only four bolts around each of the cylinders. Consequently, cylinder O-ringing is recommended in high-horsepower, supercharged, or nitrous oxide-injected applications. Conversely, because B, RB, and Hemi engines have additional head bolts, head-gasket failure is not as much of a problem on these engines. Even so, the higher the horsepower level, the greater the need for O-ringing.

Special Clearances

When you are building a custom or high-performance engine, special consideration must be given to certain clearances within the engine that are not normally checked as part of a stock rebuild.

First is the piston-to-head clearance. There must be a minimum of 0.055-inches clearance between the top of the piston and the cylinder head. This can be checked by installing the cylinder heads using old head gaskets and some modeling clay on the pistons, then measuring the thickness of the clay after rotating the engine by hand. Another method calls for setting a piston on top dead center, removing its rod cap, and then using a dial indicator to measure how far it can be pushed until the piston touches the head. To be safe, check all of the cylinders. Maintaining the same head-gasket thickness, or taking into consideration the difference in head-gasket thickness if the gasket style is to be changed, is crucial in maintaining this dimension, especially if the clearance is tight.

The second is the piston-to-valve clearance. For Hemi engines, there must be a minimum of 0.100 inches of clearance between the intake valve and the head of the piston as it rolls past top dead center for engines used with automatic transmissions. For engines used with manual transmissions the clearance must be 0.120 inches. For the exhaust valve, there must be 0.120 inches of clearance in automatic transmission applications and 0.140 inches for manual transmission applications.

Wedge engines used in conjunction with automatic transmissions can run as little as 0.090 inches of piston-to-valve clearance, but those used with manual transmissions should have a minimum of 0.100 inches clearance for the intake valve and 0.120 inches for the exhaust. To check this properly, modeling clay is placed on top of the pistons and the heads installed with old head gaskets, as described above. A set of solid lifters and adjustable rocker arms or pushrods should be installed and adjusted to zero lash. This should be done even if the engine has a camshaft meant for hydraulic lifters, for it is only being done for checking purposes. Next, rotate the engine by hand two full revolutions. Remove the cylinder heads and measure the thickness of the clay. Be sure to adjust your measurements if the thickness of the head gaskets you used for checking is not the same as the thickness of the head gaskets you plan to install in the engine.

Even if there is sufficient valve-to-piston clearance when you build your engine, changes made later – such as changing the thickness of the head gaskets, changing the profile of the camshaft, and changing the rocker arm ratio – will all affect the valve-to-piston clearance. Keep this in mind if the clearance is marginal!

The third critical clearance is valve spring coil bind. When the valve springs are compressed to the point that the coils of the spring are touching each other, the spring becomes solid, for it can't compress any further. Coil bind quickly leads to bent pushrods and broken valvetrain pieces. To be sure that this does not happen there must be at least 0.100 inches of total clearance left between the coils of the valve springs with the valves at maximum valve lift.

To check this, measure the installed heights of the springs (the distance between the spring seat on the head and the underside of the valve spring retainer). Next, subtract the valve lift specified by the camshaft manufacturer. If other than stock rocker arm ratios are being used, be sure to adjust the valve lift number before subtracting it from the valve spring installed height. Finally, compress a spring in a vise and measure its solid height. (It is best to not use this spring in the engine after you have compressed it fully in the vise.) Subtract this number from the difference listed above. There must be a minimum of 0.100 inches left. For example, say we were working on a 340:

1.688 inches installed height - 0.509 inches valve lift - 1.02 inches spring solid height = 0.159 inches clearance

Factors that will alter the valve spring coil bind clearance after the engine has been built include changing the camshaft profile, the rocker arm ratio, the valve spring retainers, or the valve springs to a different style.

The fourth clearance that needs to be measured when a high-lift camshaft is being used is the distance between the underside of the valve spring retainers and the tops of the valve guides. With the valves on their seats and the valve guide seals pushed down against the tops of the guides, measure the distance between the top of the valve guide seal and the bottom of the valve spring retainer. Subtract the valve lift specified by the camshaft manufacturer, again adjusting this number if rocker arms of a different ratio are being used. There must be at least an additional 0.050 inches of clearance between the bottom of the valve spring retainer and the valve guide seal. It is common to have to machine the valve guides to accept multiple valve springs and retainers, but if there is not enough clearance between the retainer and the seal, the guide will have to be shortened slightly, too.

NOTES

NOTES